THE COMPLETE BOOK OF BICYCLING

THE COMPLETE BOOK OF BICYCLING

by EUGENE A. SLOANE

Trident Press
New York

SBN: 671–27053–2

Library of Congress Catalog Card Number: 71–101246

Published simultaneously in the United States and Canada by Trident Press, a division of Simon & Schuster, Inc., 630 Fifth Avenue, New York, N.Y. 10020

Printed in the United States of America

THIRTEENTH PRINTING

CONTENTS

PREFACE

As the world becomes more mechanized, the need for walking diminishes to the point where we drive our cars to the corner drugstore for a gallon of ice cream or the Sunday paper. As our legs threaten to go the way of our appendix as useless appendages, the medical profession becomes increasingly alarmed at the incidence of cardiac failure due more or less directly to lack of exercise. Paradoxically, it seems that the very civilization that has brought unprecedented economic wealth to Americans has also made life so physically easy that it can be fatally disabling.

There is hope, however. In addition to other good things, such as pizza pie and continental car styling, World War II G.I.'s brought home a desire for a better type of bicycle than had been available in this country before the war—the so-called "English racer." While a far cry from an actual racer, this bicycle does have three gears and is considerably lighter than the balloon-tired seventy-five-pound monsters the G.I.'s had dragged around as children. After the war, bicycling became something grown-ups could enjoy, too. Pedaling was a lot easier, and we adults could even look dignified on a bike.

During the postwar baby boom, it became a common sight to see a child being carried on the back of its mother's bicycle to the store where she did the family shopping, or simply for a pleasant ride on a summer afternoon. Soon, entire families were pedaling around town, in the parks, and even on extended trips.

Today, thanks to the eminent cardiologist Dr. Paul Dudley White, the efforts of the entire bicycle industry (especially the Bicycle Institute of America), and to a growing realization on the part of the public of the need for regular exercise, a genuine bicycle boom among adults is here.

In this book, you will learn about quality, ultralightweight bicycles that make cycling much easier than you dreamed possible, with gears that let you take the steepest hills sitting down. We hope that by describing top-rated bicycles, we will be able to convince the novice cyclist of the worth of a good machine, whose frame seems almost alive and responsive to the thrust of the leg muscles. A fine bicycle can become a part of you, an extension of your torso and your arms and legs. Its ten or fifteen gears will shift instantly and surely, and its brakes will stop you safely and smoothly.

For experienced cyclists, the book offers tips for maintaining all kinds of bicycles, and guides to aid you in the selection of everything from the bicycle itself to accessories, tools, and camping equipment. We hope that the book will bring to the sport of cycling much the same dedication those who enjoy other sports give to equipment selection and to play of the sport itself. The chapters on camping and touring are the sum of the experiences of dozens of knowledgeable cycle tourists.

Most important, for children as well as adults, there is a chapter on cycling safety in both city and country.

And cycling is fun! This book can make bicycling a source of genuine enjoyment for you and your family, and you'll find there's much more to bicycling than just good exercise. The cyclist is open to nature, to the sound of the cricket in the field, the distant farm tractor, the wind as it rushes through a forest or field.

While much of this material has been prompted by my personal experiences, some points have grown out of other riders' years of cycling. I am particularly indebted to and want to dedicate this book to the late Oscar Wastyn, Sr., Chicago, one of the last great custom bicycle builders in the United States; Gene Portuesi of Detroit, Michigan, an American Olympic Cycling Team coach; Dr. Clifford Graves of La Jolla, California, President of the International Bicycle Touring Society; Paul Schwemler of Whittier, California, 1967–68 Southwestern Vice President of the League of American Wheelmen and a veteran camper; Dr. G. Douglas Talbott of Kettering, Ohio, Director of the Paul Dudley White Research Laboratory; Al Stiller of Chicago; Jim Rossi, twice United States national cycle-racing champion; Peter Hoffman, of *Bicycling!* Magazine (formerly *American Cycling*); Fred DeLong of Hatboro, Pennsylvania; and my good friend Robert Wahlgren of Winnetka, Illinois, whose extensive library of old books and magazines on bicycling was of inestimable help in writing the chapter on history.

THE COMPLETE BOOK OF BICYCLING

1

CYCLING YOUR WAY
TO BETTER HEALTH

The right kind of physical exercise can add years to your life. It can also make you feel better daily, and prepare you to compete in today's demanding world, where sheer stamina and resistance keep one out front.

The right kind of exercise, according to Dr. Paul Dudley White, is sustained for at least an hour and is vigorous enough to produce a mild sweat. Cycling is just such exercise.

A number of studies have been made to determine the relationship between cycling, exercise, and health. A quick review of these facts will, I'm sure, convince you of the importance of exercise.

First, however, I must say a word about conditioning. No beginner should hop on a bicycle and pedal 15 or 20 miles at top speed right away. Everyone, however, even octogenarians, can do this, if they keep themselves in good physical condition.

According to Dr. Clifford L. Graves, a well-known cycling expert, a trained cyclist in good physical condition should be able to ride 25 miles in between an hour and a quarter and an hour and a half, no matter what his age. Records of the Veterans Time Trial Association (a time trial is a race against the clock) show that 72-year-old Billy Steer rode a 25-mile time trial in one hour, fourteen minutes, seventeen seconds, and when he was seventy-four rode 190 miles in twelve hours. At sixty-four, E. A. Butt covered 439 miles in a 24-hour trial.

Every year the Cyclists' Touring Club of England holds a century (100-mile) ride for men over fifty and women over forty, in which hundreds of people participate. In 1966 the oldest rider, who was eighty-five, completed the 100-mile run without pain or strain.

"What all this amounts to," says Dr. Graves, "is that a healthy person can engage in vigorous physical activity well into his old age."

It is no coincidence that most heart attacks occur when the victim has been sedentary for a number of hours. Dr. Graves states that there has yet to be a heart attack during the thousands of time trials held by the VTTA. On the contrary, he says, "Heart attacks are much more apt to come during inactivity, because it is during inactivity that the blood pressure drops and the coronary circulation slows down."[1]

Dr. Paul Dudley White is justifiably unhappy about many Americans' lack of exercise. We spend all evening watching TV, take the car to the drug store, use electric appliances, and end our days too tired for the extra effort and exercise that could save our lives.[2]

Dr. White states that no one should sit down for more than an hour without getting up and moving about, preferably jogging in place for a couple of minutes. This is the way to keep a heart healthy and blood pressure down.

Vigorous exercise like bicycling will also:

• Improve the blood flow to the brain, keeping it operating at full capacity.
• Induce a state of *healthy* fatigue—a wonderful antidote to the nervous stress and strain of modern life.
• Reduce the possibility of a slipped disc by strengthening back muscles.
• Add as much as five years to life expectancy (according to Dr. Jean Mayer, Professor of Nutrition at Harvard University's School of Public Health).[3]
• Reduce the incidence of all types of degenerative vascular disease, responsible for or associated with heart attacks, strokes, and high blood pressure. (This accounts for approximately 55 percent of all deaths that occurred in the United States in 1968, as opposed to 18 percent due to cancer and 11 percent due to auto accidents.)[4]

---

[1] Clifford L. Graves, "A Doctor Looks at Racing," *American Cycling* (now *Bicycling!*), December, 1966, pp. 18-27.
[2] Paul Dudley White, "For Fun and Fitness Get Back on a Bike," New York: Bicycle Institute of America.
[3] American Heart Association, "Lack of Exercise and Life Expectancy," *Heart Research Newsletter,* Vol. XIII, No. 2 (Spring, 1967), p. 3.
[4] G. Douglas Talbott, "Medical and Health Aspects of Bicycling," Kettering, Ohio: Cox Coronary Heart Institute, 1967.

Fig. 1: *Famous heart specialist Dr. Paul Dudley White joins a group of congressmen for a bicycle ride to the Capitol after addressing a meeting of public service organizations in May, 1964. Dr. White is second from left.*

DR. RODAHL'S EXPERIMENT

Fred DeLong, who writes for Schwinn's (one of the most prominent domestic bicycle manufacturers) dealer publication, described, in one of his articles, the research of Dr. Kaare Rodahl, in Philadelphia. Dr. Rodahl took telemetered cardiograms of a number of men while they were cycling on a stationary bicycle, at various levels of activity. From the cardiograms, Dr. Rodahl determined each man's tolerance for exercise. Based on this tolerance level, he set up a program of hard physical exercise of varying duration for each man.

Participants in this program were executives who ranged in age from twenty-nine to forty-two; follow-up examination of each participant by Dr. Rodahl revealed that the men were rewarded for their rigorous regimen with as high as 10 percent overall increase in physical capacity. Pulse rates were better, and the executives reported that they were more alert on the job and had more energy left for home activities. They all agreed that physical deterioration so common to men over thirty had in their cases not only been checked, but reversed.

FATIGUE AND EXERCISE

We have all read about fatigue that comes about with no apparent physical cause. How many times have you come home exhausted after "a hard day at the office," where all you did was sit hour after hour at your desk? And, how often do women complain to their husbands of feeling "tired all the time"?

Nothing fights fatigue after a tension-filled day in the office or around the house better than getting on a bicycle and pedaling for all you are worth.

Dr. Theodore Klumpp, a New York specialist participating in an American Medical Association panel on geriatrics, stated, "Fatigue is the greatest obstacle to a happy, useful life for oldsters. Its best antidote is physical activity when one feels tired. Over and over again it has been demonstrated that physical activity at the end of a trying day brings a degree of freshness and renewed energy that nothing else can equal."[5]

And a recent study of fatigue[6] showed that this is a primary complaint of executives. In a survey of 165 top-level executives, 43 percent said they often feel tired. They ascribed their fatigue to job pressure (61 percent), increasing age (46 percent), and excessive work load (25 percent).

Dr. John E. Vaugh, Vice President of Fairleigh Dickinson University, observes that some executives feel thirty years old at 9:00 A.M. and sixty at 5:00 P.M. Other observers of executive life note that the ability to build up and keep a full head of steam all day long is crucial if job and career goals are to be met. Therefore, regular exercise on a bicycle not only can prolong your life; it can also promote your career.

---

[5] "Ride A Bike to Health," *New York World Telegram*, Vol. 126, No. 291 (August 29, 1959).

[6] "Get Rid of That Run-Down Feeling," *Nation's Business*, July, 1967, pp. 82-83.

A WORD ABOUT PHYSIOLOGY

Why does exercise promote health? Let's look for a moment at the heart and lungs.

The Heart

The heart is a fantastically efficient machine. It pumps 5.2 quarts of blood in a minute in a person at rest. It can pump as much as 31.7 quarts a minute during exercise. The blood is a transport vehicle that carries off wastes and supplies nutrients to muscles and other tissues.

ARTERIOSCLEROSIS AND EXERCISE

Arteriosclerosis is a disease in which the walls of the arteries become hardened and calcified. In extreme cases, the arteries become pipelike, bonelike tubes. Hardening of the arteries begins at birth, but exercise helps delay its progress. Blood that flows rapidly will not permit deposits to settle in the walls of the blood vessels as quickly as blood that flows slowly.

Take a pipe two millimeters in diameter. If this pipe can pass one cubic milliliter of water, a pipe twice the diameter (four millimeters) can pass sixteen times that amount. The resistance to flow in a pipe is inversely proportional to the fourth power of the pipe diameter, all of which simply means that *a very small decrease* in the diameter of your veins and arteries due to calcification will result in a *great decrease* in the amount of blood these vessels can carry. To compensate, the heart must pump harder and the blood pressure goes up. High blood pressure is a common cause of stroke or rupture of a blood vessel in the brain.[7]

ATHEROSCLEROSIS

Atherosclerosis occurs when fatty substances are deposited on the lining of the blood vessels. This is why a low-fat diet is advisable in middle and old age. The fatty deposit comes in contact with the flowing blood

---

[7] Arthur C. Guyton, *Function of the Human Body.* Philadelphia: W. B. Saunders Co., 1959.

and can start a blood clot which, in turn, may plug up the arteries that feed the heart. This plugging of the coronary arteries (thrombosis) is a major cause of heart attack. Such a blood clot may also block arteries that lead to the kidneys and cause kidney damage, or it may block an artery in the brain and cause a stroke.

Exercise, by keeping the blood flowing swiftly, helps prevent these dangerous symptoms.

The Respiratory System

One measure of lung efficiency is vital capacity—the difference between the maximum amount of air that can be taken into the lungs and the maximum amount forced out. Your ability to breathe deeply depends on the strength of your respiratory muscles.

Exercise strengthens respiratory muscles and, by inducing regular deep breathing, can help keep vital capacity high.

WEIGHT CONTROL

You can also use your exercise program to get rid of excess weight. The only problem here is that after a brisk bicycle jaunt, people tend to overeat. They rationalize, using the exercise as an excuse. I admit that there's nothing like a bicycle ride to make a person wolf down a meal. But, if exercise is going to help control your weight, you must use self-control. Remember that next to cycling the best reducing exercise is placing both hands firmly on the edge of your dinner table and pushing hard.

Calories and Exercise

Let's consider the relationship between caloric intake and exercise. For a medium-sized male, five feet, nine inches tall, a reasonable weight would be 150 pounds. You probably know your own best weight. Multiply your optimum weight by 20 and you have about the number of calories you should consume daily with light work or moderate exercise. For our medium-sized man, this would be 150×20 or 3,000 calories per day.

Mild cycling uses up an average of 5 calories per minute or 300 calories per hour. Vigorous cycling, which you need to do to go up a hill, will use up approximately 10 calories per minute, or 600 per hour.

CYCLING REGIMEN

As I have already cautioned, if you are not used to strenuous exercise, take it easy on bicycling in the beginning. Do not tackle a cycle tour without conditioning yourself first. Keep your bicycle in the lowest, or next to lowest, gear and ride slowly, without strain, three or four miles a day for two or three weeks. Build up your cycling stamina gradually by increasing your daily rides by two or three miles each week. If you are in good health (and you should have a complete physical every year to be sure about this), you will probably find that ten miles or so a day will keep you fit and trim.

WINTER EXERCISE

If you live in what is laughingly called the Temperate Zone, skating, skiing, and just plain dog-trotting are all fine winter workouts to keep you fit when ice and snow on the streets make cycling too difficult and danger-ous. Cycling, skating, and skiing are complementary sports, each keeping you fit for the other.

There will be days during the winter when the weather is so bad or your schedule so limited that you do not have time to go outside for exer-cise. When this happens, there are a number of good bicycle-like exer-cisers on the market. I prefer the Model 960 Ergometrecycle made by Jonas Oglaend of Sandnes, Norway.

When using this or any similar exerciser, set the load (which should be adjustable) to a level at which you can feel resistance, and pedal at your normal cadence (sixty-five to eighty-five pedal revolutions per minute) for three or four minutes. Rest for the same period, then pedal another three or four minutes. Repeat this for about twenty minutes.

Start training by following this program twice a week for two weeks; increase frequency to three times a week for the next two weeks, and, thereafter, exercise four times a week. Finish each session by flexing your muscles lightly.

Or, ride for ten or twelve minutes at a time in front of the television set. The noise level of the Oglaend unit is low enough to permit fast and furious use without interfering with TV viewing. This machine is fitted with SKP ball-bearings and a special tire to keep the noise low. The Oglaend unit costs around $50.00. Write Jonas Oglaend, Aksjeselskap, Sandnes, Norway.

Schwinn, too, makes a good bicycle exerciser, with built-in speedometer, mileage indicator, and adjustable pedal resistance. It lists for about $72.00 and is available from any Schwinn dealer.

A word of caution about home fitness equipment. Forget about any gadget that purports to condition or tone your muscles without work. Gadgets that claim to give you exercise by "remote muscle control"— electronic stimulation or motor-driven apparatus—are, in my opinion, useless. You've got to move those muscles yourself. Save the money these gadgets cost and buy a good bicycle exerciser that you pedal yourself.

If you can't find the Oglaend or Schwinn units, test out the exerciser you do find by riding it. Does it feel rickety or "junky"? Is there an easily adjustable friction or other idler to decrease or increase pedal resistance? Is it quiet? If not, keep looking.

WHAT ISN'T EXERCISE

Besides workouts on electric or motor-driven gadgets, other activities are touted as good exercise but are in fact not. Golf, for example, is not adequate exercise—not even eighteen holes. If you carried your own bag and *ran* between strokes, you might approximate a half-hour of bicycling. For youngsters, according to Dr. Dale L. Hanson, Associate Professor of Physical Education at the University of Maryland, Little League baseball involves very little exercise—"So minimal," he states, "that it should not be considered a major factor in the development of cardiovascular-respiratory fitness." Dr. Hanson reached this conclusion by telemetering the heart-rate response of players (excluding the pitcher and catcher) in Little League games. The results proved that, unlike many other sports, baseball consists of a great deal of watching and waiting.

You are not exercising either when you travel in an airplane or on a train, no matter how tired you feel at journey's end. In fact, long flights alarm Dr. Paul Dudley White, who has proposed equipping planes with a bicycle exerciser for such flights. He believes the exerciser would help keep the pilot relatively immune from heart attacks, and keen and alert enough to meet emergencies. It would also maintain circulation in the legs, states Dr. White, where blood clots sometimes form. The airlines probably wouldn't like this idea, but I am in favor of the passenger getting up and walking up and down the aisle during the flight.

Studies made by Dr. Jeremy Morris of London, England, showed that bus drivers, who work sitting down, have twice as many heart attacks as bus conductors, who go up and down the aisles and stairs to collect fares. Other studies have shown that sedentary postal employees have more heart attacks than mail carriers who walk most of the day.

If you've been reading this book for more than an hour, it's time to put it down and go for a quick bike ride!

2

PRACTICAL TIPS FOR BICYCLING SAFETY

If you read and follow the suggestions in this chapter on cycling safety, you need never have a bicycle accident. The recommendations are based on my own observations during fifteen years of city, country, night and day, winter and summer bicycling, and on those of others with the same background.

A summary of bicycle accidents is given at the end of this chapter, a review of which should show you why cycling safety is so very important.

GENERAL SAFETY HINTS

In the first place, a cyclist is far more likely to *run into* a car or other object than to have it run into him. I will begin, therefore, with a few general rules *you* should observe, which apply to all types of cycling, before getting into specifics of safety, its seasonal aspects, city versus country riding, and night versus day riding.

LEGAL ASPECTS

From the viewpoint of obedience to traffic regulations, most public officials look upon bicycles as a motor vehicle. Police regularly give tickets to cyclists who violate these regulations, and, in my judgment, they *should*.

It is tempting to run a stoplight or stop sign if there is no visible cross-traffic. You can whip a bicycle quickly around a line of stopped cars, and it can give you a satisfied feeling to leave the automobile at the light as you wend your way down the next block. But this is a hazardous undertaking; you simply cannot tell when a car might shoot out of a hidden intersection, alley, or driveway and come barreling down the street toward you. A bicycle simply cannot move out of the way fast enough. And if you are run into after having violated a traffic regulation, you will have a mighty tough time collecting on the other guy's insurance!

Here are general cycling safety tips:

- *Always ride* WITH *the traffic, never* INTO *the traffic,* unless, as in some states, the laws require that you ride into the traffic. Riding with the traffic reduces the relative speed difference between you and moving traffic, and thus reduces the impact if an accident should occur. You'll feel a bit nervous at first with all that traffic coming from behind you, but you'll get used to it.
- *Never ride on a city street where parking is not allowed!* There is simply no room for you between the traffic and the gutter on streets where car parking is forbidden. Such streets are high-traffic through-street's. Cars might drive you right into the curb, or drive behind you honking madly because your bike is moving too slowly.
- As a corollary to the above, *always ride on city streets where car parking is allowed* and, in fact, where cars are parked. By law, traffic is supposed to allow from thirty to thirty-six inches, up to a full three feet, on streets where cars are parked, to allow for the doors of parked cars to open easily. (Unfortunately, this is not always adhered to.) If you are a reasonably skilled cyclist and can ride straight, thirty inches will be all you will need. You'll even have room to spare.
- *Watch out for car doors opening ahead of you when riding on streets with parked cars!* Discourteous drivers have whipped in ahead of me, parked their cars, and opened the door on the driver's side, all in one motion, forcing me to veer out into the stream of traffic to avoid running into them. As you cycle on streets with parked cars, keep a close watch on the cars as far ahead as you can see. I have trained myself to watch parked cars for a block ahead, and to notice what's going on in all the parked cars on that block.
- *In particular, watch through the rear windows and look at the side-view mirrors of parked cars.* These will help you know if a driver or passenger is about to open a door. You may notice a driver who appears immobile and waiting, but I have found that this does not mean that he won't suddenly leap out of his car. Some cities and states have an ordinance that makes the driver liable for any accidents caused

by his opening a door on the traffic side, but you will still be better off if you can avoid running into a car door anytime. Watch out especially for children in cars; they are always unpredictable.

As you cycle, be alert for the same situations you would be concerned about if you were driving a car. These include:

- Children chasing a ball into the street.
- Adults coming out from between parked cars.
- Cars leaving a parking place without signaling.

I have found, in fact, that my extreme caution as a cyclist has made me a much safer driver of automobiles, because now, instinctively, I drive more defensively.

- *Beware of the "Sunday Driver."* Drivers who don't drive regularly can be dangerous to cyclists. Whenever I hear behind me the squeal of power brakes and wheels being turned rapidly, usually followed by a horn blowing, it almost always seems to be an inexperienced driver who cannot decide what to do about me. Watch out for these people at intersections. They may appear to be waiting patiently for you to pass, but they seem to be unaware that an experienced cyclist in good physical condition may be coming at fifteen or twenty miles an hour, and they will suddenly charge out in front of you. Also, I have found that these drivers will come uncomfortably close to me when they pass.

Men and women who drive to work every day are usually safe to be around on a bicycle. And teenagers who have taken driver education courses in high school are often safe drivers. But watch out for the suburban housewife or the older driver! Give them a wide berth. Don't rely on their hand or automatic turn signals—they are not necessarily indicative of their next move.

- *Approaching an intersection calls for judgment.* If it's a suburban through-street with a stop sign in your favor, do not assume that traffic will stop because of the sign. Sometimes drivers will barrel up to stop signs, slow to a running crawl, and speed up again, even though you as a cyclist have the right of way and are already into the intersection. Teenage male drivers are particularly untrustworthy in this respect, with or without driver education.

I have found that the safest procedure to follow upon seeing a car waiting for me to pass through an intersection, whether the car is to the left or the right, is to move over to the center of the road as I approach the corner, provided there is no traffic behind me. In this position I have a better chance of swerving right or left to avoid a collision if the driver at the intersection decides to force his way through. From the center of the road, I have room to turn the corner right or left as necessary to avoid being hit. If I were to go through the intersection next to the curb, it would be impossible to turn at the sharp right angle necessary to escape collision.

Cultivate the habit of cycling in an absolutely straight, unwavering line at all times, and continue to do so while you quickly turn your head as necessary to check traffic behind you. If there is no traffic, try cycling down the center of the dividing line on the street. You'll be surprised to find that after a little practice you'll be able to steer straight down the line. Accurate steering is vital in city cycling, because the clearance between traffic and parked cars is ample only if you can cycle straight, without weaving from side to side.

- *Watch out for child cyclists.* Children on bicycles usually weave from side to side, turn unpredictably without signaling, and cannot be counted on not to run into you even when you are passing them. I watch children on bicycles very closely as I approach them from the front or the rear, and I am ready to take evasive action at all times.

Incidentally, while cycling in the city, you should have your hands on or next to the brake levers at all times, so that you can stop instantly if you have to. Also, keep toe straps loose. I'll never forget the time I forgot to loosen my toe straps on a city ride. It was during rush-hour traffic at the major intersection in Detroit, and I came to a traffic light with cars all around me. I stopped quickly, but with my feet strapped tightly in the pedals, I toppled slowly and ingloriously to the side.

Apropos of motorists' attitudes, there seems to be a curious relationship between the time of day and the attitude of the driver toward cyclists. For example, I used to cycle from my home in Grosse Pointe Farms to my office in downtown Detroit, a distance of twelve miles. The route took me through the car factory area, and I found that if I cycled before 8:00 A.M. motorists were quite discourteous and careless about my well-being. When I left home after 8:00 A.M., however, I found everyone quite courteous.

During evening rush hours, though, no holds are barred and courtesy to cyclists doesn't seem to exist.

If you want to cycle on a Friday or Saturday evening, try to avoid main traffic routes, and watch out at all times on any roads for a drunk driver or a teenager late for a date or showing off to his girl.

- *A word about city cycling routes.* If you want to cycle to work (a good idea), I recommend that you get out a large-scale map of the city and carefully chart your route downtown. Plan to use only streets that are parallel to main arteries, so that the stop signs will be in your favor, but the streets will not be heavily traveled in rush hours.

I now ride my bicycle from my home in Evanston to my office in Chicago's Loop, a distance of about fourteen miles. I have charted a rather devious route which avoids all main arteries, yet gives me streets quite safe all the way downtown. I use it summer and winter, except when it is raining or there is snow or ice on the street. All the streets I use for this trip have parked cars on them, or permit such parking. It takes me about one hour to get to work, which is not bad when I consider that it takes nearly an hour to get there via public transportation. In my judgment, the extra time is well spent for the exercise involved.

- *Right of way.* Remember that cars on your right, at intersections, have the right of way; in any case, don't argue. Pedestrians have the right of way at all times. I would advise you to give the right of way to anyone who wants it.
- *Driveways can be a hazard,* particularly if they are hidden by shrubbery or parked motor vehicles. Women drivers in particular have a habit of shooting backward out of residential driveways into the middle of the street. So be ready to veer away. It's a good practice to look back over your shoulder frequently so that you always know the overtaking traffic situation, and whether or not it's safe to swerve to the left to avoid an accident at any given moment. Watch out especially for cars and trucks emerging from shopping-center parking lots.
- *As you approach a stoplight, watch out for cars next to you that want to turn right.* Although it infuriates drivers, I veer left into the traffic line if the traffic light turns red as I approach it, to prevent motorists from pushing me to the curb. Since there are no parked cars at intersections, right-turning cars tend to hug the curb at stop-

lights, or as they approach intersections. Once you have stopped, you can move out of the way to let traffic by when the light changes. Be especially careful about buses. Bus drivers must pull over to the curb to let passengers on and off. If you're following a bus, remember that it may stop at *any* corner, and it is definitely unsafe for you to be between the bus and the curb at a corner. Stay behind a bus, even if its diesel fumes tempt you into taking chances on passing. You can watch your opportunity and pass the bus between intersections or, if traffic permits, you can pass it on the left while it is stopped. Do this slowly and carefully, watching out for cars and pedestrians who may suddenly appear in your path from in front of the bus. Once you have passed a bus, you should be able to stay ahead of it.

- *At extremely busy intersections, if it's possible, use a truck or a bus to run interference for you.* Just stay to the right of the truck, and anyone coming from the left will run into the truck instead of you.

In my many years of cycling through city traffic, I have never had any kind of traffic accident. There was one mishap, but it was ridiculous—and my fault. I was cycling home on a pitch-black, very cold January evening about 6:30 P.M. The street was deserted, without traffic or a pedestrian in sight. Because it was ten degrees below zero, my feet were getting cold, and I looked down for a moment to check the connection between my electrically heated socks and the battery strapped to my seat post. Before I could look up, I found myself spread-eagled on the roof of a parked car. On that dark night, the black car was invisible a few feet away. I wasn't hurt, but I wrecked a front wheel rim and bent a fork. Fortunately, I was wearing a hard crash helmet, so if my head did hit anything I was not aware of it. Since that incident, I have always checked my gear while at a standstill.

- *Consider safety equipment.* A great many cities and/or states now require motorcyclists to wear approved hard crash helmets. I see little difference in falling off a motorcycle or a bicycle—you might strike your head on a concrete pavement, a curb, or any other un-yielding surface, in either case. A motorcyclist goes faster and can hit an immovable object harder, but the relative speed of impact is of little concern, since you can just as easily receive a skull fracture by falling from a stationary bicycle.

I always wear a hard crash helmet in city traffic. Sears Roebuck sells a good helmet, which has ear flaps for winter comfort, for about $25.00. You can also get a summer-weight helmet of impact-resistant plastic from Sears that resembles a sport hat with visor for about $15.00.

A new winter helmet, just on the market, offers safety protection plus warmth and good looks. This is the Trooper Cap made by Wolverine World Wide, which costs $15.95 and is currently available at a limited number of bicycle, motorcycle, and snowmobile dealers. I like this hat because it is lightweight (about fourteen ounces) and does not look like a safety helmet—it looks just like an ordinary hunting hat, with ear flaps that tie at the top. The Wolverine helmet exceeds American Standards Association Z90 Committee recommendations with regard to energy absorption that will prevent brain damage. It comes in blue, black, and international orange. The orange, of course, is extremely visible, another safety factor. I'd rather be seen and live than be an elegant corpse. If you can't find a local source for the Wolverine Trooper Cap, I am sure the company will be glad to send you the information. It is located in Rockford, Michigan 49341.

You can get by without a crash helmet in the suburbs and on country roads, but it's foolhardy to cycle in the city without head protection, unless you are out at 5:00 A.M. and off the street by 7:00 A.M. Remember, almost any part of your body can be mended, except your head.

- *Lights are a vital necessity* if you cycle at night, on any road anywhere. Rear lights are especially important, and these should be clearly visible to overtaking traffic from at least three blocks away. A wide choice of lights is available—most of them poor. (For a full discussion of bicycle lights, turn to pages 194-96, in the chapter on accessories.) Just remember that the largest tail-light is the best; it should be visible from the rear and both sides from at least 500 feet away.

   A new French-made light is available, which can be strapped to the left leg, just above the calf, below the knee. It costs about $1.50, is very lightweight, has a white front light and a red rear light, and can also be seen from the side. The up-and-down motion of the leg as you pedal adds two-way visibility to this light for the motorist, and it is an excellent back-up system to your main lights if they should fail.

• *Reflectors* are also a safety back-up to lights. The bigger the reflectors, the better. Use a three-inch-diameter round reflector. Another good reflector is Minnesota Mining's reflective pressure-sensitive tape. Stick strips of this tape on the back of cycling shoes, on fenders, belts, helmet, frame, pedals, and handlebars.

• *About horns.* A mechanical horn, such as a squeeze-bulb type, takes up too much room for the noise it makes. Tinkle bells are about all you need if you do a lot of sidewalk riding. If you really want noise, try a Freon-powered boat horn, which can be heard for ten blocks. When they were new on the market, I bought one and put it in a bottle carrier on my handlebar, where I could get at it quickly. It sounded rather like a diesel freight train coming down the highway. The first time I used it, I was between a squad car and the curb, and it caused the squad car to leap forward with dome light flashing. The second time, I tried it on a woman driver coming at me from an intersection. She came to a satisfying, screaming stop. The third time, I blew it at a driver who opened a car door in front of me, and it frightened him into closing the door rather quickly. By the time he did, I was long past him. But since I find my lung power about as good a horn as I need, I discarded the Freon horn and its pound of gas. In general, it's far better to be alert at all times to what's happening around you and be prepared to take evasive action than it is to count on a horn to get you out of trouble. In my opinion, any horn is just dead weight.

• *Cycling in parks.* Cycling at night is usually safe enough if you can be seen, but even lights won't help if you are foolish enough to cycle in city parks at night—especially in big cities like Chicago, New York, or San Francisco. Avoid dark parks, ill-lighted streets, and shore paths where police protection is spotty or nonexistent. On my first trip to Chicago, I was foolish enough to be lured by the summer evening solitude of a lakeshore park area and, in one wooded section, I was confronted by a gang of young hoodlums. Fortunately I had my Freon-powered boat horn with me, so I simply bent over the handlebars to get up speed, and when I was a few feet from them, I sounded the horn. The sudden blast made the kids leap out of the way as though I were firing a machine-gun. I was no more than ten feet away when they realized they had been had, but by that time, I was doing thirty miles an hour.

• *Making turns on a bicycle* is a bit different than in an automobile. If there is traffic around, you should, of course, signal turns. A left turn from a busy street or at a busy intersection can be made in two ways. The safest method is to cross the street to the other side of the intersection, stop and wait for the light to turn, and walk across with pedestrians. This is the way children should be taught to cross. Never attempt to make a left turn from the right curb position; this is as bad as trying to turn left in a car from the right lane of a four-lane highway.

I prefer to make my left turns by moving to the center of the road as I approach the intersection, signaling my intention, and making sure traffic will permit this move. I either make my left turn at once, if coming traffic will permit, or I wait at the intersection until the traffic clears. If the traffic is extremely heavy, I go to the far side of the intersection, wait until traffic clears, and turn left in the pedestrian cross-lane. Again, letting a truck run interference on a left turn is a good protective measure.

• *About clothing.* Clothing worn on any type of bicycle trip should, ideally, be brightly colored. International orange is a good color if it's a bright, clear shade; a light windbreaker of this color is ugly but ideal. You can also buy jackets made of light-reflective or light-phosphorescent safety orange of the color you see on traffic police gloves, school crossing-guide belts, or roadworkers' vests. For availability, check with any safety supply store listed in the classified directory of the telephone book. These phosphorescent vests glow when light strikes them, so they are particularly useful at night.

I always wear gloves when cycling. One fall without gloves removed some skin from the palm of my hand and taught me never to go out without gloves of some sort. If your bicycle has tubular tires, you should wear Italian cycling gloves in the summer and ski mittens in the winter. Italian gloves have double thick palms so that you can reach down and brush off any glass or other impedimenta your tires may have picked up. It's a good idea to do this whenever you think you have run over something that could cause a flat. I prefer ski mittens to ski gloves for winter cycling because mittens are much warmer, yet not too bulky for gripping brake levers.

WINTER CYCLING COMFORT

The only mystery to winter cycling that appears to puzzle noncyclists is how to keep warm. Feet particularly seem to be a problem. I do a lot of riding in all weather, and as the temperature drops I pile on more clothes, starting with thermal underwear.

Some years ago I conceived the brilliant idea that if the electrically (battery-) heated socks sold in sporting goods stores solved the cold-feet problem for hunters, football spectators, hikers, and the like, surely they could be ideal for winter cyclists too.

I have been wearing these socks for three years now, and I find they work well. Of the brands I've used, the "Rechargeable Electric" socks made by Northern Electric Company, 5224 North Kedzie Avenue, Chicago, Illinois 60625, seem to work best. The socks use a rechargeable battery which, at full charge, will last for four hours. The battery itself can be recharged about eighteen times, which gives you something like seventy-two hours of warm feet. The socks, with battery, battery carrying case and battery charger cost around $25.00 and are available from sporting goods stores. Your feet are the part of your body which is most vulnerable to cold, yet feet are used the most in cycling. Warm feet make a happy cyclist.

The next best foot warmer to electric socks is a pair of double-layer thermal socks intended for skiing, and a pair of lightweight, fleece-lined low-cut boots such as "Hush-Puppies."

The ideal shoes for winter cycling, of course, would be the weather-proof and fleece-lined short boots, made with reinforced inner soles for cycling. Conventional summer cycling shoes are made this way, with four-point steel shank supports to minimize foot fatigue over long distances. I have not been able to locate a winter cycling shoe in the United States, but after a good deal of searching and correspondence with European sources, I finally found one.

The winter cycling boot I like is a short boot, chukka style, completely fleece lined, including the inner sole and uppers. The entire shoe is water-proofed, has a medium heel, and is cut and styled to permit free ankle movement. This little boot costs, with duty and postage, about $15.00— a reasonable price for warm feet in cold-weather cycling, in my opinion. These shoes can be obtained from W. F. Holdsworth, Ltd., 132 Lower Richmond Road, Putney, S.W. 15, England.

ABOUT IMPORTING PARTS

Occasionally I have mentioned an overseas source for bicycle components and accessories, but I have only done this when no domestic supplier carries a specific item. This does not mean that I could encourage anyone to buy everything from overseas suppliers. Unless you live in a port-of-entry or near one, and can go down to the dock and clear the item through customs yourself, you probably will find that hiring a broker to handle all the paperwork for you will involve brokerage charges as great, or greater than, the cost of the item itself. Stick to domestic suppliers when you possibly can, unless you are planning a trip overseas. Then you can order by mail for personal pickup in the country of origin.

For the hands, double-palmed ski mittens are about as warm as electrically heated gloves. The rest of a good winter cycling outfit consists of Italian-made wool shorts with chamois lining in the crotch, overlaid with thermal underwear, followed by a cotton track suit. A sweater or two and a leather jacket, a hard helmet with earflaps or a knit cap with ear muffs, and a scarf complete the outfit.

What about snow? You can ride in snow if you're careful. For winter snow cycling I use 27-inch x 1¼-inch tires rather than thinner tubulars. The thicker and wider tread gives a bit more road-holding stability. Of course, this means a complete change of wheels, because tubulars and tube tires are not interchangeable on the same rim.

Do not ride on light snow with ice underneath, or on ice-covered streets. You can ride in snow until it gets up to about two inches deep, after which the going gets a bit rough. The roads are usually plowed soon after most snowfalls, so if you get up early enough in the morning, you can ride down the center of the road until traffic becomes heavy.

RIDING IN THE RAIN

Riding in the rain can be fun if you're equipped for it. When I think it's going to rain, I take along a light rain outfit, cape, or poncho.

Cycling in the rain is safe enough if you don't try to take corners too fast. Pavements are especially slippery when the rain has just begun to fall. In the autumn, when leaves begin to drop, remember that the only thing slicker than wet leaves is wet ice. You can take a rather nasty spill if you try to cut around a corner fast and run into a patch of wet leaves.

Remember, too, that you are going to be less visible to motorists when it's raining or snowing. Therefore, you should be doubly careful to stay away from high-traffic streets and roads, to listen for oncoming traffic, and to be alert at all times.

An inexpensive pair of light blue or yellow sunglasses will keep rain out of your eyes, if you don't wear glasses. I prefer light yellow glasses; they make dark days look a lot cheerier.

WATCH OUT FOR STORM SEWERS

Storm sewers with grated street covers are a little-recognized but very real hazard in city cycling, particularly in suburbs. Many makes of these drains are designed with sufficient width between the grating members to permit a bicycle wheel to drop down between them (Fig. 2). Some of these gratings are round, and it would be a simple matter to have them all turned with the grating perpendicular to the curb. This danger should be pointed out to the city street and road commissioner, or a similar official.

If the grating is not round or square, and the openings are parallel to

Fig. 2: *This is how you can get hurt on the grated storm sewer covers found in many cities in the United States. If you or your children should happen to run into such a storm sewer grating, be sure to get the name of the grating manufacturer for use by your attorney. Many large bridges have similar hazards in the form of an expansion joint, that is, the point at which road meets bridge.*

the curb, the best thing to do is to inform the police or fire department, or whichever local agency issues bicycle permits, so those who apply for bicycle licenses can be warned about the danger. A cyclist going at fifteen or twenty miles an hour can be seriously injured if his front wheel drops into a storm-sewer grating.

BRIDGE EXPANSION JOINT HAZARDS

I found myself in a predicament similar to the sewer-grating situation on my first trip over the bridge between Detroit and Windsor, Canada. I didn't notice it going over, because I had a bad head wind and was going fairly slow. But on the way back, with a strong tail wind, a steep hill, and the bridge arched down to meet the land, I barely had time to swing my wheel to the slight angle needed to avoid dropping the wheel between the bars of a grated expansion joint, where two sections of the bridge meet. Afterward, Gene Portuesi, former Olympic team cycling coach, told me that on the day the bridge opened many years ago, unsuspecting cyclists were thrown and hurt when they passed over this grating at high speed.

So, watch out for expansion joints on bridges, especially suspension bridges over wide rivers. *These joints usually run the entire width of the bridge.*

COUNTRY RIDING

Never, but never, ride on freeways, toll roads, or major arterial highways. I know there are a number of touring cyclists who argue that it is perfectly safe to cycle on interstate highways because the shoulder is broad enough to keep them away from the main traffic stream. No doubt this is true—the shoulder is wide enough, and it is paved. The trouble is that should an accident occur anywhere near you at the seventy-mile-an-hour-plus speeds common to interstate routes, you could be involved. At those speeds, it would take only a passing brush by a motor vehicle to send you spinning off into the wild blue yonder. Also, highway shoulders are frequently littered with broken glass and other hazardous material.

There are other tips on country cycling in the chapter on touring (pages 122-43). Here, let me just say that you should plan your route using roads parallel to main routes. You will be amazed at how well paved many of the less-used back-country roads are, and these roads have little traffic and almost all the beauty. In general, avoid any road bearing a state or federal route number. Many states have cross-state bicycle routes, which are simply hand-picked, well-paved roads bearing little motor traffic. (See Chapter 7.)

If you have to ride on dirt roads, be very careful about cornering on sandy or pebbly surfaces, watch out for potholes that can send you sprawling and bend a wheel, and keep your eyes and ears open for on-coming traffic.

Country riding does have one special hazard: people who habitually drive on back-country roads are almost never alert for cyclists, or, for that matter, for any other traffic. Consider the sight of a silo or a barn to be a danger signal, and be alert for a truck or tractor to come right out on the highway from a hidden intersection, without regard for oncoming traffic, including cyclists. Farmers seem to regard the roads in front of their homes as their personal driveways, and they are prone to drive in and out of their property as though no other traffic exists.

On any country road, whether paved or not, keep your ears open for traffic coming in either direction. It's quiet in the country, and you can hear motor vehicles coming from at least a mile away. And on dusty dirt roads, you can often see as well as hear evidence of approaching traffic. Rural drivers may be on any part of the road as they approach you, so if you have just rounded a corner and you hear a car coming up fast behind you, either stay on the far right side of the road or ride well to the left, on the shoulder, to let the car by. If you're cresting a hill, keep alert to traffic behind you. After you pass the crest, if there is no oncoming traffic, cross to the left side of the road for a block or so, so upcoming cars won't zoom over the hill into you, since your presence cannot be observed below the crest.

Rural Intersections

Where two rural roads meet, any stop signs generally are not observed, so be prepared to stop as you approach intersections. Be aware, at all times, of the surrounding territory so that you will know the best place to go to steer yourself out of trouble.

For example, if as you approached an intersection a car suddenly shot out at you from the right, where could you go? There's usually a ditch at these intersections, with little or no shoulder. Or, if there is no other traffic, you could cross the lane or even make a 180-degree turn.

If you're with a group of cyclists, it's wise to have an experienced rider at both ends of the line. The rear cyclist can listen for and size up potential hazards from oncoming traffic, and the lead rider can analyze the situation from up front, such as intersections, approaching traffic, curves, and hills.

If you're cycling in mountainous terrain, or plan such a trip, double check the maintenance of brakes beginning on page 250. Be sure your brake cables are in good shape, brake blocks are fresh and new, and brakes properly adjusted, with levers where you can grab them quickly.

RADIOS NOT RECOMMENDED

Because ears as well as eyes must be used in any type of cycling, I definitely do not recommend listening to a radio while cycling. I have seen cyclists pedaling along with a tiny earpiece plugged into one ear, completely oblivious to the sound of traffic around them. A radio takes away from cycling enjoyment, in any case. In the country especially, how can one possibly enjoy the sound of the wind and the birds, or simply the wonderful silence, when a radio is on?

SAFETY TIPS FOR YOUNGSTERS

The following tips could save your child from serious injury or worse. Insist that he or she learn these rules and observe them without exception:

- Ride only on streets where cycling is permitted, never on streets where signs say cycling is not allowed.
- Never ride on a street unless there are parked cars in evidence, and then watch out for car doors opening in front of you.
- Never ride at night without a good headlight and a good tail-light.

The rear light should be visible to motorists from two to three blocks away. Your bicycle should also be equipped with a two-to-three-inch-diameter reflector.

- Brakes should always be in good working condition.
- Always signal your turns. Left arm straight out with index finger straight out means left turn; left arm straight up means right turn.
- At street intersections, give everyone the right of way, including cars, trucks, buses, and people.
- Never turn left, while mounted, at a *busy* intersection, or at one where there is a stoplight. *Always* dismount, walk to the far side of the street, across the intersection, wait till the light turns, and *walk* your bicycle across in the pedestrian lane.
- Obey all stoplights, stop signs, and other road signs, just as though you were driving a car.
- *Never* try to hitch a ride by holding onto a truck. You never know which way the truck will turn or how suddenly it will stop. Trucks often have air brakes that enable them to stop so fast that you would not be able to hold on. If the truck stops that quickly, there is probably an emergency reason which would also apply to you. The truck driver may not realize you are hanging on, and brush you against an object such as a parked car.
- Never ride two on a bicycle unless you have a tandem. Riding two on a bicycle built for one makes it hard to see where you are going, hard to stop, and easy to spill.
- Always go *with* the traffic, not against it. When you ride along with the traffic, you give the drivers of cars behind you a better chance to steer out of your way, and they're more likely to see you than if you unexpectedly appear in front of them going the wrong way.
- Steer straight; don't weave all over the street; stay close to parked cars at all times.
- *Don't fool around on a bicycle.* Many boys and girls think it's fun to rear the bicycle back on the rear wheel and go off down the street with the front wheel off the ground. Fun and games and trick riding on a bicycle can be dangerous if you are thrown off balance into the path of a car, or if you fall and strike your head on a concrete curb. You can have fun on small-wheeled bicycles, because they're so maneuverable, but I would advise playing bike polo or bike hockey only on a school parking lot.

ABOUT DOGS AND OTHER ANIMALS

A dog may be man's best friend when both are afoot, but there's something about a man on a bicycle that brings out the worst in a dog. For years I have been wondering what it is about a man on a bicycle that turns friendly dogs into snarling beasts. Perhaps the bicycle emits some infuriatingly high-pitched sound that only a dog can hear. Or it may simply occur to the dog that he has a human being at a disadvantage.

Whatever the reason, you should always be on the alert for an attack by a dog of any size, shape, and description, at any time, in any place. I find myself reacting instantly to the tinkle of a dog collar and watching shrubbery and front yards in the suburbs and farm yards. All dogs are potential enemies. In the country, you can usually outrun a dog, which is the best advice I can give you, if this is possible. But if the dog comes at you from the front, or cuts across a yard as you round a corner, you might be in for a bad bite.

The dog problem is a serious one for cyclists, and it occupies a lot of space in bicycling magazines published in both this country and abroad. Reviewing the experience of a number of cyclists, the best defense, if you are not able to get away, seems to be a slender whip fastened to the handlebar stem, somewhat like an old-fashioned buggy whip. A cyclist can have it in his hand in an instant. One quick blow across a dog's nose will make even the most vicious animal think twice about further pursuit.

You can also buy a small aerosol spray can of "dog repellent" for about $2.00 from most hardware stores, which can shoot a thin stream of chemical about ten feet. The active ingredient in the spray is Oleoresin Capsicum, a pepper derivative. The trouble with this protection is that by the time you fish the can out of your pocket, aim it, and press the button, you could already be bitten. However, if you have time to stop, and the dog is close enough, the spray will discourage him from any further interest in you. Incidentally, although the effects are potent, there is no permanent damage done to the animal.

The old adage that barking dogs don't bite cannot be trusted, I have found, but, be doubly suspicious of the dog that comes up to you silently and stands there looking at you. He's just waiting for you to get back on the bicycle so he can get you at a disadvantage. A friend of mine who is an experienced cyclist spent two months in the hospital because of just such an incident. One evening she was cycling alone about thirty miles from home. A snarling dog chased her down a dead-end street, where she dismounted. The owner of the dog was in his yard nearby, but made no move to call the animal back. The dog waited until my friend had climbed back on the bicycle and, as she was mounting sank his teeth in her calf, penetrating all the way to the bone, through heavy jeans. Not realizing how serious the bite was, my friend rode home and attempted to treat it herself. By the time she got to her doctor, the wound was so badly infected that she not only had to be hospitalized for two months, but she has suffered minor but permanent impairment of leg movement, which affects her riding ability.

My heart goes out to children who are chased by dogs and badly frightened—or bitten. Most cities do not permit dogs to be at large anymore; they have to be either tied up or penned in the yard. In the country, of course, farm dogs are seldom tied and are almost always ready and willing to attack the passing cyclist.

To avoid a painful series of rabies inoculations, if you are bitten, remember to try to find out who owns the offending animal. Your child should be instructed to do the same thing if he is bitten. A dog will usually run home after an assault, and if you can manage it, and there is no one in the immediate vicinity who can tell you who owns the animal, try to follow it home. You can then warn the owner to keep the dog locked up for the period of time recommended by your doctor. If at the end of that time the dog has not developed rabies, you or your child will not need rabies shots.

If you are in the country and are bitten, and you cannot follow the animal to its home, try to memorize what he looks like: his size, shape, markings, and general appearance. A neighbor in the vicinity may recognize your description and help you locate the dog and avoid rabies inoculations.

In any case, if you are bitten by a dog, *always* get immediate treatment as soon as possible from a doctor. Then call the dog warden and your lawyer, in that order. You have all the legal redress in the world, because people should keep a dog that will attack a cyclist under restraint. Even if you yourself aren't bitten, you will be doing a favor to the rest of the cycling fraternity if you take note of the address where the chase began as the probable home of the animal, and call the dog warden as soon as you get home. I think dogs attack out of a sense of duty, feeling that the territory around their house is their exclusive property.

Other animals sometimes bite, too, though more rarely than dogs. Squirrels, woodchucks, and raccoons, if they think they are cornered, or are crazed by rabies, will bite. If you can't immediately kill an animal who bites you, and I don't see how you can do this from a bicycle, you are probably in for a series of rabies inoculations. But do try to kill these pests if you can. You will save yourself the ordeal of injections if the animal is not rabid, and prevent the spread of rabies if it is. A doctor can quickly analyze a carcass for rabies.

If you camp out on a bicycle tour, observe all the usual precautions about snakes and other animals. Keep a simple first-aid kit with you. If you fall, clean your scratches and cuts with tap water from a canteen or flask, and apply antiseptic ointment. Then bandage lightly. If the cut did not cause a lot of bleeding or sever a muscle, there's no need to end the trip or wait for the wound to heal. If you want to cycle-tour, you'll have to get used to a few bumps and bruises and take them in stride.

CARRYING A CHILD SAFELY

There are a number of good seats especially designed to permit you to carry a small child on a bicycle, as long as he can sit up. Be sure to use a seat that is fitted with side rails and a restraining strap. (See pages 197-98 in the chapter on accessories for full details on child seats.)

A word of caution: I do not recommend a child-carrier seat that fastens to the handlebars. The weight of a child on the handlebars creates a dangerously unbalanced bicycle and makes accurate steering practically impossible. In the event of an accident, the child has no protection. When the child is in a rear-wheel carrier, you are between him and any object ahead.

What I have noted about carrying a child also applies to packages. Use baskets or panniers to lug groceries or carry gear on a trip. If you must carry more than will fit into your carriers, be sure to use a bag especially designed to fit handlebars, with a front spring-clip carrier to support its weight. (See pages 130-31.)

CYCLING SAFETY STATISTICS

The nationwide statistics on bicycle accidents that follow come from the National Safety Council.

Country More Dangerous than City

In the United States, in 1967, there were 750 fatalities as a result of collisions between bicycles and motor vehicles (up 10 percent from 1966). Four hundred of these accidents occurred in urban areas, 350 in the country. Considering that there are vastly greater numbers of both bicycles and motor vehicles in the city than the country, the fact that the accident rate is nearly the same in both locations points up the greater danger involved in country cycling. Rural bicycle–motor vehicle collision fatalities were up 15 percent in 1967, over 1966, whereas urban accidents of this nature rose only 4 percent during this period.

Children More Accident-Prone than Adults

In 1964, 34,000 cyclists were injured more or less seriously in nonfatal accidents. Of the 690 fatalities in that year, two-thirds of the deaths and four-fifths of the injuries were among children five to fourteen years old, and 15 percent were in the fifteen-to-twenty-four-year age group.

Where and When Accidents Occur

According to a National Safety Council Survey, instances of collisions between vehicles and bicycles occurred about as follows:

- Well over half at intersections.
- Seven out of ten during daylight hours.
- Four-fifths involved a violation on the part of the motor vehicle operator.
- One out of five bicycles involved had some mechanical defect.

Most common traffic violations by bicyclists are:

- Failure to yield right of way. (In most cases, the cyclist did not see the car; in others, he simply infringed on the motorist's right of way.)
- Riding in the center of the street.
- Speed too fast for conditions.
- Disregard of traffic control devices.
- Riding against the flow of traffic.
- Improper turning.

Injuries, not involving motor vehicles, were caused by falls on ice or otherwise slippery or bumpy roads, or by a defective mechanical condition of the bicycle, improper use of the bicycle, and/or overloading.

3

SO YOU WANT TO
BUY A BICYCLE!

Now you've made up your mind. You want to buy a bicycle. But what *kind* of bicycle should you get? New or secondhand? Coaster brakes or caliper brakes? A three-speed "racer" (Fig. 3) or one of those fancy jobs with turned-down handlebars (Fig. 4) and lots of gears and things hanging from the rear wheel? Where should you buy your bicycle? Do you go to a discount house or a bike shop? How about a take-apart bicycle (see Fig. 22, page 81)—handy to store in the trunk of the car, neat, too—very "camp." And how can you tell a top-grade bicycle from a piece of junk that will give you nothing but trouble and needless expense?

This is going to be a difficult chapter for me to write. I have tried everything—the cheap new three-speed, the better new three-speed, the really expensive three-speed "English racer," and the moderately priced ten-speed turned-down handlebar job. I have finally found the only bi-

Fig. 3: *Three-speed bicycle, the so-called "English racer," which it definitely isn't.*

Fig. 4: *This ultra lightweight bicycle is popular with many cycling fans.*

cycle I can live with—the best one money can buy (but not the most expensive). I would have saved a lot of money, and enjoyed cycling a lot more from the beginning, had I not had to learn from experience the shortcomings and deficiencies of all the various makes and models.

Over the years, I have tried all these bicycles, for both short and long trips. Now I know that I would never invest in anything but a good quality ten-speed or, for long trips and in mountainous country, fifteen-speed bicycle, with turned-down "racing" handlebars.

But I don't want to scare you away from cycling altogether, or have you put down this book right now and write me off as just another cycling nut. I must confess that, at first, the idea of paying $120.00 to $180.00 for a bicycle with dropped handlebars, complicated gears, and apparently flimsy wheels and frame seemed to me to be sheer madness. But I want to tell you immediately that if you intend to get serious about cycling, for health, for the pure pleasure of getting out of doors, or for family trips and touring, you will eventually wind up paying *at least* $120.00 for a new ten-speed machine. I recommend therefore, that you seriously consider this purchase now. Cycling as a fun thing to do may not appeal to you at first, but I warn you, once you start, you'll more than likely be bitten by the bug.

Today, almost 60 million Americans own bicycles and, presumably, ride them occasionally. Bicycle sales practically doubled between 1960 and 1966. According to the Bicycle Institute of America, sales rose from 3.8 million bicycles in 1960 to 6 million in 1966. It looks like bike sales are going up a lot faster than the rate of population increase.

Part of this upward trend in bike sales can be attributed to the publicity surrounding President Eisenhower's first heart attack, and subsequent statements by his physician, Dr. Paul Dudley White, who encourages daily bicycle riding to promote good health (see the chapter on health for a full discussion, pages 11-19).

I am convinced that the 35 percent of the bicycles sold today to adults are purchased mainly for health reasons. And there's no telling how many grown-ups sneak their child's balloon-tired monster out of the garage and wheeze it around the block a few times an evening. But this type of cycling—on the heavy, rusty, rattling monstrosity that passes for a bicycle in America—may keep you from truly enjoying cycling, which is the best argument for you to try this growing sport on a good machine.

But you may not want a bike for yourself. You might want to buy one for your child. What type, size, and make should you buy? Far too often I have seen children completely frustrated by a bicycle that is too large, too complicated, and too unwieldy for their age and physique. A ten-year-old should not be expected to be able to mount and ride a twenty-six-inch wheel, three-speed, caliper-brake (handlebar-mounted brake levers) machine. The frame is too big for him to get up on the saddle easily, and when he does, he can't reach the pedals. And once in motion, he can't stop because he's too weak to grasp the brake handles.

Further on in this chapter (Table I, pages 52-53), you will find a selection of bicycles for children from ages five to twelve, based on size, design, and price. But first, let's look at a few problems that are common to any bicycle purchase.

WHERE TO BUY A BICYCLE

First, let me recommend categorically that you buy a bicycle *only* in a bicycle store. Let me tell you why. I have spent a good many hours examining bicycles in discount shops and department stores. Although you *can* save a few dollars in such places, chances are that if the bike's not a cheap brand that will fall apart within a year, you will spend far more time getting it ready to ride than you will have saved.

For one, I have never seen a skilled bicycle mechanic on duty in a discount or department store. The assembly job that store clerks do is mute testimony to this fact. Wheels are badly out of line, caliper brakes unworkable, and handlebars askew. If the bicycle on display is the best the store's "mechanic" can do, then what will the bicycle you buy be like, if the store assembles it for you? And if the store does not assemble it for you, and it comes "almost fully assembled" in a carton, you will have a long, difficult task ahead when you try to put the bicycle into riding condition.

To prove my point, I am going to tell you what happened when I chose, at random, a "fully assembled" cartoned bicycle from the stock of a discount house, indicating the time I spent making it ready for the road. (Remember, I can work a bit faster on bikes than the average person; I have the correct tools, some experience, and a lot of interest.) Here is what I found in the carton:

- Frame and fenders covered with protective gum tape, which I had to remove. (eight minutes)
- Front wheel badly out of alignment. One spoke nipple stripped, spoke loose. Had to remove tire, replace broken spoke, replace tire, realign wheel. (thirty minutes, including trip to bike shop for new spoke)
- Front-wheel hub cones binding, wheel hard to turn. Readjusted hub cones. (fifteen minutes)
- Rear wheel badly out of alignment; realigned. (fifteen minutes)
- Gear-shift handle not installed. Gear-shift cable not installed. Rear three-speed hub not adjusted because cable not installed. Installed and adjusted gear shift and cable. (twenty minutes)
- Fenders not installed, (fifteen minutes)
- Front light not installed; no batteries. (eight minutes)
- Pedals on backward. Normal for shipment, but had to remove and reinstall correctly. (eight minutes)
- Caliper brakes not set correctly. (ten minutes)
- Bottom bracket (crank) bearings binding; chainwheel turned tightly. Readjusted bottom bracket cone. (six minutes)

- Front fork binding. Readjusted headset cone. (five minutes)
- Handlebars and seat not adjusted for rider. (fifteen minutes)

Assembly time totaled two hours and forty minutes, which, at $7.50 an hour, the going rate for bicycle mechanics, amounts to nearly $20.00.

Bicycle stores, on the other hand, will sell you a bike that is fully assembled and ready to ride safely. And if it isn't in tip-top shape, there's always a trained mechanic on hand to fix it. In addition, under the warrantee you can always take a bicycle back to a bicycle store for small adjustments. Department and discount stores cannot honor a warrantee because usually they have no one on hand to repair a bike.

Further on in this chapter I am going to give you pointers on what to look for when you buy a new bicycle, in terms of both quality and the method for checking, to make sure all is in good working order before you leave the store.

ALL ABOUT FRAMES

This information on frames is rather technical, but it will be valuable for the cycling enthusiast who wants to get the best possible frame construction.

Bicycle frames are made of a number of different kinds of steels and tubing. The garden-variety, inexpensive, coaster-brake or three-speed bicycle is usually made of seamed tubing—a strip of steel wrapped into tubular form by rollers and then automatically welded electrically into a tube. Such tubing is straight gauge, meaning that it is not reinforced where it joins other parts of the bicycle. Typically, the tubes of this type of frame are simply stuck into each other and welded at the joints. The problem with a frame of this sort is that electric welding is done at high temperatures, which causes stresses at the joints that can weaken them. Simply sticking frame members into each other and welding them makes the weakest type of frame construction. Unfortunately, the vast majority of bicycles are made this way.

The best bicycles are made with Reynolds double-butted, cold-drawn, seamless manganese-molybdenum steel. This tubing combines lightness with high strength and resistance to "fatigue," and high tensility for maximum resilience with a feeling of "liveliness" in the frame.

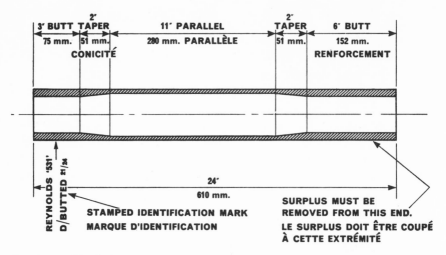

Fig. 5: *Best bicycle frames are made of Reynolds "531" double-butted tubing, shown here. See Figure 16 for a complete description of various types of Reynolds "531" tubing.*

The average cyclist cannot tell if a frame is double-butted just by looking at it. Double-butting means that the metal is thickened at both ends where maximum stress occurs, without changing the outside diameter of the metal tube (Fig. 5).

There are a number of different combinations of Reynolds "531" tubing, so a Reynolds decal on a frame does not necessarily mean that it is a superior bicycle. Read the label or decal carefully to know exactly what you are buying.

Here is what the various Reynolds labels or decals (Fig. 16, page 66) mean:

The label that says "Reynolds '531' Frame Tubing" means that the top tube, seat tube, and down tube are made of Reynolds "531" plain gauge (*not* double-butted) steel.

The decal or label that says "Guaranteed built with Reynolds '531' plain gauge tubes, forks, and stays" means that all the tubing in the frame is Reynolds "531" *plain* gauge (*not* double-butted) steel.

The decal that says "Guaranteed built with Reynolds '531' butted frame tubes" means that the top, seat, and down tubes of the frame are of Reynolds "531" double-butted tubing.

The label that says "Guaranteed built with Reynolds '531' butted tubes, forks, and stays" means that the frame is all Reynolds double-butted. This is the most costly and best frame you can buy. But even this type of frame is not the best possible one unless it is welded properly, and finest quality, precision-made, hand-filled lugs are used.

The Reynolds manufacturer specifies that the best welding is done by hand, using low-temperature bronze brazing materials with a melting point no higher than 850 degrees Centigrade. Look for bicycle frame specifications that say "all-lugged, low-temperature, bronze-brazed" or words to that effect. High-temperature brazing makes joints brittle at the point of stress, which can negate the good tensile qualities of the Reynolds steel.

HOW TO CHECK YOUR NEW BICYCLE'S CONDITION

Whether you buy a new or a used bicycle, there are certain things you should look for to make sure the bicycle will be safe to ride and will give you reasonable satisfaction. Gene Portuesi, who has his own bicycle shop in Cadillac, Michigan, says that even top-quality imported machines must be removed from their cartons, assembled, adjusted, and then disassembled and repacked before shipment to the customer.

Points for you to check are:

Wheels: Spin wheels. Put a finger or pencil on the frame while wheels turn; watch for out-of-roundness. Pay no attention to tire, watch rim only. Wheels should be perfectly true from both side-to-side and concentrically as to roundness. In checking display bicycles, I found that 90 percent of them had wheels out of round.

Spokes: "Pluck" spokes or "twing" them as you would strings on a guitar. Spokes should give about the same musical pitch all around, and should show the same degree of tightness. Even if wheels are aligned, loose spokes will cause them to go out of round soon.

Hubs: Spin wheel slowly. Wheel should come to a stop gradually. Put wheel with valve at three o'clock position and let go. Wheel should move clockwise under weight of valve alone. If wheel stops suddenly or won't move under weight of valve, hub cone needs readjustment.

Grasp wheel between fingers and, holding the bicycle frame firmly, move wheel from side to side. If wheel has side play, hub cones are too loose.

Brakes: Test coaster brakes on an actual ride. They should grab enough under back pressure to make wheel skid.

Check caliper hand brakes. Brake block should grab wheel rim squarely and evenly. When hand lever is released, brake blocks should be clear of rim sides and not rub. Test on a ride, trying front and rear brake alone. Each should show about the same degree of braking ability. Levers should be adjusted to fit your hand (cable adjustment). Brakes should stop evenly and smoothly, even when gripped tightly, and should not "shudder" or grip unevenly.

Gears: See trouble-shooting section on both hub gears and derailleur (ten-speed gears on pages 259 and 234.) A bicycle should exhibit none of the defects listed and should operate smoothly through all the gear changes. Make sure gear hub is lubricated before riding because oil evaporates in storage and in transit.

Frame: Sight down fork and frame for alignment. Check frame where fork goes through; look at the paint. If paint is wrinkled slightly where top tube and steering head meet, the bicycle has been in an accident and frame has probably been bent. Wrinkled paint indicates metal movement under stress, such as collision with a brick wall.

Fenders: Should be on tight and not rattle. Try a road test. In fact, on a road test nothing should rattle, and when you coast over a bumpy road all you should hear from the bicycle is the sound of the wind in your ears and the slight click of the freewheel pawls from the rear, as you coast.

Chainwheel and bottom bracket: Check bottom bracket adjustment by slipping chain off chainwheel and spinning the assembly. Chainwheel should come to a stop gradually, move easily and freely. It should not come to a stop suddenly, or "bind." Have someone hold the frame steady and push cranks from side to side. You should be able to feel or see no side play. If any of these defects are present, the bottom bracket cone should be readjusted. (See pages 286-90 for more information.)

Pedals: Should turn freely, not bind, and should have no side play.

Handlebars and Saddle: Should be adjusted to fit the rider, and be tight. (See pages 91 and 99 for details on fitting.)

General check: Just because a bicycle, of any make or model, is brand new, right out of a crate, and you have bought it from a bicycle dealer, you have no guarantee that nothing can go wrong (or is wrong) with it.

The sad fact is that you or your bicycle dealer *must* check *every* bolt, nut, cable adjustment, derailleur adjustment, and everything else that can come loose or go out of whack, before you ride the new bicycle out of the shop. This is true regardless of *how* much the bicycle costs or *what* make it is.

Let me give you an example. Recently I bought a fine, rather costly, derailleur-equipped bicycle expressly designed for touring. After giving it a most cursory inspection, I set off on a short trip. After a few miles, while I strained up a steep hill, the chain suddenly slipped off the center of the three chainwheels. I was mildly annoyed at the time, but if I had given it proper thought, I would have stopped cycling right there and walked home. (A chain does not simply slip off the center chainwheel! Off the smaller or larger wheel, possibly, if the front derailleur is maladjusted. But slipping off the center chainwheel meant that something was drastically wrong.) All I did, however, was slip the chain back on the wheel (which was rather difficult because it had gotten firmly wedged between the center and outer chainwheel). About fifty feet farther, the chain slipped off again. This time I studied the chainwheel closely, and I found, to my horror, that a center bolt, spacer, and nut had fallen out entirely in two places out of the five, and the other three bolts were loose. This time the chain was wedged in firmly, and the center chainwheel was badly warped from the wedge pressure of the chain.

To give you another example, a friend of mine rode a brand-new expensive bicycle out of a showroom, and after cycling about five miles, the rear derailleur cable had slipped right out of the derailleur cable clamp. The clamp bolt had fallen out as well, which meant a long ride home over hills in top gear.

These are trivial mechanical troubles in the showroom, but on the road, they can spoil a trip. Replacement parts can be obtained only in the bike shops specializing in high-quality bicycles. Parts for these machines are almost always made in Europe and nuts are threaded on the metric standard. So check *everything* before you leave the bicycle store.

One final word of advice. If the mechanic needs any special tools to remove the freewheel or adjust the derailleur, for example, buy the tool while you are in the shop. (See pages 231-233 for a list of tools you should always carry.)

THE CHILD AND THE BICYCLE

It is very important to fit a bicycle to a child—to buy him one that fits him, and that he can handle safely and pedal easily. Beyond that, you should consider how much bicycle you get for your money, and here it is very easy to go wrong.

To help you make the right decision, I have carefully examined and reviewed the specifications of dozens of makes of bicycles, ending up with a selection of those makes that I believe represent the most bicycle for the least money. There are less expensive bicycles on the market, but the models I have recommended will, with reasonable care, greatly outlast less costly makes. For this reason, it is worth investing a few dollars more.

Table I (pages 52-53) gives you bicycle selections for the five-to-seven, seven-to-nine, and nine-to-twelve-year-old child, respectively. Models for both boys and girls are included. But before you buy a bicycle, I urge you to study the following general recommendations for type of bicycle by age group. They will help you understand why the particular models in each table were selected.

Children from Five to Seven

Because, with proper care, a relatively inexpensive bicycle can last for five or six years, even when subjected to the rigors of a child's use, it pays to ignore the toy-like fixed rear hub, solid tire bicycles and start with a fairly decent bicycle your child can grow with. (After all, the seat and handlebars can be raised as your child grows.)

For children aged five to seven, therefore, I recommend a 10- to 20-inch-wheel bicycle with a coaster brake (Fig. 6). Definitely do *not* get your small child a gear-shift bicycle with hand-lever caliper brakes. He hasn't the strength to operate either, and you'll only frustrate him.

Fig. 6: *For the child from five to seven, this 20-inch-wheel bicycle with coaster brake is ideal.*

I also do not recommend that children from five to seven have a bicycle with "high-riser" handlebars. (In fact, I deplore high-rise handlebars for anybody; they're awkward, hard to use, and lead to an unbalanced situation, which makes them downright dangerous.)

You can start your child with training wheels. If he is five years old, he should not need them after about three or four weeks. If at first he can't reach the pedals, pedal blocks will help. (See Table I for a selection for children from age five to twelve.)

Remember, until your child is a mid-teenager (fourteen and up), a bicycle is basically a toy. If he wants a fake motorcycle engine, banana seat, or fake motorcycle tank, humor him. It's a cumbersome toy, but at least it's a safe one, if he stays off the street and rides on the sidewalk only. And 20-inch x 1¾-inch balloon tires can take quite a lot of punishment.

Children, thanks to grown-up advertising, think of a bicycle as something like an automobile; hence, bicycle manufacturers use names such as "Roadmaster," "Jet Pilot," and "Sport Shift." These bicycles should cost no more than $30.00 to $35.00.

Table 1 • Bicycles for Children

AGE CHILD	MAKE AND MODEL	SPECIFICATIONS	LIST PRICE (Approx.)
5–7 Boy	Schwinn "Skipper" Model L35-7	13½-in. seamed tubing frame. 20-in. x 1¾-in. tires. One-piece cranks, axle, and chainwheel. Training wheels (removable). Coaster brake.	$43.00
5–7 Girl	Schwinn L85-7 ("Lil' Miss")	Same as above, except girl's frame.	$43.00
5–7 Boy	Raleigh Mountie Model DL-79	Cantilever lugged and brazed 14-in. frame, 10-in. wheels. Coaster brake. Four-piece chainwheel, cranks, and axle.	$44.95
5–7 Girl	Raleigh Mountie Model DL-79L	Same as above, except girl's frame.	$44.95
5–7 Boy or Girl	Raleigh "Winkie" tricycle	No ordinary tricycle. Has chain drive, 16-in. wheels, ball bearings throughout, hand brake, and cushion tires. Has fenders on all three wheels, chain guard, kit bag, and basket. Ideal to pass down from one child to the next. Well worth the money.	$37.95
7–9 Boy	Schwinn "Typhoon" Model L 22-6	15½-in. frame, seamed tubing, 24-in. x 1¾-in. tires, coaster brake, and kickstand. One-piece axle, cranks, and chainwheel.	$47.00

7–9 Girl	Schwinn "Hollywood"	Same as above, except girl's frame.	$47.00
7–9 Boy	Raleigh DL-54 "Space Rider"	16-in. frame, lugged and brazed. 24-in. wheels, coaster brake, four-piece chainwheel, axle, cranks.	$48.00
7–9 Girl	Raleigh DL-54L "Space Rider"	Same as above, except girl's frame.	$48.00
9–12 Boy	Raleigh DL-58 "Colt"	Choice of 18-in. or 20-in. frame, lugged and brazed. 26-in. wheels. Coaster brake.	$59.95
9–12 Girl	Raleigh DL-58L "Colt"	18-in. frame only. Other specifications same as boy's model above.	$59.95
9–12 Boy	Schwinn L12-6 "Typhoon"	17½-in. cantilever frame. One-piece crank, axle, and chainwheel. 26-in. wheels. Kickstand. Chromed fenders.	$48.00

Touring and 10-Speed Models

12 and older, both boys and girls	See adults' bicycles. Children over 12 should be able to handle any adult bicycle with or without caliper brakes, three-speed hub, or even derailleur ten-speed.

Fig. 7: For children from seven to nine years of age, the 24-inch-wheel bicycle shown here, with balloon tires and coaster brake, is just right.

Children from Seven to Nine

For children from seven to nine, I recommend a 24-inch-wheel bicycle with 1¾-inch tires and coaster brakes on the rear wheel, as shown in Fig. 7. Such a bicycle should cost, at the most, about $55.00. You can find cheaper models, but the quality will be inferior, and if you have younger children who will want to use the bicycle later on, the better model will still be around when the first child graduates to something bigger.

Children from Nine to Twelve

The small, 20-inch frame, 26-inch-wheel bicycle with a three-speed rear hub and caliper brakes front and rear, is a nice little machine for the nine-to-twelve age group (Fig. 8). This bike should have 1¾-inch tires. Again, though, I'd avoid high-rise handlebars; they are really dangerous. Because hands must be raised elbow high to steer, good balance is hard to hold and the bicycle isn't easy to steer.

The 26-inch bicycle should cost no more than $48.00-$60.00.

Children from Twelve to Fifteen

I am assuming that your child is not particularly interested in cycling as a hobby or a sport, and that he still regards his bicycle as a toy and a regrettable substitute for a sports car. Chances are, if your child is like mine, he won't be seen dead on a bicycle after he gets into high school.

But he may still want one to get around the neighborhood. He may never go any farther on it than to school, the nearest candy store, or to a friend's house nearby. For this kind of cycling, and considering the fact that the teenager can't seem to learn to bring his bicycle in out of the rain, ride it gently over curbs, or otherwise treat it as a fine machine, the best route for you as the purchaser is (up to a limit) the least expensive.

I will assume that you want the bicycle to last longer than six months or a year. This means that you should plan to spend a bit more for it and get a fairly well-built machine.

For the average teenage child, the best bet is a 26-inch-wheel "tourist" bicycle with a three-speed rear hub and caliper brakes (Fig. 9). Tires should be 26-inch x 1⅜-inch wired-on tube type (see pages 205-28 for a discussion of tires). If your boy is going to carry a heavy load, however—if he's a newspaper boy, for example—better get him a bicycle with heavier, 26-inch x 1¾-inch tires.

Fig. 8: *This 26-inch-wheel, small-frame bicycle, with three-speed rear hub and caliper brakes front and rear, will suit children from nine to twelve.*

Fig. 9: *For the average teenager, the best bet is a 26-inch-wheel bicycle (with a frame size to suit his body—frames can vary from 19 inches to 24 inches), considering the solicitude with which so many teenagers treat mechanical possessions. Though far from a true racing bicycle, this machine is well built, sturdy, and fine for about-town use, though a bit heavy for longer trips.*

You can buy a new bicycle like the one described above, starting at $50.00 and for as high as $100.00.

A word about lights. If he's a teenager, you are not going to be able to keep your child off the streets after dark. Therefore, any bicycle you buy him should have a good front and a good rear light. I recommend the generator light for a child's bicycle because it eliminates the possibility of a dead battery. The generator is ready to provide light at all times. For the really fine bicycle, however, where long after-dark trips are involved, the matter of lights is a separate problem altogether. (See pages 194-96 for a discussion of lights.)

For a young person who has the inclination and the mechanical ability to take proper care of his bicycle, you might spend a bit more and buy him a five-speed derailleur bicycle for around $68.00 (Fig. 10). (See Table II, page 58.)

HOW TO FIT THE BICYCLE TO THE CHILD

Since twenty-six-inch-wheel bicycles come in a variety of frame sizes, ranging from eighteen inches to twenty-four inches, you should try to fit the bicycle to the child. By age fourteen, for example, your child will be almost fully grown, as far as his legs are concerned. The simplest way to fit a bicycle to a boy is to buy the largest size frame he can straddle comfortably with both feet on the ground and crotch over the top tube (the bar running from handlebars to seat). For a girl, buy the frame size that, with seat properly adjusted (see page 87), will permit her to get on and off the bicycle easily.

A WORD ABOUT QUALITY

There are several bicycle manufacturers in the United States, and large numbers of bikes are imported from England and Japan. It is interesting to note that there is quite a variety in quality, but not much difference in price, between domestic bicycles and imports. Let me tell you a few

Fig. 10: *There are some teenagers who take pride in their possessions and who will properly care for a good bicycle. For them, an inexpensive five-speed lightweight bicycle, as shown here, is a good investment.*

Table II • Top-Quality "Tourist" ("English Racer"-Type) Bicycles*

MAKE AND MODEL	SPECIFICATIONS	LIST PRICE (Approx.)
Schwinn Deluxe Racer (U.S.)	26-in. wheels, 26-in. x 1⅜-in. nylon tires. Three-speed Sturmey-Archer rear hub, handlebar trigger gear shift, side-pull caliper brakes. Frame sizes 19 in., 21 in., and 23 in. One-piece cranks. Men's and women's models.	$60.95
Raleigh "Superbe" (Great Britain)	Dynohub generator built into front-wheel hub, headlight, three-piece cranks, tail-light. Lock fork with keys, leather saddle. 26-in. wheels, 26-in. x 1⅜-in. tires. Caliper brakes. Brazed-up frame with cutaway lugs.	$79.95
Dunelt Model CM-26** (men's) or CL-26 (women's) (Great Britain)	Sturmey-Archer three-speed rear hub, trigger handlebar gear shift. 26-in. x 1⅜-in. tires, brazed-up frame with cutaway lugs, side-pull caliper brakes. Men's 21-in. and 23-in. frame sizes, women's in 19-in. size only.	$47.50
Raleigh "Tourist" Model DL-1 (for tall people) (Great Britain)	Special touring cycle for tall people. Specifications similar to Raleigh "Superbe" above, except has 24-in. frame in men's models and 22-in. frame in women's. Both frames come with 28-in. wheels. Only bicycle of its size available in U.S. (Caution: On special order only. Buy two extra sets of tires and tubes because 28-in. tires are ordinarily unavailable in U.S.)	$69.00
Peugeot "Steyr" (France)	Men's 21-in. and women's 19-in. frame only. Lugged and brazed-up frame. Four-piece crank, chainwheel, and axle assembly. Side-pull caliper brakes. Kickstand.	$50.00

* All have fenders and conventional handlebars.
** Available from most of the bicycle mail-order houses, if you can't find it locally (see page 317).

things to look for to help you select the best quality for the least money. (You can skip this section if you are interested in a really top-quality machine for long rides, club tours, and general cross-country cycling for pleasure and health, because none of the bicycles so far discussed are really suitable for this type of cycling. I will discuss quality in fine machines in detail further on.)

THE FRAME: Where frame tubes meet, they should be brazed into lugs at their joints (Fig. 11). Frame construction where tubes are inserted into each other (Fig. 12) is not nearly as strong as the lugged and brazed frame.

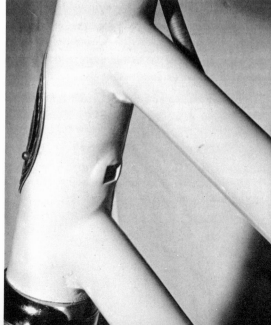

Fig. 11. *The hallmark of a good bicycle is a lugged frame, as shown here. A lug is a fitting into which frame tubes are fitted and brazed.*

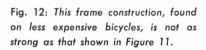

Fig. 12: *This frame construction, found on less expensive bicycles, is not as strong as that shown in Figure 11.*

CALIPER BRAKES: Presently most popular are the "center-pull" type (Fig. 13) rather than the "side-pull" (Fig. 14). Center-pull brakes have a wire attached to the center, and as the brake lever is squeezed, the brake arms and shoes close evenly. Side-pull brakes pull up from one side only.

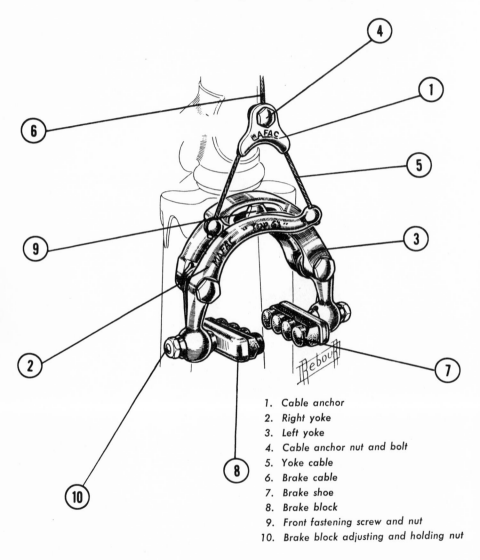

1. Cable anchor
2. Right yoke
3. Left yoke
4. Cable anchor nut and bolt
5. Yoke cable
6. Brake cable
7. Brake shoe
8. Brake block
9. Front fastening screw and nut
10. Brake block adjusting and holding nut

Fig. 13: The best type of brakes are of the center-pull design, because they stop more evenly.

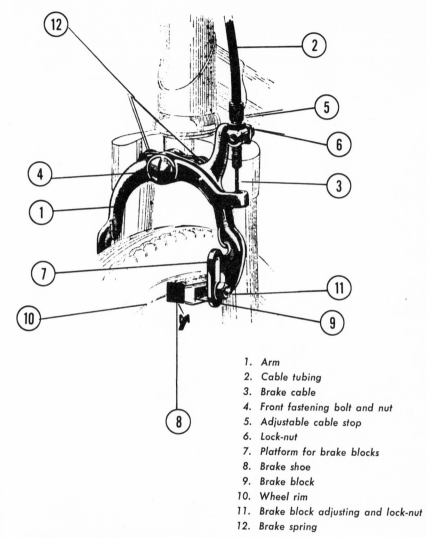

1. Arm
2. Cable tubing
3. Brake cable
4. Front fastening bolt and nut
5. Adjustable cable stop
6. Lock-nut
7. Platform for brake blocks
8. Brake shoe
9. Brake block
10. Wheel rim
11. Brake block adjusting and lock-nut
12. Brake spring

Fig. 14: *Side-pull caliper brakes*

Side-pull brakes are usually found on less costly bicycles, hence are more widely used. To adjust, loosen lock-nut (6.), turn cable stop (5.) so brake blocks (9.) barely clear rim. Give wheel a twirl. If wheel rim is badly out of line, straighten it by adjusting spoke tension (see page 304 for instructions on wheel alignment). Otherwise wheel will bind at spots where it rubs on brake blocks. Retighten nut (6.). If only one brake block contacts rim when brake lever is squeezed, tap down lightly on brake spring (12.) opposite side where block binds. Brake blocks must not touch tire when brake is applied!

HUBS: Should be one-piece machined. Avoid the stamped-metal type.

WHEELS: Should have thirty-six spokes in the rear wheel and no less than thirty-two spokes in the front wheel, except English bicycles with three-speed rear hubs, which have forty spokes in the rear and thirty-two in the front. Other lightweight models have thirty-six spokes front and rear. An exception are the smaller bicycles, twenty-four-inch wheels and down, where twenty-eight spokes front and rear should be installed. Any fewer number of spokes than those listed above will give you a weak wheel that won't stand up under rough handling. Spokes should be double-butted, which means they should show a slight thickening at both ends, for added strength.

WEIGHT: Fully equipped, should be around thirty-six to forty pounds. Anything heavier is just too much dead weight for anyone to push around. The better quality road-racing and touring machines (described further on), weigh around twenty-two to twenty-three pounds, which is quite an energy-saver on long rides. The finest, hand-made track-racing bicycle, without brakes and stripped to the limit, weighs from eighteen to twenty pounds.

BICYCLES FOR ADULTS

There are only two types of bicycles for adults, with a wide range of quality and prices within these types.

There is the so-called "tourist" bicycle (see Fig. 3) which is really the common, garden-variety bicycle one sees all over Europe, ridden by men and women around town and to and from work, and by rural policemen and mail carriers on their appointed rounds. The tourist model is also the bike the American Youth Hostel cycle shops and other cycle shops usually rent out. This machine is one step away from the balloon-tired heavy-weight bicycle so popular among children in the United States. It is also known as an "English racer," though as a racing machine it's about as suitable as a wheelbarrow.

For the adult who wants a reasonably reliable bicycle for tootling around town, the English racer is quite adequate when it is equipped with a three- or five-speed rear hub and caliper brakes.

However, for really serious cycling fun and for long trips, the ten-speed, derailleur-equipped bicycle with turned-down handlebars is a must. If you think there's a lot of performance difference between the fifty- to sixty-pound balloon-tired monster and the English tourist racer, then you're in for a delightful surprise when, after riding the forty-five-pound English racer, you try a twenty-two-pound high-performance road bicycle with a good selection of derailleur gears (Fig. 15). You'll find, as I did, that there's by far more difference between the English racer and the ten-speed job than there is between the English racer and the balloon-tired bicycle. It's like changing to a hot sports car from a worn-out, six-cylinder, cheap compact car. Actually, I think the difference is even greater than that, but the novice may not appreciate such a tremendous improvement. Perhaps the best way to test this difference is to go on an all-day jaunt with a friend riding the twenty-two-pound, ten-speed bike and you the forty-five-pound, three-speed English tourist type. If you are both in about the same physical condition, the first hill you meet is going to see

Fig. 15: For the cycling enthusiast, this high performance, precision-made bicycle is well worth the extra investment.

you down at the bottom while your friend is sailing over the top, and after about ten miles, you'll want to rest while your friend cycles around you in circles.

At this point, swap bicycles with your friend. You'll find the fine steel frame of the ten-speed feels like a spirited colt after the heavy frame of the tourist. Also, the ten-speed bicycle goes exactly where you want it to in contrast to the imprecise steering of the tourist model. And when you shift down to low speed on the first steep hill and find you can go right up the grade sitting down, you'll wonder how you ever finished ten miles on the tourist. Also, you'll find your cycling efficiency increased by about 30 percent because of the "rattrap" toe clips that enable you to pull up with one foot while you push down with the other. More about toe clips later.

While the turned-down handlebars on the ten-speed may worry you at first, you will quickly discover that it's actually more comfortable than the conventional tourist handlebars. When you bend over slightly instead of sitting straight up, you cut wind resistance considerably. Also, this new position lets you use your back and stomach muscles in addition to your arm and leg muscles. Later on, I will discuss dropped or turned-down handlebars versus conventional handlebars again, because you can get either kind with any type of bicycle.

If your limited cycling needs will be satisfied with a tourist or English racer type of bicycle, I have listed several good ones in Table II, with their specifications and approximate prices. I have checked these models, and they will all give you excellent service. Some are a bit better than others, with better brakes, seat, and frame; in general, the more expensive models will last longer and need less maintenance.

A note about the various makes of bicycles I mention in this chapter. By no means do they represent all the fine makes available. I have had to limit my list to a few bikes in each category, and have tried to pick those makes which are made in quantity and are generally available throughout the country. Also, the market changes every day, with new models and parts being introduced constantly. If your bicycle store does not carry these particular makes, or if you are interested in buying a specific bike which is not listed here, you can use the specification tables to check the quality of the bike you are interested in. A great variety of machines can be bought in this country. Some of the better makes, in addition to those mentioned in the tables, are Masi, J. R. Jackson, Bianchi, Gitane, Mercier, Viking Hetchin's, Renè Herse, Pogliaghi, Mercian, and Allegro. Your bicycle dealer should be able to describe the specific differences between these makes.

DERAILLEUR TEN-SPEED BICYCLES

When you take your first look at derailleur-equipped bicycles, you will probably be puzzled at the broad price range (from $85.00 to $250.00), since all these bicycles look pretty much alike.

The old saw, "you get what you pay for," applies here. The price depends on the quality of steel used in the frame and the type of equipment the maker selects to hang on the frame.

Therefore, in buying a derailleur-equipped bicycle, you should examine its specifications *very* carefully. Below are a few pointers to guide you in your selection. You won't always find the parts equally matched; for example, you may find a frame of the very finest steel equipped with low-cost components, a selection of gears you don't particularly want, or tube tires when you prefer tubular tires.

Later on in this book (page 118), you'll find a complete discussion of gears and gear ratios to help you in selecting the right combinations for the type of cycling you want to do, and to fit your own physical ability. You might read this data now before making your final decision.

THE FRAME: The best quality bicycles use Reynolds "531" tubing. The Reynolds trademark (Fig. 16) bearing this number will be on the frame and fork. Reynolds "531" metal is made only in Great Britain, but it is used by top bicycle manufacturers all over the world (including the U.S.S.R., which ordered a carload to make its own track bicycles for the 1964 Olympic races).

RIMS: The best rims are made of aluminum. Mavic, Weinmann, and Fiamme are all high quality. Steel rims are a sign of lower quality. Generally, special orders aside, machines with tubular tires (sew-ups) indicate a more expensive machine.

Only the Top Tube, Seat Tube and Down Tube of a frame with this transfer are made from REYNOLDS 531 Tubing—plain gauge.

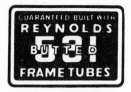

The Top Tube, Seat Tube and Down Tube of a frame which bears this transfer are REYNOLDS 531 BUTTED tubing.

All the tubing in a bicycle with this transfer is REYNOLDS 531—Frame Tubes, Chain & Seat Stays & Fork Blades, but it is all plain gauge tubing.

This transfer signifies that the bicycle is an aristocrat, a thoroughbred—made throughout of REYNOLDS 531 tubing BUTTED for lightness with strength.

Fig. 16: *Any bicycle made with any grade of Reynolds "531" tubing is better than one made with any other kind of tubing. But Reynolds "531" tubing varies by type and use. Study this illustration and the remarks made about each grade of tubing to understand what you are getting when you buy an expensive bicycle. The best bicycles, of course, come with the bottom decal transfer signifying that top-grade Reynolds "531" is used throughout. See also page 45 for more data on frame steels. Please note that Columbia tubing, used on some Italian bicycles, is comparable to Reynolds.*

HUBS: Campagnolo hubs (Fig. 17) are generally considered the highest quality, although Normandy, Simplex, and Cinelli hubs are good. All are one-piece, machined aluminum. Quick-release hubs are found only on the best road and touring bicycles. These have hollow axles which permit the quick-release skewer to pass through the hub and lock both sides to the frame. With quick-release hubs, wheels are easy to release, in seconds, without tools, which is helpful for a quick change in case of a flat.

LUGS: Lugs are the sleeve braces by which the tubes of the frame are joined together (Fig. 18). The trade name "Nervex" indicates high quality.

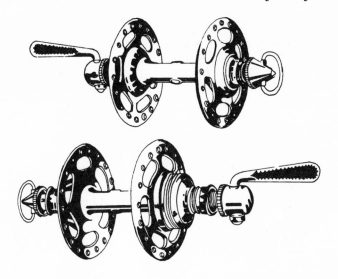

Fig. 17: Campagnolo hubs, the finest money can buy, are a hallmark of quality in any bicycle, are used for both track and road racing and are also found on fine touring bicycles.

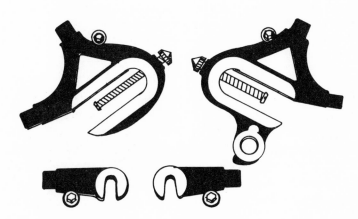

Fig. 18: These Campagnolo fork (bottom) and rear frame tips (top) are brazed into fork blades and seat and chain stays, respectively.

DERAILLEURS: Campagnolo is the best quality and the most expensive, with the quickest, most positive shifting and the widest range. Campagnolo derailleurs come in three grades, listed here in order of quality, starting with the best: "Record" (Fig. 19), "Gran Sport," and "Sportsman." Next in order to quality, in my opinion, is the Simplex "Prestige" derailleur, followed by the Huret "Allvit."

CRANKS AND CHAINWHEEL ASSEMBLY: Again, Campagnolo is the top line, followed by Stronglight, T. A., and Williams. In general, top-grade cranks and chainwheels are made from aluminum alloy and are of cotterless design. Cottered cranks, using a key to hold steel cranks on crank axle, indicate a lower quality bicycle, although this should not be the only criterion in judging a machine.

BRAKES: Center-pull design brakes are the most popular because they work more smoothly and more evenly. The best center-pull brakes, in my

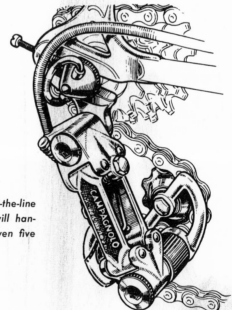

Fig. 19: This Campagnolo top-of-the-line "Nuovo Record" rear derailleur will handle 13- to 30-tooth rear gears, even five or six speed freewheels.

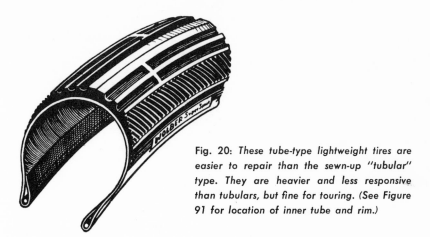

Fig. 20: *These tube-type lightweight tires are easier to repair than the sewn-up "tubular" type. They are heavier and less responsive than tubulars, but fine for touring. (See Figure 91 for location of inner tube and rim.)*

opinion, are Mafac "Racer" brakes, which are made from aluminum alloy, and permit the brake shoe to be adjusted three ways. Weinmann center-pull alloy brakes are also good.

TIRES: In general, you will find the more expensive, higher quality bicycles fitted with 27-inch wheels and tubular (sew-up) road-racing tires. But you can, if you wish, specify tube-type (Fig. 20) 27-inch x 1¼-inch wheels and tires. Tubular tires are more prone to flats in city-street cycling, and they are more difficult to repair because the casing is sewn up all the way around. But they and the wheels they are used on are lighter and more responsive, making cross-country pedaling easier and more enjoyable. Tube-type wired-on tires and the wheels they are used on are heavier. However, tube tires are easier to repair because the tube is readily accessible. On the other hand, tubular sew-ups can be changed in seconds, and they are so light that several spares can be carried compactly. Repairs can always be made after a trip.

PEDALS: Again, Campagnolo pedals indicate highest quality. The Lyotard platform pedal, which is one of the better, all-purpose models of the Lyotard line, is excellent too. It is very sturdy and less expensive than the Campagnolo. Fig. 21 shows three basic types of pedals.

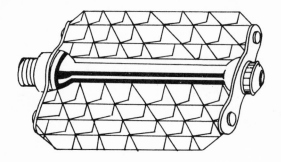

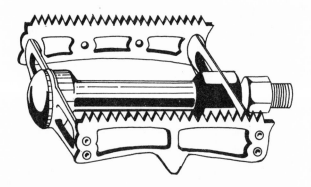

Fig. 21: The three basic types of pedals. Top, conventional rubber tread pedal, for city and knock-about use; center, road-racing pedal, also fine for touring, and bottom, track-racing pedal, lightweight, with teeth for gripping shoes.

SELECT THE BICYCLE YOU WANT

Only you can select the right bicycle to fit your purse and the kind of cycling you plan to do. However, to help you buy the best machine, I have selected, from the hundreds of makes and varieties of derailleur bicycles available today, a few of the best models in three price ranges: fairly good-quality, low-priced models (Table III); higher-quality, medium-priced machines (Table IV); and top-quality, precision-made bicycles where price isn't a factor (Table V).

If you can't find your choice of bicycle in your local bicycle shop, you can buy it from the dealers and wholesalers listed below:

Louison-Bobet: Cyclo-Pedia, 311 North Mitchell, Cadillac, Michigan 49601.

Peugeot: For local dealer, write Franklin Imports, 106 West 81st Street, New York, New York 10024.

Raleigh and Carleton: For local dealer, write Raleigh Industries of America, Inc., 1168 Commonwealth Avenue, Boston, Massachusetts 02134.

Gitane: Wheel Goods Corporation, 2737 Hennepin Avenue, Minneapolis, Minnesota 55408. (Also sells Raleigh and Dunelt by mail.)

Schwinn: Dealers are everywhere, but in case you can't find one, write Schwinn Bicycle Company, 1856 North Kostner, Chicago, Illinois, 60639.

Table III • Low-Cost, Quality Derailleur Bicycles

SPECIFICATIONS	*Peugeot UO-8*
FRAME	Seamless lightweight tubing, special lugs, chrome fork, tips, and head
FRAME SIZE	21 in., 23 in., 24 in., and 25 in.
DERAILLEURS	Simplex "Prestige" No. 537
CRANKS	Nervar, steel, cottered design
CHAINWHEEL	10-speed 36 x 52 teeth mountain gear; steel; double chainwheel
HUBS	Normandy dural wide flange with Simplex quick-release axles and skewers
FREEWHEEL	Atom 14, 16, 19, 22, and 26 teeth
RIMS	Rigida dural rims, 27 in. x 1¼ in.
SPOKES	Double-butted stainless steel
TIRES	Hutchinson 27 in. x 1¼ in. tube type
HANDLEBARS	AVA alloy stem, MAES bar (drop)
SADDLE	Black butt leather racing type
BRAKES	Mafac center-pull "racer" with covered levers
PEDALS	Lyotard No. 36 rattrap
ACCESSORIES	Pump, Mafac toolbag, tools
WEIGHT	27 lbs. complete
LIST PRICE (APPROX.)	$90.00

Louison Bobet "Sports"	*Raleigh "Record" DL-73*
High-tensile seamless steel, lugged and brazed; brazed-on pump pegs and cable guides; half-chrome fork ends	Good quality steel frame, lugged, butted, and brazed up
20½ in., 21⅝ in., 22⅞ in., 24 in., and 25½ in.	22½ in. frame size only
Huret "Allvit"	Huret "Allvit"
3-pin chrome steel	Steel, cottered design
15-speed triple steel chainwheel with wide range gears	Double chainwheel of steel, 40 and 52 teeth
Dural wide flange, quick-release axles with skewers	Wide-flange, alloy
Cyclo five gear	Five-speed (with double chainwheel makes 10-speed)
Steel, 27 in. x 1¼ in.	Steel, 27 in.
Double-butted stainless steel	Double-butted
Hutchinson 27 in. x 1¼ in. tube type	27 in. x 1¼ in.
Dural Sport drop bar with dural stem	Dropped, steel
Butt leather road-racing type	Brooks racing, leather
C.L.B. dural "racer" center-pull, rubber hooded levers	Center-pull
Rattletrap Tourist with toe clips and straps	Toe straps, rattrap
Pump, tool bag, tire irons, aluminum fenders	Stamina bottle, fenders (alloy) fender flap
29 lbs. complete	About 28 lbs.
$85.00	$95.00

Table IV • Moderate Cost, Good Quality Derailleur Bicycles

SPECIFICATIONS	*Louison Bobet C-34*
FRAME	Reynolds seamless "531" (not double-butted); fine-grade detailed lugs; low-temperature brazing
FRAME SIZE	20½ in., 21⅝ in., 22⅞ in., 24 in., 24¾ in., and 25½ in.
CRANKS	Stronglight 3-pin steel
CHAINWHEEL	Chromed steel chainwheel, removable; double chainwheel
HUBS	Normandy quick-release high-flange alloy
DERAILLEURS	Campagnolo 10-speed "Gran Sport"
FREEWHEEL	Competition grade
RIMS	Mavic dural tubular "Sports"
SPOKES	Robergel stainless
TIRES	Tubular road racing, 27 in.
HANDLEBARS	Dural road racing, dural stem, turned-down bars
SADDLE	Ideale #41 road-racing butt leather
BRAKES	Mafac "Racer" center-pull dural, hooded levers
PEDALS	Lyotard, with toe clips and straps
ACCESSORIES	Dural pump
WEIGHT	24 lbs.
LIST PRICE (APPROX.)	$115.00

Raleigh "Carleton" DL-100

Reynolds "531" tubing with Capella professional lugs (not double-butted)

21½ in. and 23½ in.

Cottered cranks 6¾ in. (steel)

Williams 40–52-tooth chainwheel (double chainwheel) or Metuar 52–40-tooth (steel)

Normandy quick-release high-flange alloy

Simplex "Prestige" 10-speed

14–28 teeth

27-in. Weinmann dural or Dunlop dural

Double-butted

27-in. x 1¼-in. tube type

Alloy turned-down road-racing bars and stem

Brooks B-15 leather racing saddle

Weinmann or G. B. Synchron center-pull, hooded levers

Toe clips, straps

Alloy half-fenders, plastic chainguard

About 26 lbs.

$120.00

Table V • Highest Quality Derailleur Bicycles

SPECIFICATIONS	*Louison-Bobet Pro C-35*
FRAME	Reynolds "531" double-butted seamless tubing; Nervex lugs; Campagnolo rear drop-out; Reynolds "531" fork
FRAME SIZE	20¼ in., 21⅝ in., 22⅞ in., 24 in., 24¾ in., and 25 in.
CRANKS	Stronglight Super 63 Competition cotterless dural
CHAINWHEEL	Double Stronglight dural
HUBS	Campagnolo Record dural; high-flange with quick-release
DERAILLEURS	Campagnolo Record
FREEWHEEL	Competition grade—to specification
RIMS	Mavic Professional dural alloy, 27 in.
SPOKES	Robergel high-tensile
TIRES	27-in. tubular road-racing
HANDLEBARS	Dural road-racing bars and stem
SADDLE	Unica Model 63 with dural micro-adjusting post (or Brooks B-17)
BRAKES	Mafac TOP 63 forged dural center-pull; hooded levers
PEDALS	Campagnolo #1037 road-racing dural with toe clips and straps
ACCESSORIES	Dural road-racing pump
WEIGHT	22 lbs.
LIST PRICE (APPROX.)	$225.00

Peugeot PX-10E	*Schwinn Paramount P-13*
Reynolds "531" double-butted seamless tubing; Nervex lugs; Simplex ends	Reynolds "531" double-butted seamless tubing; Nervex lugs; Campagnolo Gran-Sport rear drop out; Reynolds "531" butted oval to round fork blades; Nervex Pro crown and Campagnolo Gran-Sport fork tips
21 in., 23 in., 24 in., and 25 in.	20 in., 21 in., 22 in., 23 in., 24 in., and 25 in.
Stronglight Super 63 Competition cotterless dural	Campagnolo Record alloy 6¾ in.
Double Stronglight dural, 45 and 52 teeth	Double Campagnolo, 49 and 52 teeth; tools
Normandy luxe competition alloy; Simplex high-flange with quick-release	Campagnolo Record, high-flange with quick-release
Simplex Prestige 537	Campagnolo Record, rear and front
Competition grade, 14, 16, 19, 20, and 23 teeth	Regina, 14, 16, 19, 21, and 24 teeth
Mavic Montlhery, reinforced spoke holes, 27 in.	Weinmann aluminum alloy
Robergel double-butted	Not specified
27-in. tubular road-racing	Dunlop road-racing 27 in. x 1¼ in. (wired-on type)
AVA dural bars and stem	Aluminum alloy drop with Maes-style bend, steel stem
Brooks Professional with Simplex seat post	Brooks Professional with Campagnolo seat post
Mafac Racer center-pull, alloy; Hooded levers	Weinmann Vanquer 999 center-pull with quick-release levers except 19 in. and 20 in. frames have side-pull brakes
Lyotard 45CA dural with toe clips and straps	Campagnolo Gran-Sport with toe clips and straps
Dural road-racing pump	Extra-cost options include tubular tires, handlebar controls, custom-sized frame
About 21 lbs.	25¾ lbs. with tubular wired-on tires
$160.00	$245.00

Table V • Highest Quality Derailleur Bicycles (*Continued*)

SPECIFICATIONS	*Cinelli*
FRAME	Columbus double-butted tubing throughout. Nervex or Campagnolo lugs
FRAME SIZE	20½ in. to 25 in.
DERAILLEURS	Campagnolo Nuovo Record front and rear
CRANKS	Campagnolo cotterless dural cranks
CHAINWHEEL	Campagnolo double chainwheel, dural alloy. Gears to specification
HUBS	Campagnolo high-flange with quick-release
FREEWHEEL	Competition, gears to specifications
RIMS	Fiamme "Red Label"
SPOKES	Robergel high tensile
TIRES	Tubular Clementi Criterium or your specification
HANDLEBARS	Alloy bars and stems
SADDLE	Unica leather-covered nylon, or Brooks B.15
BRAKES	Universal center-pull
PEDALS	Campagnolo 1037
ACCESSORIES	To your order
WEIGHT	About 23 lbs.
LIST PRICE (APPROX.)	$255.00

Falcon	*Frejus*
Reynolds "531" double-butted tubing throughout; Prugnat lugs; Campagnolo headset and micro-saddle post	Similar to the Falcon, except that it can be purchased with Columbus double-butted tubing throughout or with the three main tubes, or "diamond," made of Reynolds "531" tubing. Campagnolo micro-adjusting seat post, headset, and lugs
20½ in. to 25 in.	20 in. to 25 in.
Campagnolo	Campagnolo
Campagnolo dural cotterless; gears to specification	Campagnolo dural cotterless
Campagnolo quick-release dural	Campagnolo quick-release
Campagnolo Record, front and rear	Campagnolo Nuovo Record, front and rear
Competition grade, gears to specification	Competition grade, gears to specification
Fiamme "Red Label" alloy	Fiamme "Red Label" alloy
Robergel high-tensile or similar	Robergel high-tensile or similar
27-in. tubular road-racing or wired-on, to specification	27-in. tubular road-racing
Alloy bars and stem, road-racing type	Alloy bars and stem, road-racing type
Brooks B-15 or to specification	Brooks B-15 or to specification
Weinmann 999, center-pull	Mafac center-pull
Campagnolo #1037 or to specification	Campagnolo #1037 or to specification
To specification	To specification
About 23 lbs.	About 22 lbs.
$225.00	About $215.00

MINI-BIKES—NOTES AND COMMENTS

A few years ago, a British engineer named Alex Moulton invented the "mini-bike." It was enthusiastically received by the buying public, whose interest was heightened by the claim that several road-racing records had been broken by cyclists using this machine.

Let's set the record straight. According to Gene Portuesi, the only records that were broken were done so on carefully selected courses in England, involving records which had been set over fifty years ago and had not been challenged since.

These bicycles are not suited for long-distance touring; to use them for racing of any type is ridiculous. The typical Moulton-type bicycle is perhaps best represented by the Raleigh version, the Model RSW-16 (Fig. 22), which weighs in at a rather heavy forty-three pounds.

But let's review the pros and cons of the mini-bike.

Advantages

PORTABLE: Mini-bikes take up little room. Many of them can be taken apart and carried in the trunk of a car.

PRACTICAL: They can carry a lot of groceries and other packages, and they are easy to ride and turn about in small spaces.

Disadvantages

BALANCE: Small wheels (sixteen-inch or twenty-inch diameter) make these bicycles quite unstable. They are likely to spill a rider on any skiddy surface such as a gravel road.

USE: Heavy weight and general design make them unsuitable for anything but short trips around town.

EXPENSE: Mini-bikes are rather expensive for the quality of ride and general utility they give. The Peugeot D-22 take-apart bike costs $89.50; the Raleigh lists at $79.95.

STOPPING POWER: Braking leaves something to be desired. I have found that even with center-pull brakes, it is impossible to come to a reasonably quick stop in wet weather.

Fig. 22: *This English small-wheel folding bicycle is easy to knock down, but rather heavy for general cycling; weighs a hefty forty-three pounds. By comparison, good lightweight machines weigh about twenty-one to twenty-four pounds.*

OTHER KINDS OF BICYCLES

The Tandem

A little further on I will discuss the various types of tandems, but let's look at them for a minute, and consider some of the advantages and disadvantages of tandem cycling.

First, the advantages. One of the difficulties in family cycling is that too often one member of the family is less expert than the other and can't keep up. One person always lags behind, and the good cyclist is forced to slow down his pace in order to stay within shouting distance. Tandems end this problem, although there are certain back-seat driver situations that can take its place. Tandem riding lets you and your partner chat about the day and the scenery, and the fun of working together as a team in cycling can add to the enjoyment of family life in general.

The major drawback of a tandem, however, is its awkwardness. Especially when one rider is not skilled, it is difficult to manipulate a tandem rapidly and precisely through a stream of traffic or other bicycles. Consequently, tandems are not as safe as individual bikes. Also, the stronger rider must work twice as hard to compensate for the fact that the other rider is putting out less energy per pound of body weight. In effect, the strong rider is carrying the weight.

Two skillful, strong riders, on the other hand, can really make a tandem scoot for long distances, because there is twice the power and the same frontal area (breaking wind) as with a single bike. Also, there is less bicycle weight per pound of body weight. (They do have only two wheels, although the frame is a little heavier than a single bicycle, as are the extra cranks and chainwheel.)

If you want a tandem, and togetherness is a good reason to buy one, you should get a tandem you can enjoy. I would buy only a tandem built as a high-quality ten-speed derailleur machine, with ten-speed gear shift and lightweight road-racing wheels and tires. This machine will weigh about forty-three or forty-four pounds, compared to the eighty-nine or ninety-pound weight of a balloon-tired tandem, and will be much easier to pedal.

Good tandems are expensive, though. Two very fine ones are made by Jack Taylor of Great Britain and are available from Wheel Goods Corporation (see Appendix for address). The "Sports Tandem" sells for $209.50 and has these specifications:

Frame: 22-inch front, 21-inch rear. Reynolds "531" finest grade seamless tubing.
Fittings: Stronglight headset and T.D. cross-bottom brackets.
Wheels: 27-inch Endrick rims.
Tires: 27-inch x 1¼-inch tube tires.
Handlebars: Alloy Maes turn-down bars with chrome steel stems.
Brakes: Mafac Tandem Criterium. (On a tandem, good brakes are a must and these are excellent.)
Saddles: Choice of Brooks B.15 standard or racing saddle.
Chainwheels: Williams D.34.
Derailleur gear: Cycle Benelux five-speed.

The Jack Taylor Touring Tandem, which sells for $349.50, has many of the above specifications, plus much better brakes, built-in lighting, rear luggage carriers, and a set of fifteen-speed derailleurs which a tandem *should* have for long-distance touring. Generally, better equipment is used on this model, such as dural cotterless Williams cranks and chainwheels. Also, a rear hub brake is fitted to this machine for safer cycling down steep mountain hills. This is the machine I'd recommend for touring.

For short trips, however, you can buy a less expensive model than either of these, which will be satisfactory. This is the Gitane Tandem, which costs $149.50. It has a front man's style and lady's rear style frame, and comes with a Huret ten-speed derailleur set, front turn-down and rear conventional alloy handlebars, 27-inch x 1¼-inch tires and wheels, and Mafac brakes. Also, I understand that Schwinn has a new touring tandem on the market. This bike retails for about $395.00, if you would prefer to buy an American-made machine.

Adult Tricycles

If you're beyond the age when you think you can learn how to ride a bicycle, or if, for some reason, you cannot or should not balance yourself on one, adult tricycles might be the answer for you.

There is a wide variety of these tricycles, however, and it's important to get a good one, because with these bikes, the best costs so little more. In this market, you're paying a larger price because of the small demand and limited production.

Actually, a good tricycle isn't much less efficient than a good bicycle. In England, there have been racing events in which tricyclists have gotten up to speeds of forty miles an hour or better.

The real difference between a bicycle and a tricycle of equal quality lies in the greater maneuverability of the two-wheeler and the consequent greater skill it takes to ride one.

Still, rather than give up the joy of outdoor pedaling, a tricycle can be an excellent compromise. One sees great numbers of tricycles in retirement areas.

There are several types of tricycles you can buy. The best I have found that is readily available in the United States is a three-speed model which has a Huret Allvit derailleur shifter and a Cyclo three-speed freewheel. This unit is especially built for those who need low-gear ratios to pedal up steep driveways or slight inclines. Other specifications include lugged and brazed frame construction, a three-piece crank with precision-ground hanger axle and cups, a forty-eight-tooth chainwheel, 26-inch x 1⅜-inch wheels and tires and caliper front, and a cable-operated brake. This tricycle comes with spring mattress saddle, saddlebag, tools, and pump. Seat, handlebars, stem, and seat are adjustable.

In addition to the three-speed model, you can buy a tricycle with a fixed gear, which means you can't free-wheel down a hill, though. But you can pedal backward as well as forward with this model, and since the pedals turn as long as the tricycle moves in either direction, and you can help stop forward motion by back-pedaling, the fixed-gear model is a better choice. If you plan to cycle in the city, and maneuver in tight places where the ability to pedal backward as well as forward would be useful, this is the model to get.

One additional recommendation for a fixed-gear tricycle: if you have limited movement in your legs, the forward momentum of the trike will pull the pedal around the 360-degree arc for you. You may not, for example, be able to put pedaling pressure right at the top of the stroke or at the bottom one-fourth. If you had a freewheel tricycle, you'd have to kick the pedal around somehow, which is difficult if leg muscles or ligaments are limited in movement. Remember, a fixed gear is one that involves rotation of the pedals whenever the wheels move, and you can't coast when you are holding the pedals in one position. As I mentioned above, you can back up with a fixed-gear trike by simply standing up and putting your weight on the pedal at the top of the stroke. If you live in flat country, such as Florida, urban Arizona, or Southern California, and you want a tricycle with which to get some outdoor exercise without having to climb hills, I recommend the fixed-gear machine.

You can buy a derailleur (ten- or fifteen-gear) tricycle from several European manufacturers, for example, Holdsworthy of England (see ⋀ppendix for address).

A freewheel lets you stop pedaling and coast. The three-speed model is $130.00 and the single-speed model, either freewheel or fixed gear, is $120.00 from Cyclo-Pedia (see Appendix for address).

Converting a Two-wheeler to a Three-wheeler

You can also convert your two-wheeler into an adult three-wheeler with a precision rear-axle assembly. For safe cycling, such a conversion should be attempted only with a bicycle already fitted with a front-caliper hand-brake.

The lightweight model conversion kit for 27-inch wheels is $55.00. For 26-inch x 1⅜-inch wheels, the price is $72.50, which includes tires, tubes, and wheels. Both kits are available from Cyclo-Pedia.

Less expensive tricycles for adults can be bought, but I don't recommend them. If you need a tricycle, you should have the easiest to pedal, and the other tricycles and conversion kits available in this country are heavy, cumbersome things.

Unicycles

Strictly in the gimmick and toy area is yet another cycling variation, the unicycle. This is a one-wheeled cycle with a banana seat, which children seem to be able to ride with great facility for short distances, and with a lot of fun and enjoyment. Personally, I'd rather try a delayed parachute fall—at least I'd have a chance for an easy landing.

But, if your child wants a unicycle, and you can afford the $35.00 they cost, I'd recommend a Columbia Unicycle. Columbia furnishes a four-page instruction manual on how to ride the thing, which may ease the pain of the learning process. The Columbia model also seems to be the best made and comes in a twenty-inch or twenty-four-inch wheel size, the choice of which depends on your child's age, or your own size, if you're the one who wants to learn this circus trick. The manufacturer calls this "A new fun fad . . . ," which I suppose it is.

4

FITTING YOUR BICYCLE TO YOU

Perhaps the most vital step in bicycle selection is proper frame size. As the bicycle comparison charts on pages 72-79 show, frames come in a variety of sizes, from twenty and one half to twenty-five and one half inches. The English "bobby's" bike frame is about twenty-eight inches, and custom-made bikes can be made with even bigger frames.

Frame size is measured from the seat lug (a.) at the top of the seat tube to the center of the bottom bracket at the bottom of the seat tube (b.) (Fig 23).

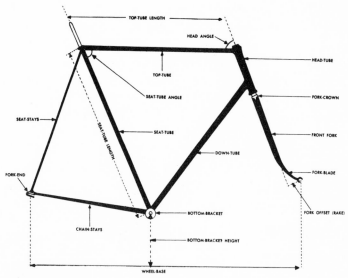

Fig. 23: *Fitting the bicycle frame to your own frame—your body—is a vital first step in selecting the right machine for you. Measure frame size by checking length of seat tube from seat post lug at top to center of bottom bracket, as shown above. You can buy a custom-made bicycle with frame made just to suit you (any good frame-maker in England or France, such as Rene Herse in Paris, makes beautiful frames, even complete bicycles, but be ready to shell out $300.00 or more).*

It is vital that you select a frame size that permits you to straddle the top bar with comfort, so that you can mount and dismount without difficulty (or injury). In general, you should select a frame size that measures nine to ten inches less than your inseam, as measured in your stocking feet.

If you are buying a bicycle in a bicycle store, take off your shoes, straddle the top tube (the horizontal bar from head stay to seat tube), and make sure you can stand up comfortably. I made the mistake, many years ago, of buying a bicycle with a frame too large for me—it was a bit hazardous coming to stops in the city. I had to lean sidewise to get my foot on the ground. Riding that bicycle was not only dangerous but decidedly uncomfortable.

HANDLEBARS

There are two basic types of handlebars, and a number of variations within each type, in use today. The more common are the upright or flat handlebars (Fig. 24) used with three-speed or coaster-brake bicycles. High-rise handlebars, a variation, force a child (no adult would use them) to ride with his hands at chin height, hardly a safe position or one which permits precise steering. Young children like to copy older children, though, so you do see many bikes with motorcycle-type high-rise handlebars on sixteen- and twenty-inch Sting-Ray bikes.

The second kind of handlebars is the dropped or turned-down type (Fig. 25) used on good (and some not-so-good) ten-speed derailleur lightweights and on the no-speed fixed-gear track-racing bicycles.

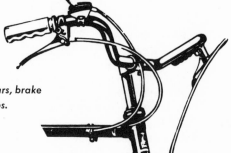

Fig. 24: On conventional "flat" handlebars, brake levers are located under handlebar grips.

Fig. 25: Here are the three basic types of turned-down handlebars: Left, Randonneur; center, Maes; and right, Pista. Randonneur is favored for cycle touring because it offers more hand positions.

Most adults who are interested in cycling express concern about dropped handlebars. They say that the crouch position (about forty-five degrees from upright position) must be uncomfortable, and that it must be difficult to see where one is going. But dropped handlebars have been preferred for over forty years by experienced cyclists in both this country and abroad for short- and long-distance touring. Flat handlebars are inefficient, uncomfortable, and tiring.

Dropped versus Flat Handlebars

There are so many reasons why dropped handlebars are better than flat bars for any kind of cycling that it would take ten pages to explain them fully. I hope this quick summary will sell you on the dropped bars, because I'm confident you'll be happier and more comfortable with them.

Obviously, you must crouch down at about a forty-five-degree angle with dropped bars (see racing photos in Chapter 8). This position is actually more effective and healthier. It cuts down wind resistance, which can save a lot of energy, particularly when you are pedaling into a fifteen- or twenty-knot wind. Also, with your back arched slightly, you can use more muscles, more effectively, for a longer period.

Try this demonstration to prove the muscle-using efficiency of dropped bars. Sit upright in a chair, with both feet flat on the floor in front of you. Try to stand up. Now sit back as before, and bend over about forty-five degrees and try to stand up. You have now positioned your body so that you can put some of those powerful back and thigh muscles to work.

A great deal of medical research has been done on the use of dropped handlebars and the human back, and the conclusions show that the bent-over position is better for the back than the sitting-up position.

An interesting article by Fred DeLong,[1] points out that

at the small of the back the spine curves backward and the discs and vertebrae are pinched together at the rear. Upper body weight tends to further
compress this region; excess weight accentuates the condition, and road impact compounds the problem. On the front of the spine, the ligaments which
hold the spine from collapsing become strained.

When leaning forward, however, the back relaxes and extends and the
vertebrae separate, relieving the pinching, permitting absorption of impact
without damage. If you will have someone measure with a tape you'll find
that your spine will actually lengthen as much as two inches when you bend
forward from the erect to the dropped bar position.

Physicians also point out that the bent-over position is easier for breathing because, as you lean over on the dropped handlebars, part of the body
weight is supported by the arms, which allows the chest to expand and
contract more readily.

Riding is also a lot more comfortable with the dropped bars because
body weight is more evenly divided between saddle and bars. This is
particularly noticeable on long rides and bumpy roads. When the going
gets rough, you can lean forward a bit, or even ease your weight off the
saddle and onto the handlebars to reduce road shock. I recommend you
do this when riding over railroad tracks, through intersections, or over
very rough roads. This will spread the shock evenly over front and rear
wheels and protect the wheels as well as yourself from the impact.

Types of Dropped Handlebars

As you browse through bicycle parts catalogs or watch other cyclists
go by, you will see a great many shapes of dropped handlebars. The three
most popular types (Fig. 25) are the Pista, the Maes and the Randonneur.
The Pista have curves which bend quickly away from the main stem. This
type may be fine for track racing, but they are no good for touring because
there's no room to rest the hands at the top of the bars (the favorite position in distance cycling). The Maes offer just about the best combination
of curvatures. They have a long, flat top bar section that permits the rider
to ride gripping the top bar (a very comfortable position), yet bottom
sections are readily available for dropping quickly to the low position for

---

[1] *American Cycling* (now *Bicycling!*), April, 1966, p. 16.

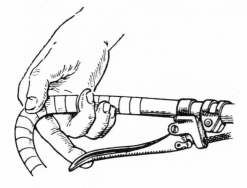

Fig. 26: *Touring handlebars fitted with brake levers at top section of bars.*

maximum energy exertion on hills, or for sprinting. Also, the curvature of the Maes bars permits plenty of variety in placing brake levers.

The Randonneur-type handlebars are best suited to persons with short arms, especially if the rider finds it consistently difficult, after a long trial period, to reach brake levers on Maes-type handlebars. French-type brake levers, located at the end of the stem just under the center section of the top bars, make it easier to grip brakes quickly from the top of the bar position (Fig. 26). The Randonneur are also well suited to women (or men) with short fingers.

Fitting the Handlebars to You

A tiny off-adjustment in handlebars can make all the difference in the world to your cycling comfort, especially on a long trip. Therefore, handlebar adjustment is extremely important because no two persons have exactly the same arm and torso length. Handlebar height and stem length must be accurately selected for comfort.

The stem is the part of the frame that rises up from the steering head, to which handlebars are fastened. Stems come in various lengths (Fig. 27), the usual variation being 1¾ inches, 2 inches, 2¾ inches, 3½ inches, and 4 inches. You can see that there's plenty of variation to bring handlebars as close to you or move them as far away from you as necessary.

The problem is that you cannot always tell what stem length you need, and at $5.50 each, you don't want to spend a lot of money trying out various stem lengths. If there are a number of people in your family who are planning to cycle seriously, it might be a good idea to invest in an adjustable stem, which can quickly adjust handlebars closer to and away from a rider. These stems are available for approximately $7.50, and a family can use one to establish correct handlebar horizontal adjustment for each person.

The first rule of thumb for approximate or rough handlebar adjustment is to raise the bars until the top bar is level with the nose of the saddle.

The second handlebar adjustment is stem length. You cannot change stem length unless you have an adjustable stem (Fig. 27), which must be purchased separately (or buy a new stem, as noted above). You can help make the handlebars come closer to you, however, by moving the saddle horizontally. Loosen the saddle clip nut and slide the saddle forward or backward. This adjustment is strictly limited, though, because if you move the saddle too far off the correct position (see pages 99-103), you will impair your pedaling efficiency. The saddle nose should be about 1¾ to 2½ inches behind the crank hanger, if you were to draw a vertical line from the saddle to the hanger. The variation will depend on your height. (A saddle position a bit to the rear will give you better "ankling" efficiency; see pages 105-06 for a description of ankling.)

A good way to find a correct handlebar horizontal length is to measure the distance from your elbow to your outstretched fingertips. This should be the distance from the very rear edge of the center part of the handlebars to the nose of the saddle.

Another way to check handlebar or stem length is to sit on the bicycle,

Fig. 27: Be sure to select the right handlebar stem for your arm length. They come in lengths from 1¾ inches to 4 inches. Or, unless you are competing, you can use an adjustable stem (upper left).

assume your usual riding position, and, with someone holding you, re-move one hand from the handlebars and rotate the arm freely, without stretching, until it comes back to the bars. If, as the hand comes back to the bar top, it is behind or in front of the other hand, you should adjust your stem length.

In fact, I would recommend that you use either or both of the hori-zontal fitting methods when you buy a new bicycle so that you will have at least approximately the correct stem length. Bicycles are fitted with stems for the *average* rider, so if you are a short woman with short arms, or a tall man with a long torso and long arms, the stem that comes automatically with the bicycle will probably never give you the correct horizontal handlebar adjustment. A good dealer, who specializes in high-quality machines, will have a selection of stem lengths in stock and will be able to fit your particular physique.

Once you have made these rough adjustments in the saddle and handlebars, do not make any further changes until you have given them a good trial (about fifty miles).

There is another handlebar adjustment, applying only to dropped handlebars, that has to do with the tilt of the dropped part of the bars (Fig. 28). You can alter tilt by loosening the stem nut and rotating the

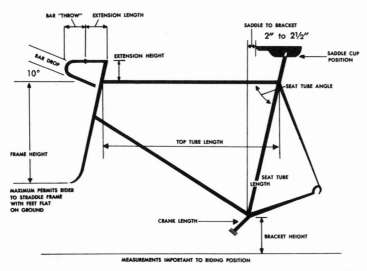

Fig. 28: *Tilt of the handlebars is important. It can be varied, but about ten degrees is commonly used, as shown here.*

bars. For a first adjustment, which is the position that suits most people, tilt the lower section of the bars about ten degrees downward. Then, as you ride, drop your hands to this lower position to check how comfortable it is for you. If it doesn't feel right, change the angle of the dropped section until it suits you. But do this only after you have made all other adjustments on the saddle and handlebars.

Position of Brake Levers Is Important

Chances are that when you buy a new ten-speed bicycle or some other type of bicycle, the dropped bars will already be taped and the brake levers will be tightened in position. This should not deter you from removing the tape and shifting the brake-lever position so you can reach the levers quickly from any riding position, no matter where your hands happen to be located on the bars. Quick stopping is vital in an emergency. Brake levers should be somewhere on the curve of the bars (Fig. 29), but the best position for you will depend on how easy it is for you to grab them.

I always tape my handlebars, and I believe you will find taping a must on long trips. Taping gives you a better grip. Sweaty palms and light aluminum alloy are a slippery combination. I prefer the nonsticky plastic tape, which can be applied and removed easily.

Taping Handlebars

Before taping, be sure the brake levers are in the position that suits you best.

Most manual instructions call for beginning the taping job after leaving a space of about two inches between the stem and the top of the bar. I do a lot of riding in cold weather, so I prefer to tape right up to the stem. This provides a layer of tape between my gloves and the cold alloy of the bars.

In taping, first pull the tape taut then pass two or three layers over each other so that the first layer will hold in place. Tape the bars as you would a baseball bat, overlapping the tape about an eighth of an inch. When you reach the brake levers, tape right down to where they are fastened to the bars, then pass behind the levers and continue taping. Leave two or three inches of tape beyond the end of the bars, and push

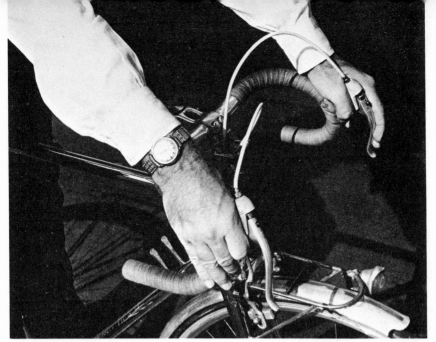

Fig. 29: *Locate brake levers where you can reach them by extending one or two fingers from top of the bar position and you'll be able to grab them quickly with the entire hand in an emergency. The position of brake levers probably won't be just right for you when the bicycle is brand new. You'll have to experiment.*

this excess tape into the bars with your finger. Then plug the end of the bars with a bar plug (Fig. 30). Even if you don't tape your bars, you should use bar plugs as a safety measure. The open unplugged end of the bars could give you a nasty gash in a spill.

If you use the push-on kind of bar plug (the type without an expanding screw), you can cut a small hole in it and use it to hold spare light bulbs (the glass part of the bulb inside the plug).

TOE CLIPS

Toe clips are both an important safety feature and a major contributor to cycling efficiency. Clips with straps will keep your feet from sliding off the pedals when you need to accelerate quickly, or keep them from sliding off accidentally at any time, causing you to lose control of the bicycle. Toe clips also permit you to pull back and up with one foot while you are pushing down and forward with the other. This can increase your cycling efficiency 40 to 50 percent.

Fig. 30: *How to tape handlebars. (Courtesy of Wheel Goods Corporation)*

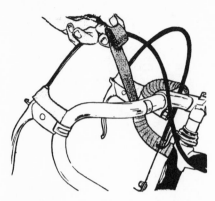

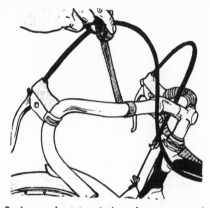

1. Both plastic and cloth tape have their advantages; which tape you use is entirely up to you. If the cloth is adhesive, start at the bottom and work upward; if not, it will have to be plugged into the end of the bars with a rubber or plastic bar plug; starting at the top of the bars is necessary.

2. Leave about two inches of space on each side of the bar extension clip. Stick the end of the tape to the bars with a small piece of adhesive tape or paper. Then work downward toward the brake lever, making sure not to leave any unsightly gaps of metal between each twist of the tape.

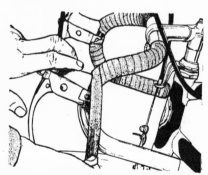

3. Tape over the lever (useful for added comfort if the lever is not fitted with a honking rubber) or (as illustrated) loosen the lever, tape the bars inside it and over the clip, then screw the lever tightly back.

4. When you reach the end of the bars, push about two or three inches of tape inside the end of the bars with your fingers. Then check to see that you have left no gaps through which metal is showing.

5. Finally, plug the end with a bar plug, which will secure the tape and complete a workmanlike job.

For the beginning cyclist, the major concern about toe clips that are tightened with straps is that he will not be able to pull his foot out fast enough if he has to stop quickly. Let me say that no cyclist should ride with straps tightened firmly in city traffic anyway, but you can pull your foot off the pedal, with or without straps, if you have to stop fast and support yourself.

It is important to get the right size toe clips. Toe clips come in three sizes—small, medium, and large. The toe of your shoe should not touch the inside edge of the clip; if it does, it could cause uncomfortable chafing, which could be troublesome, especially on a long trip. If toe clips are too long, the top edge will hit your shoe tongue and chafe the top part of your foot. In general, men who wear American shoe sizes from six to eight should use the small size toe clips; shoe sizes from eight and a half to ten, the medium size; and over ten, the large clips.

SHOE CLEATS AND SHOES

I also recommend using shoe cleats (Fig. 31). Cleats give you more cycling efficiency because they fit firmly into the pedal and let you pull back and down without allowing your foot to slip out of the pedal. You should also consider investing in Italian or Belgian cycling shoes. They have long, built-in steel shanks, which keep the steel pedal and your innersole apart, allowing you to put more even pressure on the pedals.

Italian cycling shoes are fine if you have narrow feet, but if your feet

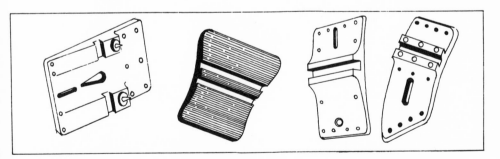

Fig. 31: *Shoe cleats, for use only with road- or track-racing shoes made for this purpose. Cleats fit into rattrap pedals, permit you to pull pedals up and push them down, and keep feet from sliding off pedals. Shoe cleat at left is for cycle-cross racing; next, a model used for touring; third; a track cleat, and on the right, a road cleat.*

are broad in the toe and the arch areas, by all means use Belgian shoes. They offer a wider last.

When you first buy cycling shoes, do not attach cleats to them until you have pedaled about a hundred miles. This amount of cycling on the bare pedals will make an imprint on the leather sole of the shoes, which will show you exactly where to mount the cleats. When you mount the cleats, the cleat tunnel should be exactly on top of and aligned with the mark made by the pedal on the shoe sole. Any shoemaker can tack the cleats onto the cycling shoes.

Cycling shoes (Fig. 32) cost anywhere from $8.50 to $15.00 and can be purchased from cycle shops specializing in the sale and repair of high-quality bicycles, or from any of the bicycle mail-order shops listed on pages 317-18.

If you order shoes by mail, be sure to indicate your correct size. You can do this by putting on a pair of lightweight socks and standing on a plain piece of paper and tracing the outline of your left foot, or your right, if it's larger. Send this outline to the mail-order shop. Cycling shoes should always be a little tight when new. They will loosen considerably with use.

Whatever you do, do not wear tennis shoes on a long cycling trip. Rubber shoes are no protection from rattrap pedals; after a few hours you will feel as if you were pedaling with bare feet. Ordinary shoes are not much better; they aren't flexible enough for efficient ankling. Cycling shoes are light, flexible, steel-shanked (as already noted), and very comfortable.

Fig. 32: Top, racing or touring cycling shoe. Bottom, winter touring boot. Bicycle shoes are recommended for the serious cyclist.

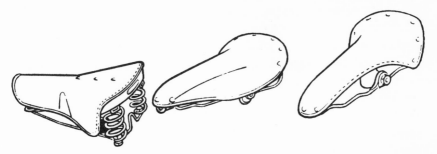

Fig. 33: *Typical road saddles. Left, mattress saddle; right, touring saddles. (For the rac-ing cyclist, many different makes and styles of saddles are available.) Reprinted with the permission of the English Universities Press Limited from "Teach Yourself Cycling" by Reginald C. Shaw.*

SADDLE ADJUSTMENT

Proper adjustment of the saddle (or seat) is very important to riding comfort. But first, let's review quickly the various types of saddles (Fig. 33).

The mattress-spring, wide saddle, which is found on conventional three-speed bicycles, is fine for that type of machine. The three-speed bicycle has conventional handlebars, so most of the rider's weight is on the saddle.

The smaller, lighter, and more compact saddle found on better ten-speed derailleur bicycles may look uncomfortable at first. However, an experienced cyclist knows that with dropped handlebars, the body is bent forward and the hands are on the bars, so that his weight is distributed more or less evenly between the seat and the handlebars. A wide saddle would interfere with thigh movement. Also, the mattress springs in the wide saddle absorb a great deal of energy that an experienced cyclist would much prefer to apply to the pedals.

Actually, the narrow, racing-type saddles can be very comfortable, particularly on long tours. The narrow saddles are made of either saddle leather or nylon. Nylon is lighter and fine for racing. For touring, how-ever, I prefer leather because it will absorb moisture, so there is less sliding about, particularly in hot weather.

Saddle height is important because leg muscles can only be used effi-ciently with correct saddle height, and everyone has different leg lengths.

Most cyclists ride on saddles that are far too low for comfort and pedaling efficiency. You have seen cyclists on any city or suburban street pedaling madly (but slowly), with their knees practically touching their chins and their bicycles wobbling from side to side. Parents hop on their child's bike, and sometimes take it for a four- or five-mile ride without ever considering saddle height. Many bicycle dealers don't give this a thought either. A discount house or department store will offer you no choice; all adjustments are strictly do-it-yourself.

While sitting on the saddle, you should be able to just reach the pedals comfortably with the heels of your feet. At first, you might feel it a bit awkward when you raise the saddle to its proper height, but after about a mile of cycling you will find that pedaling is a great deal easier, and that you are actually balanced on the seat better. You will be able to turn around occasionally to check traffic without losing your balance.

Saddles can be adjusted by loosening the screw and nut located at the bottom of the seat pillar, and pulling the saddle and saddle pillar up or down as needed.

A saddle can be repositioned toward or away from the handlebars by loosening the nut on the saddle clip (Fig. 34) and moving the saddle in either direction. While individual preferences vary according to arm length, the average rider is best fitted when the nose of the saddle is between two and three inches behind a vertical line drawn through the center of the bottom bracket (see Fig. 23). Or, for a rough fit, adjust the saddle so that its center bisects the center of the seat post. Make no further adjustments until you have ridden the bicycle for at least two

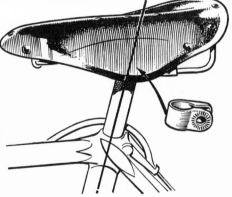

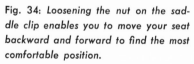

Fig. 34: *Loosening the nut on the saddle clip enables you to move your seat backward and forward to find the most comfortable position.*

miles, after which fine adjustments should be made to comply with individual differences in arm and body length.

When you loosen the saddle clip nut, you will also be able to tilt the saddle up or down. A saddle should have a very slight upward tilt—its forward peak slightly higher than its rear—for best distribution of weight between legs and arms.

All of the above instructions apply to both men and women.

Scientific Saddle Height Adjustment

Experiments conducted at Loughborough University, England, illustrate the importance of saddle height to cycling efficiency.[2]

The experiments, which used well-known racing cyclists and a bicycle ergometer (a stationary bicycle) with a harness to hold the rider in position, showed that cycling energy output varies significantly with minor changes in saddle height. Tests proved that alterations in saddle height of 4 percent of inside leg measurement affected power output by about 5 percent. Experimenters also concluded that the most efficient saddle height is 109 percent of inside leg measurement.

These are average values, however, and it must be expected that some minor variations will be necessary for individual builds and preferences. But it is interesting to note that recent studies of racing cyclists reveal that the better racers tend to have their saddle height conform to this formula.

How does one adjust saddle height to 109 percent of leg length? The method is easy:

First, measure the length of your leg *on the inside*, from the floor to the crotch bone, while standing erect and without shoes.

Then, multiply this length as measured in inches by 109 percent. Let's say, for example, that your leg measures forty inches from floor to crotch. Multiply $40 \times 1.09 = 43.6$ inches (or approximately 43½ inches). With the crank parallel to the plane of the seat tube (Fig. 35), measure or adjust the saddle so that the top of the saddle is 43½ inches from the pedal spindle.

---

[2] Vaughn Thomas, "Scientific Setting of Saddle Position," *American Cycling* (now *Bicycling!*), June, 1967, p. 12.

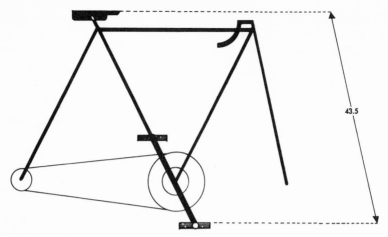

Fig. 35: A scientific method of adjusting saddle height is measuring leg height from floor to crotch, on inside of leg, and multiplying this measurement by 1.09. Result should equal length from top of saddle to pedal spindle, as shown above. If leg measures 40 inches, saddle height should be 43.6 inches (make it 43½ inches).

Some cyclists will not want to follow this formula because they feel more comfortable at some other saddle-to-leg length ratio. But you should bear in mind that saddle height is something one becomes accustomed to, and any particular saddle adjustment is not necessarily the most efficient because it is, at the moment, the most comfortable. The beginning cyclist who adjusts his saddle according to the formula above will, in my opinion, be more likely to wind up a more efficient cyclist than the experienced cyclist who departs from this formula.

Few people are more opinionated than racing cyclists, or more concerned with the minute details of technique and equipment. Yet, when this formula for saddle height adjustment was announced in 1967, a fierce controversy arose and many skeptics protested. The furor appears to have died down, and many professional cyclists, as well as their coaches and scientists who are interested in cycling, have adopted the formula.

Don't forget that this formula is the result of tests on 100 racing cyclists, ranging from beginners to the late world champion, Tommy Simpson. Four hundred readings were obtained at four different saddle heights— 105, 109, 113, and 117 percent of inside leg measurements. These measurements were made from the top of the saddle to the pedal spindle at the bottom of the stroke, with the *crank* aligned with the seat tube.

If you find that there is a great difference between the formula height and the present height of your saddle, I would suggest that you make the adjustment gradually, in increments of a quarter-inch, over a period of several months. This will give you time to adjust to the new setting, and give the formula a fair try. If you boost or lower the saddle height an inch or so to adjust to the formula at one time, you might find the new setting uncomfortable. Saddle height, as I said above, is something one can adjust to.

I have tried this formula on long trips. Once I had gotten used to the minor change I had to make, I found my cycling more efficient.

Saddle Height Affects Muscular Power Output in Cycling

Muscles have ranges of optimum stretch. They will stretch only to a limited degree. Experts say that leg muscles can exert more power as they approach the fully extended position—one reason why people who use a child's bicycle without readjusting the saddle huff and puff so ridiculously. But, if leg muscles are stretched beyond their maximum capacity by a saddle that is too high, fluidity of leg movement will be disrupted.

The saddle height of 109 percent of leg measurement seems to give the best combination of maximum muscle stretch and maximum fluidity.

5

ANYONE CAN RIDE A BICYCLE— HOW TO DO IT

If you don't know how to ride a bicycle at all, the best way to start is with a twenty-six-inch-wheel, three-speed bicycle with seat and handlebars adjusted to fit, as discussed on pages 91-94 and 99-103 (see Fig. 3). Have someone hold you up as you sit on the bicycle until you get the feel of the machine and can balance a little. Most people have a pretty good sense of balance, and with an hour's practice you should be able to wobble around your block.

Even if you think you *know* how to ride a bicycle already, chances are that unless you've ridden a lot with experienced cyclists, you don't know the technique that will send you soaring over hilltops while others are struggling behind.

Let me tell you a story that Keith Kingbay, Cycling Activities Director of the Schwinn Company, likes to relate. Keith and his wife, Rosetta (a young-looking grandmother), were visiting friends in Florida, when a young man (let's call him Jack) dropped in, on his weekly sixteen- to twenty-mile bicycle trip into the country. Keith told Jack that he and Rosetta would like to go along, to which Jack replied that they were welcome, if they could keep up. Keith said he thought they could. Keith let Rosetta set the pace, and to Jack's surprise, after a few miles he was gasping for breath. By the time they reached their destination, some twenty miles away, Jack was virtually exhausted and suggested a lunch stop. Rosetta blandly said that she was just warming up and that if they turned right around, they'd be just in time for a late lunch at the home of one of their friends.

Obviously, there was quite a difference between the cycling techniques of the young, muscular rider and the older man and woman. (They all had the same type bicycle.)

Proper cycling technique is the secret to tireless long cycling trips and real bicycling enjoyment. Naturally, the bicycle itself makes a big difference; you can't pedal a fifty-pound, balloon-tired machine as long as a precision-built, twenty-one-pound bicycle.

"ANKLING" TECHNIQUE

The most important first step in learning to cycle efficiently is to "ankle" correctly (Fig. 36). Ankling simply means efficient pedaling. If your bicycle is a conventional three-speed machine with rubber pedals, start by cycling *only* with the ball of your foot. *Never* place your arch on the pedals; you'll never be able to use your leg muscles effectively that way. When you use rattrap, all-steel pedals and toe clips, you have no choice; the toe clips keep the ball of the foot on the pedal correctly.

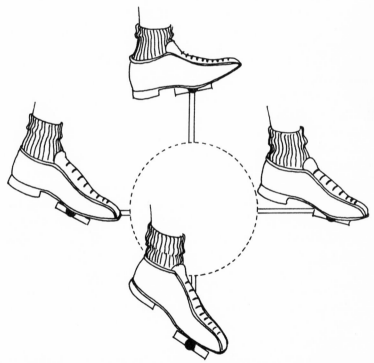

Fig. 36: Never pedal on your arch. For maximum efficiency, use ball of foot. Then ankle correctly to get maximum pedaling action, as shown here. Correct ankling technique involves ankle positions with toe pointing slightly upward at top of stroke to push pedal forward and down; downward at bottom of stroke to force pedal back and up.

To learn how to ankle properly, ride your bicycle someplace where you can watch your ankles as you ride, without having to beware of traffic or obstructions. A bicycle exerciser is an excellent way to practice ankling. Or a country road or school parking lot will do.

With the pedal at the top of its stroke (the twelve o'clock position), push forward with your foot. Toes should be up slightly, heels down. As the pedal descends, follow it with your foot by pushing your toe downward until just past three o'clock. Continuing this motion, the heel should be up and toe down at the six o'clock position (just the reverse of the top position).

Ankling or stroking should not be jerky. You should apply a steady pressure from the top of the stroke all the way to the bottom, with your ankle following the arc or angle of the pedal from top to bottom of the forward stroke. Try ankling with one foot only. Racing cyclists wear shoe cleats that fit into the steel pedal and are held on by toe straps, and they ankle "around the clock." As the pedal reaches the six o'clock position, the heel is up, the toe down, and you can actually *pull* the pedal back around to the ten o'clock position.

To review the ankling technique, at the twelve o'clock position, the heel is facing slightly downward with the toe up. At the four o'clock position, the toe is slightly downward and the heel upward. At the bottom or six o'clock position, the heel should be facing upward at an angle of about forty-five degrees, the toe should be down. The foot should be held at nearly this angle to the ten o'clock position.

Racing cyclists, wearing toe clips (Fig. 37), straps, and shoe cleats (see Fig. 31), can also continue ankling around the clock by pulling the foot straight upward from the six to the twelve o'clock position.

Practice ankling correctly until you do it automatically, and you will find cycling much easier and more enjoyable. A good way to practice is to put the gears in the highest ratio so that the pedals move as slowly as possible to permit you to watch your ankling technique. If you wear straps, keep them tight, but not fully strapped, so you can release them quickly, if necessary.

THE IMPORTANCE OF CADENCE

The next step in attaining cycling efficiency is pedaling "cadence." Cadence means pedaling at a relatively constant crank rotation speed,

Fig. 37: Toe clips are essential for any kind of distance riding, particularly for cycle touring. Only with toe clips and rattrap pedals can you ankle efficiently through 360 degrees of the pedal movement. Keep toe straps tight when touring, but loose in city traffic so you can draw foot out quickly when stopping for any reason.

changing gears only when pedaling becomes too hard in one gear, or so easy that cadence cannot be maintained.

We all have different natural cadences, or pedaling revolutions per minute, at which we feel most comfortable. For most of us, from sixty-five to eighty-five pedal strokes per minute is the pace we can maintain most comfortably for the longest period. The reason for gear changes on a bicycle, then, is not only to help you climb hills or go down grades faster; they also help you maintain your natural pedaling cadence at all times.

The mistake most beginning cyclists make is to think of bicycle gears as being like automobile gears, with their bodies as the engine. The fault in this thinking is that whereas you can advance gears on a car and the engine will push the car faster, on a bicycle, you can advance gears without getting much speed at all. As an engine your body is severely limited. And if you are thinking that you can travel faster and longer in high than low gears, then you are wrong, at least if you are an average cyclist and not a trained racing champion. You would actually penalize yourself by riding in high gears for long distances; although you might be able to maintain your natural cadence for a short time, you would find your pedal revolutions per minute slowing down bit by bit until you were literally forcing your feet around the pedaling arc and making your body wobble from side to side with the effort.

Cycling should be fun, not strenuous. Find your natural cadence and shift gears only to maintain it.

As soon as it becomes work to maintain good cadence, shift down. When you find your feet zipping around the arc without resistance, shift up. Beginning cyclists should stick to the lower gear range until they find their natural cadence. On a three-speed bicycle, stay in low or second gear. On a ten- or fifteen-speed bicycle, stay in the next to lowest gear ratio for the first 100 miles. This will establish and help you to get used to your natural cadence pedaling rpm. Then you can change gears when necessary, according to the vagaries of wind velocity, road grade, your current physical condition, or a load you may be carrying.

Do not change through the whole ten gears at once. Shift from one gear range to the next until you feel comfortable at your natural cadence.

HOW TO CHANGE GEARS—THREE-SPEED HUBS

To change gears on a three-speed internal rear hub, such as the Sturmey-Archer, ease off pedaling, pedal gently, and snap the gear quickly into the new gear. You can change gears at a stoplight, going to the lower gear for a quicker getaway. If you change gears when the bicycle is stopped, rest the weight of your foot on the higher pedal (at the two o'clock position) while you make the change. This will allow the internal gears to rotate and change easily.

HOW TO CHANGE GEARS—DERAILLEURS

Before you ride your new ten- or fifteen-speed derailleur bicycle, hang it by the handlebars and seat from the ceiling, or have someone hold the rear wheel off the ground while you turn the cranks by hand and move the gear levers from one position to another. Watch how the front and rear derailleurs work, as they change gears by derailing or moving the chain from one gear to the other.

If you have a ten-speed, you will find five rear gears and two front chainwheels. If you have a fifteen-speed, you will find five rear gears and a triple chainwheel. Any gear position of any of the front chainwheels is intermediate to any two rear gears. (See the full discussion of gear ratios and their meaning on page 118.)

As you change gears while moving the pedals by hand, you will note that there are no notches or other fixed positions of the gear-shift levers to tell you exactly what gear you're in, or when to stop the lever for a particular gear position. You will simply have to get used to shifting gears by the feel of it. Try changing gears. Watch how the chain moves from one gear to the next as you move the gear lever. You might note that the chain does not always go perfectly from one gear to the next, but seems to rub on an adjoining gear, and that sometimes you hear a grinding noise. This noise means that the gear-shift lever is not in the right position; you should readjust it in one direction or the other until you do not hear this noise. This is very important, for if you get into the habit of careless shifting, and ignore grinding noises, you will be in for trouble, such as a broken chain and marred gear teeth. If as you shift, the chain rubs against the spokes in the low-gear position or the chain stays (fork section holding wheel axle) in the high-gear position, readjust the derailleur mechanism as outlined on pages 233-49.

Let me make one point perfectly clear. *You must never shift derailleur gears unless you are pedaling. The cranks must be moving when you shift.* If you stop pedaling, change gears, then start pedaling again, you might tear up the chain or the teeth and possibly damage the derailleur mechanism.

Good ten-speed derailleur-equipped bicycles are still enough of a novelty to tempt itchy-fingered young children (and some adults) to play with the gear-shift levers, if you park your bicycle where they can get at it. If someone has moved your gear-shift levers from the position they were in when you parked your bicycle, and you unsuspectingly climb on and start to ride, you may also damage gears and derailleur, just as if you shifted gears improperly without continuing to pedal. So, always, after you have left your bicycle unattended for a while, start riding very gingerly, applying very gentle pressure to the pedals. If the gear levers have been moved, very gentle pedaling will at least permit the derailleur to work without tearing up the works. Another technique is to hoist up the rear wheels by the seat with one hand and twirl the crank with the other. This will let the chain move to another position without damaging it. Then you can mount, ride, and return the chain to the gear combination you prefer. (For a full discussion of gearing, see Chapter 6.)

RIDING THE STRAIGHT AND NARROW

Part of correct riding is to be able to ride and steer accurately. With a little training and attention to correct riding technique, you should be able to steer right down a yellow dividing line (a path about four inches wide) and stay on it. This is important to safety, as we have already discussed.

Meanwhile, remember that good riding is easy riding. You should ride relatively relaxed, without your muscles being all knotted up.

TIPS FOR EASY CYCLING

There are six positions (Fig. 38–Fig. 43) for riding bikes with dropped handlebars; shifting from one to another will help you beat fatigue on a long trip.

On tours, do not try to be the first in line, unless you're in top physical condition. If you stay behind the leader, or behind two or three other riders, they will "break the wind" for you, and you will be able to ride farther before tiring.

Watch yourself as you ride. Make sure you do not wobble from side to side, bend your back up and down as you pump, or pump with leg muscles. Learn to use your stomach, back, ankle, thigh, and leg muscles as a team to help you cycle smoothly, without tiring.

I have spent hours watching highly trained road and track cyclists riding their bicycles, trying to learn their technique. These cyclists are a symphony of effortless motion. They ride true as an arrow, with absolutely no side wobble, legs pumping like smooth-functioning pistons, and the ankles and feet like wrist pins. It looks so easy, until you mount your bicycle and try to fall in behind them. You discover that while the racing cyclist looks like he is just loafing along, he is actually pedaling away at about thirty miles per hour, and you will probably not be able to catch up to him, or, if you do, not for long.

I am not trying to make a racing cyclist out of every overweight adult American, though. I am just simply showing you how proper technique will make cycling more fun, even if to learn this technique takes practice. Once these good riding methods have become a habit, cycling will really be a joy for you, and perhaps someday you will surprise all your friends by doing the century (100-mile) tour in a single eight-hour day. There are hundreds of others—fathers, mothers, grandfathers, grandmothers—who do the century run regularly every year.

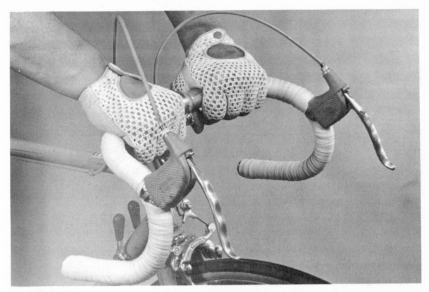

Fig. 38: *There are six basic positions for placing hands on handlebars, which you can vary from time to time to change cycling position on long rides. In this position, hands are at top of handlebars, next to stem.*

Fig. 39: *Hands at end of bars, just above brake levers. This is the usual position most riders seem to prefer.*

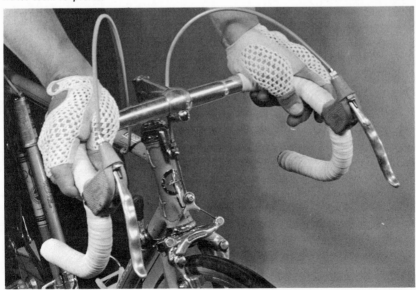

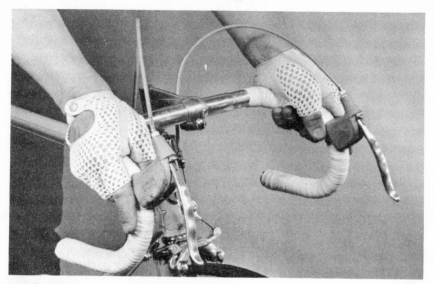

Fig. 40: *In the same position as in Figure 39, but with thumb and forefinger extended downward.*

Fig. 41: *Base of thumb and forefinger rest on brake levers, providing support for forward weight of upper torso. This is a particularly restful position to adopt on long downhill "coasts," with the added safety factor of allowing you to reach brake levers quickly and conveniently.*

Fig. 42: *This position is used frequently when the going is hard, as on an uphill climb.*

Fig. 43: *And ths is the work position, when the rider is bent as far forward as possible to minimize wind resistance and get as much speed as possible out of the bicycle. (Figures 38 through 43 courtesy Schwinn Bicycle Company.)*

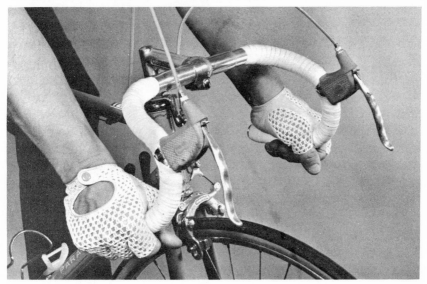

MOUNTING

I prefer cleated cycling shoes to toe straps because they increase pedaling efficiency about 30 to 40 percent, but you might not like them. Whatever you prefer, if you do use rattrap pedals with straps, you will have to learn how to mount the bicycle and how to insert one foot into the pedal quickly and safely. Once under way, you won't have time to fuss and look down, trying to fit your foot into the pedal; you must keep your eye on the road. You should practice slipping your free foot promptly into the pedal.

Try this mounting technique. Straddle the bicycle, put one foot in a toe-clip pedal, and pull the pedal up to the one o'clock position. One foot is in a pedal; the other is on the ground. Use the foot on the ground to shove you off and get you moving, while in one graceful, quick motion you pull yourself up into the saddle by pushing down on the other pedal and hoisting yourself up by pressure on the handlebars. The foot that pushes down the pedal should get you 90 percent of the way into the saddle and, at the same time, get you going forward quickly. Hold the pedals still a moment while you insert your toe and then your foot into the empty pedal. Practice this technique until it's as easy as rising from a chair to walk around the room. Mounting your bicycle this way will distinguish you as an experienced cyclist, at least to other experienced cyclists.

6

GEARS TO FIT THE RIDER
TO THE ROAD—
ALL ABOUT BICYCLE GEARING

The whole subject of gear ratios may seem complicated or even trivial to you. If your interest in cycling is confined to using a no-gear coaster-brake monster, or a three-speed hub utility bicycle, then you should skip this chapter.

But, if you have a ten- or fifteen-speed derailleur-equipped bicycle, and are interested in cycle touring as well as around-the-block jaunts, gear ratios are important because they can mean the difference between efficient or wasted use of the muscles you have with the wheels you push with them. If you want to become a road, track, or cross-country racer, an avid and dedicated interest in gear ratios is a "must."

Let me explain why. Automobiles have engines of a fixed horsepower and wheels of a fixed size. Given these fixed factors, the car designer selects gears of specific ratios for maximum or at least relatively efficient performance. The gear ratios he selects are based on the horsepower available to him.

When you go into a bicycle store to buy one of the popular American-made, low-cost, ten-speed derailleur-equipped machines, you don't have to worry much about gear ratios, because manufacturers have long since learned that the average buyer is usually a long way from being as physically strong and as competent a cyclist as the really experienced bicycle enthusiast. You'll find that the gear ratios on the less expensive models jump from high to low in fairly substantial ratios, so that you have a pretty wide range of gears to shift from on the road.

If you spend a little extra money, however, and buy a really fine machine, you'll more likely than not get a bicycle with close gear ratios, so that the difference between the highest and the lowest gear selections is much smaller than on the lower-cost machines. The reason for this difference is that all the finer machines except the Schwinn Paramount are European-made, and European manufacturers make bikes for the more dedicated and therefore, presumably, the more physically fit and competent cyclists, who will want closer gear ratios for maximum speed and performance. This should be a word of warning for you, because you might buy a higher-priced bicycle with ten-speed derailleur gears, and should not be too surprised to find that on steep hills the difference between the high and low gear ratios isn't as great as you might have imagined. In other words, if you want a good machine but aren't as experienced or as physically fit as you will be later on as you continue to cycle, you should specify gear ratios more in keeping with your needs. The dealer who sells you a good bicycle will most likely be among the rare few who knows how to change gears cogs on freewheels, and he will be able to select wider ratios for you very easily.

For example, the Schwinn Paramount, which is Schwinn's top-line model and just as good as the best European bicycles (though more costly), comes with a rear sprocket cluster of 24, 21, 18, 16, and 14 teeth and with front chainwheels of 49 and 52 teeth (a fairly close-range selection). Schwinn's lower-priced models, however, come with rear sprocket clusters of 28, 24, 20, 16, and 14 teeth and with front chainwheels of 39 and 50 teeth (a very wide range). For the average rider who wants a good bicycle but wants (and needs) a wide gear ratio selection, the 28–14 rear cluster and 40–50 front chainwheel combination is just about right. Only the well-seasoned and experienced cyclist can do without wider ratios.

For the beginning cyclist or for one who is about to graduate from the heavy three-speed rear hub twenty-six-inch wheel bicycle to a really efficient, lightweight, ten- or fifteen-speed derailleur-equipped machine, this is about all you'll need to know about gear ratios. But, if you want to make sure you have the correct gear ratios for your physical condition, here are a few tips, and some simple tables on how to figure out ratios.

Before you buy your good machine, count the number of teeth on each of the gears on the rear derailleur. For example, the freewheel gears on the usual fine machine will start with 23 teeth on the large gear and work down in two-tooth jumps to 15 teeth on the small gear, so that you will have gears of 23, 21, 19, 17, and 15 teeth. This is a close ratio freewheel that I do not recommend for the average cyclist for cross-country tours, or for riding about in hilly country, because there is not enough variation in gear selections. You can have your bicycle dealer install a set of gears with a wider range. I recommend a rear freewheel gear cluster with these teeth: 28, 24, 20, 17, and 14, with double chainwheel of 40 and 50 teeth.

ABOUT TRIPLE CHAINWHEELS

If you are planning to pack a thirty- to forty-pound load for cross-country distance touring, you will need a wider range of gears. I'd keep the wide-range rear freewheel cluster as described (28, 24, 20, 17, 14) and change over to a three-speed triple front chainwheel. There are a number of makes of good triple chainwheels of lightweight dural metal (aluminum alloy) with cotterless cranks.

Remember, though, to order the same make of triple chainwheel as the double chainwheel you now have. You will also need a longer axle (also of the same make) to accommodate the extra width of the third chainwheel, although you can use the cones and bearings you had on your double chainwheel. Before you do any changing over, be sure to review the instructions for chainwheel and axle maintenance, assembly, and disassembly, on pages 286-95, including the tools required.

THE IMPORTANCE OF DERAILLEUR CAPACITY

Also, before you start changing freewheel and chainwheel gear ratios, remember that the ability of rear derailleurs to cope with wide variations in gear ratios is strictly limited. You may have to change your derailleur to one with more capacity. Rear derailleur capacity is measured by the maximum-minimum teeth it will handle. For example, let's say your large front chainwheel has 49 teeth and your small chainwheel 44 teeth. That's a pretty small range, and the five-tooth difference falls well within the range of all derailleurs. But if you install a 34-tooth front third chainwheel and have a 28-tooth rear gear, you may have trouble using both lower gear ratios, unless you get a wide-range derailleur such as the Campagnolo "Record" derailleur, which will accommodate even the new six-gear cluster freewheels.

A WORD ABOUT GEAR RATIOS

All I've said about gear combinations applies only to 27-inch wheel bicycles with derailleurs and 6½-inch cranks. I do not consider 26-inch, three- or even five-speed rear hubs much use for touring long distances. These bicycles are too heavy, gear ratios aren't wide enough, and the whole machine is too clumsy for anything but around-the-block riding. This does not mean that you cannot tour across the country with heavier machines; you can, but you will pay a stiff penalty in weight, inefficiency, reduced daily mileage, and time.

Gear ratios simply mean those combinations of gears (number of teeth) which cover the distance traveled with one revolution of the pedals. For your convenience, a gear table (Fig. 44) is given on page 119. To find what gear ratio you have with any combination of the gears on your bicycle, use the chart as follows. Let's say you have a chainwheel with 50 teeth and use 27-inch wheels and a rear sprocket with 20 teeth. Look under the chainwheel column until you find 50 th, which means 50 teeth. Now move down the far lefthand column, under "sprocket size," until you come to the number 20. Follow this line to the right until you intersect with the 50 th, 27-inch-wheel vertical column. The number you will find is 67.5, which means your gear ratio with a 20-tooth rear sprocket, a 50-tooth chainwheel, and 27-inch wheels is 67½. In other words, with this combination of front and rear gears, for every revolution of the crank, your bicycle will travel forward 67½ inches.

THE MEANING OF CADENCE

Now that you know how to find gear ratios, and understand that the term simply means those combinations of gears, crank length, and wheel diameter which will move your bicycle forward a specific number of

Fig. 44: To find out what gear ratios you have, use this table as follows: Take any front ➤ and rear gear combination. Let's say the rear gear has 20 teeth, the front chainwheel 50 teeth, and you use 27-inch-wheels. From the table, running down the 50th column under 27-inch-wheel, you'll find your gear ratio to be 67.5. Courtesy: Cyclo-Gear Co., Ltd., Birmingham, England.

CYCLO'S GEAR CHART. 26" & 27" WHEELS

CHAIN WHEEL 24th – 44th

sprocket size	24th 26in	24th 27in	26th 26in	26th 27in	28th 26in	28th 27in	30th 26in	30th 27in	32nd 26in	32nd 27in	34th 26in	34th 27in	36th 26in	36th 27in	38th 26in	38th 27in	40th 26in	40th 27in	42nd 26in	42nd 27in	44th 26in	44th 27in
12	52.1	54.1	56.3	58.5	60.6	63.0	65.0	67.5	69.2	72.0	73.8	76.5	78.0	81.1	82.4	85.5	86.7	90.0	91.0	94.5	95.3	99.0
13	48.0	49.8	52.0	54.0	56.0	58.1	60.0	62.3	64.1	66.4	68.0	70.6	72.0	74.7	76.0	78.9	80.0	83.1	84.0	87.2	88.0	91.4
14	44.7	46.2	48.2	50.1	52.0	54.0	55.7	57.8	59.5	61.7	63.1	65.5	66.8	69.5	70.6	73.3	74.3	77.1	78.0	81.0	81.7	84.9
15	41.6	43.2	45.0	46.8	48.5	50.4	52.0	54.0	55.6	57.6	59.0	61.1	62.4	64.8	65.9	68.4	69.3	72.0	72.8	75.6	76.3	79.2
16	39.1	40.5	42.2	43.7	45.5	47.2	48.7	50.6	52.0	54.0	55.2	57.2	58.5	60.9	61.8	64.1	65.0	67.5	68.3	70.9	71.5	74.3
17	36.7	38.1	39.7	41.2	42.8	44.4	45.8	47.6	49.0	50.8	52.0	54.0	55.0	57.2	58.1	60.3	61.2	63.5	64.2	66.7	67.3	69.9
18	34.6	36.0	37.5	39.0	40.5	42.0	43.3	45.0	46.2	48.0	49.2	51.0	52.0	54.0	54.9	57.0	57.8	60.0	60.6	63.0	63.6	66.0
19	32.9	34.1	35.5	36.8	38.3	39.7	41.0	42.6	43.8	45.5	46.5	48.2	49.2	51.1	52.0	54.0	54.7	56.8	57.5	59.7	60.2	62.5
20	31.2	32.4	33.8	35.1	36.4	37.8	39.0	40.5	41.6	43.2	44.2	45.9	46.7	48.7	49.4	51.3	52.0	54.0	54.6	56.7	57.2	59.4
21	29.7	30.8	32.1	33.4	34.6	36.0	37.1	38.6	39.7	41.1	42.0	43.7	44.5	46.4	47.0	48.9	49.5	51.4	52.0	54.0	54.5	56.6
22	28.4	29.4	30.7	31.9	33.0	34.3	35.4	36.8	37.9	39.2	40.2	41.6	42.5	44.2	44.9	46.6	47.3	49.1	49.6	51.5	52.0	54.0
23	27.1	28.1	29.3	30.5	31.6	32.8	33.9	35.2	36.2	37.5	38.4	39.9	40.6	42.4	43.0	44.6	45.2	47.0	47.5	49.3	49.8	51.6
24	26.0	27.0	28.1	29.2	30.3	31.5	32.5	33.7	34.7	36.0	36.8	38.2	39.0	40.5	41.2	42.8	43.3	45.0	45.5	47.3	47.7	49.5
25	25.0	25.9	27.0	28.0	29.1	30.2	31.2	32.4	33.4	34.6	35.4	36.7	37.4	38.9	39.5	41.0	41.6	43.2	43.7	45.4	45.8	47.5
26	24.1	24.9	26.0	27.0	28.0	29.0	30.0	31.2	32.0	33.2	34.0	35.3	36.0	37.4	38.0	39.5	40.0	41.5	42.0	43.6	44.0	45.7
28	22.3	23.1	24.1	25.0	26.0	27.0	27.8	28.9	29.7	30.8	31.6	32.8	33.4	34.8	35.3	36.6	37.1	38.6	39.0	40.5	40.9	42.4

CHAIN WHEEL 45th – 56th

sprocket size	45th 26in	45th 27in	46th 26in	46th 27in	47th 26in	47th 27in	48th 26in	48th 27in	49th 26in	49th 27in	50th 26in	50th 27in	52nd 26in	52nd 27in	53rd 26in	53rd 27in	54th 26in	54th 27in	55th 26in	55th 27in	56th 26in	56th 27in
12	97.5	101.2	99.7	103.5	101.8	105.7	104.0	108.0	106.1	110.2	108.3	112.3	112.7	117.0	114.8	119.3	117.0	121.5	119.1	123.7	121.3	126.0
13	90.0	93.4	92.0	95.5	94.0	97.6	96.0	99.7	98.0	101.8	100.0	103.9	104.0	108.0	106.0	110.0	108.0	112.1	110.0	114.2	112.0	116.3
14	83.5	86.7	85.4	88.7	87.3	90.6	89.1	92.6	91.0	94.5	92.9	96.4	96.6	100.3	98.4	102.2	100.3	104.1	102.1	106.0	104.0	108.0
15	78.0	80.9	79.7	82.8	81.5	84.6	83.2	86.4	84.9	88.2	86.7	90.0	90.1	93.6	91.8	95.4	93.6	97.2	95.3	99.0	97.0	100.8
16	73.1	76.0	74.6	77.6	76.4	79.3	78.0	81.0	79.6	82.7	81.3	84.4	84.5	87.8	86.1	89.4	87.7	91.1	89.3	92.8	91.0	94.5
17	68.8	71.5	70.4	73.1	71.9	74.6	73.4	76.2	74.9	77.8	76.5	79.4	79.5	82.6	81.0	84.1	82.5	85.7	84.1	87.3	85.6	88.9
18	65.0	67.5	66.4	69.0	67.9	70.5	69.3	72.0	70.7	73.5	72.2	75.0	75.1	78.0	76.5	79.5	78.0	81.0	79.4	82.5	80.8	84.0
19	61.7	64.0	62.9	65.4	64.3	66.8	65.7	68.2	67.0	69.6	68.4	71.1	71.2	73.9	72.5	75.3	73.9	76.7	75.2	78.1	76.6	79.5
20	58.5	60.8	59.8	62.1	61.1	63.4	62.4	64.8	63.7	66.2	65.0	67.5	67.6	70.2	68.9	71.5	70.2	72.9	71.5	74.5	72.8	75.6
21	55.8	57.9	57.0	59.1	58.2	60.4	59.4	61.7	60.6	63.0	61.9	64.3	64.4	66.9	65.6	68.1	66.8	69.4	68.0	70.7	69.3	72.0
22	53.1	55.2	54.4	56.5	55.5	57.6	56.7	58.9	57.9	60.1	59.1	61.4	61.5	63.8	62.6	65.0	63.8	66.2	65.0	67.5	66.1	68.7
23	50.8	52.8	52.0	54.0	53.1	55.2	54.3	56.3	55.4	57.5	56.5	58.7	58.8	61.0	59.9	62.2	61.0	63.6	62.1	64.5	63.3	65.7
24	48.6	50.7	49.9	51.8	50.9	52.9	52.0	54.0	53.1	55.1	54.0	56.2	56.3	58.5	57.4	59.6	58.5	60.7	59.5	61.8	60.6	63.0
25	46.9	48.6	47.8	49.7	48.9	50.8	49.9	51.8	51.0	52.9	52.0	54.0	54.1	56.2	55.1	57.2	56.1	58.3	57.2	59.4	58.2	60.4
26	45.0	46.7	46.0	47.8	47.0	48.8	48.0	49.9	49.0	50.9	50.0	51.9	52.0	54.0	53.0	55.0	54.0	56.0	55.0	57.1	56.0	58.1
28	41.8	43.4	42.7	44.4	43.6	45.3	44.6	46.3	45.5	47.2	46.4	48.2	48.3	50.1	49.2	51.1	50.1	52.0	51.0	53.0	52.0	54.0

inches per crank turn, the next logical step is to ask yourself, "How fast can I travel in miles per hour at various crank revolutions per minute, at different gear ratios?" Or, to put it another way, "How fast can I go with the gear ratios I have, at various crank revolutions?"

First, let's establish what cadence means. Cadence is the pedaling or turning of the crank arm at more or less constant revolutions. It is important to understand this concept, because a regular cadence is necessary for smooth, long-distance cycling. You should try to pedal at the same rate of crank revolutions per minute all the time, varying your gear ratio to suit wind and road-grade conditions. For example, let's say you establish that a good cadence for you is between 60 and 75 turns of the crank per minute (for somebody with strong legs it may be 80 revolutions per minute and for a racing cyclist at high speed it may be 100 to 120, or more). You may be using a gear ratio of 87.8 (rear 16-tooth sprocket, front 52-tooth chainwheel). How fast will your bicycle move at a cadence of 60 crank revolutions per minute? To figure this out, just take a look at the handy cadence chart (Fig. 45). All you do is find the closest gear ratio to yours in the lefthand column (88), and move to the right one column under a cadence of 60. You will find that you should be traveling at 15.7 miles per hour.

Taking this chart one step further, you will recall that I recommended a combination of rear freewheel with 28, 24, 20, 17, and 14 teeth and a double chainwheel with 40 and 50 teeth. I am not going to figure out how fast you can go in all ten combinations of these gears; you can do this using the gear and cadence charts in this book. However, the 28-tooth rear sprocket and the 40-tooth chainwheel will give you a gear ratio of 38.6 with 27-inch wheels, and at a cadence of 60 you will travel at the lightning speed of 6.8 miles per hour (which is all you can expect on a steep grade). At another extreme, the 14-tooth rear sprocket and 50-tooth front chainwheel will give you a ratio of 96.4, and at a cadence of 60 will jet you along at around 17.5 miles per hour. And if you can beef up your cadence to 75 crank revolutions per minute, you'll be traveling at nearly 22 miles an hour. Of course, going downhill with a stiff wind behind you, you should be able to sustain a cadence of 90 to 100 revolutions per minute, and at the 100 figure with the top gear ratio of 96.4, you'll be whizzing along at around 30 miles an hour (watch out for sandy spots on turns!). It's not uncommon to find oneself going 40 miles an hour or even faster, down long, steep hills—coasting, though.

CADENCE CHART

GEAR RATIO	REVOLUTIONS PER MINUTE OF THE CRANK ARM										
	60	75	80	90	100	120	130	140	150	160	
38	6.8	8.5	9.06	10.2	11.4	13.6	14.7	15.85	17.0	18.2	MPH
40	7.15	8.95	9.55	10.7	11.95	14.3	15.5	16.7	17.8	19.1	MPH
42	7.50	9.40	10.0	11.25	12.55	15.0	16.30	17.5	18.7	20.1	MPH
44	7.85	9.85	10.5	11.8	13.15	15.7	17.0	18.3	19.6	21.0	MPH
46	8.21	10.3	11.0	12.32	13.72	16.4	17.8	19.2	20.5	22.0	MPH
48	8.51	10.72	11.45	12.88	14.32	17.15	18.6	20.0	21.40	22.9	MPH
50	8.94	11.2	11.9	13.4	14.9	17.9	19.4	20.8	22.3	23.85	MPH
52	9.3	11.68	12.4	13.95	15.5	18.5	20.2	21.65	23.2	24.9	MPH
54	9.65	12.1	12.9	14.5	16.2	19.3	20.9	22.5	24.1	25.9	MPH
56	10.0	12.5	13.4	15.0	16.7	20.0	21.7	23.4	25.0	26.75	MPH
58	10.36	12.95	13.82	15.55	17.3	20.7	22.5	24.2	25.9	27.6	MPH
60	10.75	13.4	14.3	16.1	17.9	21.4	23.25	25.0	26.8	28.7	MPH
62	11.1	13.85	14.8	16.6	18.5	22.2	24.0	25.85	27.7	29.6	MPH
64	11.43	14.3	15.3	17.2	19.1	22.9	24.8	26.7	28.6	30.5	MPH
66	11.8	14.64	15.65	17.7	19.7	23.6	25.6	27.5	29.6	31.5	MPH
68	12.12	15.2	16.3	18.2	20.3	24.3	26.4	28.4	30.5	32.45	MPH
70	12.51	15.65	16.7	18.75	21.0	25.0	27.1	29.2	31.3	33.4	MPH
72	12.87	16.1	17.2	19.3	21.5	25.7	27.9	30.0	32.2	34.4	MPH
74	13.2	16.58	17.7	19.8	22.1	26.55	28.7	30.9	33.0	35.3	MPH
76	13.6	17.0	18.1	20.4	22.7	27.2	29.4	31.7	34.0	36.3	MPH
78	13.9	17.4	18.6	20.9	23.4	27.9	30.2	32.6	34.8	37.2	MPH
80	14.3	17.9	19.1	21.45	23.9	28.6	31.0	33.3	35.8	38.2	MPH
82	14.62	18.35	19.5	22.0	24.5	29.4	31.8	34.2	36.65	39.1	MPH
84	15.0	18.8	20.0	22.6	25.1	30.0	32.6	35.0	37.6	40.0	MPH
86	15.4	19.2	20.55	23.0	25.75	30.7	33.4	35.9	38.4	41.1	MPH
88	15.7	19.7	21.0	23.6	26.3	31.5	34.15	36.8	39.3	42.0	MPH
90	16.1	20.2	21.5	24.2	27.0	32.2	34.8	37.5	40.2	43.0	MPH
92	16.44	20.6	22.0	24.65	27.45	32.8	35.6	38.3	41.3	43.9	MPH
94	16.8	21.0	22.45	25.2	28.1	33.6	36.4	39.2	42.0	44.9	MPH
96	17.15	21.5	22.95	25.75	28.7	34.3	37.2	40.0	42.8	45.8	MPH
98	17.5	21.9	23.4	26.2	29.25	35.0	38.0	40.8	43.8	46.7	MPH
100	17.9	22.4	23.9	26.8	29.95	35.75	38.8	41.7	44.8	47.8	MPH
102	18.2	22.8	24.4	27.3	30.45	36.55	39.6	42.6	45.7	48.8	MPH
104	18.6	23.25	24.85	27.9	31.0	37.25	40.4	43.4	46.7	49.6	MPH
106	18.9	23.7	25.3	28.4	31.3	37.9	41.3	44.2	47.5	50.6	MPH

CYCLO-PEDIA Cadence Chart. Calibrated by Professor Paul R. ''Pop'' Kepner.

Fig. 45: *This cadence chart puts meaning into gear ratios, telling you how fast you'll travel in any gear ratio, given a steady cadence or revolutions per minute of the pedal cranks. For example, find your gear ratio from Figure 44. Let's say it's 68.5. Find the closest ratio (68) in the left hand column under "Gear Ratio." Then determine how fast you can comfortably pedal at this gear ratio. Let's say it's 75 pedal crank revolutions per minute. Moving down the 75 column to the 68 gear-ratio column at left, you'll find the number 15.2, which means you pedal 15.2 miles per hour with a 68 gear-ratio at a pedal cadence of 75 revolutions per minute. Courtesy of Cyclo-Pedia and Professor Paul R. "Pop" Kepner.*

7

CYCLE TOURING AND CAMPING—
A FUN WAY TO
SEE THE WORLD

Sooner or later, if you have bought one of the better ten- or fifteen-speed derailleur bicycles described in Chapter 3, you'll want to do more than just pedal around the block. And you will never experience the real fun of cycling until you take weekend jaunts, or longer tours.

If you are thinking about taking a bicycle trip, and I urge you to do so, there are a few things you should know.

In the first place, your trip should be planned in meticulous detail with regard to route and equipment. If you plan to stop at motels, you can get by with a minimum of gear. But if you want to camp out, you will need a lightweight tent and sleeping bag, cooking gear, and other equipment that should be selected with careful attention to utility and portability.

Let's start with the trip itself. The American Youth Hostels regularly schedule bicycle trips of various distances and duration from most major cities. There are AYH chapters in most cities, which you may join even if you don't live in the particular city. Or you can be a member-at-large, and select the group you want to travel with. Don't let the word "youth" fool you. American Youth Hostels members are of all ages, although, naturally, the majority of cyclists are under thirty. The AYH maintain hostels all over the United States, and as a member, you will be entitled to a list of them. All you have to do to use the facilities is to bring either your own sheet (lightweight nylon is preferable) or a sleeping bag or both.

A big advantage of joining an AYH cycle-touring group is that you will be under the watchful eye of an experienced leader, who will make sure that the day's journey is within your physical capacity, and that you can handle the average speed of the group. Many AYH groups bring along a car-pulled "sag-wagon" for those whose ambitions are stronger than their legs. And there's usually someone in the group who is an expert in repairing broken chains, flat tires, busted spokes, and those problems which always seem to occur on long trips.

This reminds me to advise you strongly to have your bike overhauled before you take off on a trip. (Review the chapter on maintenance in this book first.) Check brake blocks, all cables, tires, wheel alignment, and the condition of pedals and spokes. Your seat and handlebars should be properly adjusted for comfort and cycling efficiency.

About family touring: Many experienced European cyclists take small children on long trips in specially rigged child-carriers. But such families were raised on bicycles and carrying heavy burdens is second nature to them. I have children, and I have toured with children, but I would hesitate before taking a small child on a trip. On one trip our family took, my then-eleven-year-old youngster struggled manfully to stay with the group for a fifty-mile jaunt, strenuously resisting the ignominy of the sag-wagon. This was not one of my more successful trips. He was pretty tired and cranky for quite a while afterward. I don't think it is a good idea to take youngsters under fifteen along on a long trip; I prefer to keep the minimum age to around eighteen. There's a certain amount of individual responsibility and self-discipline involved in cycle touring that you cannot expect from youngsters.

I should also mention here that Asa Warren, Western Regional Director of the American Youth Hostels, has recently published a *North American Bicycle Atlas* which contains detailed routes and maps of bicycle tours throughout the United States and Canada. The tours are graded by length and difficulty. Easy trips are rated from eight to fifteen miles over fairly flat terrain, whereas rugged trips may contain hard mountain passes, unpaved roads, and go up to 100 miles a day. Mr. Warren's book is a handy and complete touring guide, and can be bought for $1.95 from your nearest AYH chapter.

The League of American Wheelmen is another old cycling club, whose members include some of America's most dedicated cyclists. The LAW has chapters in most large and medium-sized American cities, and chapter members are usually quite willing to aid travelers and fellow LAW members.

Dr. Clifford Graves, a surgeon, President of the International Touring Society, and one of our most experienced cycle tourists, regularly heads up cycle tours in the United States and abroad. Many businessmen, housewives, and professional people join him on these tours, which are fairly deluxe trips, with most meals eaten in restaurants and with evening lay-overs in hotels.

Other cycle-touring groups that travel abroad are listed in the Appendix. The Cyclists' Touring Club of England, for example, conducts world-wide tours. I would urge you to join this club if you are interested in cycling in Europe. The club magazine *Cycle Touring* will come with your membership. Or I would recommend that you join a "Huff-'n-Puff" tour sponsored by the International Bicycle Touring Society.

The British publication *Cycling and Sporting Cyclist* is a biweekly magazine which contains many excellent articles on cycle touring in England, Wales, Scotland, Ireland, and the Continental countries. (Subscriptions cost $16.00 a year or $41.00 for three years. Write to the publication at 161-166 Fleet Street, London, E.C.4, England 5011.) This publication caters to the racing cyclist as well as the tourist, which is about the only place I can think of that cycle racing and touring ever meet. Racing cyclists don't care for touring any more than a drag racer would care about auto touring. Racing is an arduous, highly competitive, complicated sport with a technique that has nothing in common with the leisurely pace and benign outlook of the average touring cyclist.

THE TOURING BICYCLE

As I mentioned at the beginning of this chapter, you will need a good bicycle if you want to take long trips. People do travel on three-speed English racers, but they pay a terrific penalty in the extra fifteen pounds or so of weight and the inefficient mechanism of these machines.

The ideal touring bicycle has downturned handlebars, a Reynolds tubular seamless steel frame throughout, high-quality fittings, and gears with ten- or fifteen-speed gear selections. Fifteen gears (using a triple chainwheel) are useful only if you plan to climb mountainous terrain. As I mention in the chapter on gears, any fifteen-speed gear selection is a compromise at best. For example, you won't be able to use the large chainwheel and the large rear gear. Which is to say that the only reason for fifteen gears is to let you use the small front chainwheel and the big rear gear together for steep grades. If you plan to climb the Rockies or do much touring around San Francisco, then a fifteen-speed combination is handy. Dr. Graves recommends (and I concur) a rear gear cluster of 14, 16, 19, 23, and 28 teeth and a front dual chainwheel of 32–48 teeth. For the fifteen-speed gear combination, use a triple chainwheel of 30, 40, 50. The 28-tooth rear gear and the 30-tooth front chainwheel give you a gear ratio of 28.9 with twenty-seven-inch wheels. Translated into speed, this ratio means that if you pedal at a steady cadence of sixty revolutions per minute of the crank arm, you'll travel around five miles per hour. Not a fantastic speed, by any means, but pretty good if you're crawling up the Rocky Mountains with a forty-pound pack on your bicycle.

Readers who are technically oriented might be interested in reading what Gene Portuesi says about fifteen-speed gears in his *Cyclo-Pedia* (see Appendix page 317):

> A fifteen-speed derailleur system utilizes a longer bottom bracket axle to accommodate the third chainwheel 3 mm further to the right than on the normal ten-speed. Let us assume that the cycle has a triple chainwheel of 32 x 46 x 52 teeth or a similar combination, and the freewheel range is 13 to 30 teeth. When trying to run the chain from the 52-tooth front chainwheel to the 30-tooth rear cog, the angle of the chain is very acute. The tension is at a maximum, and so is friction. Chain also tends to hang on top of the 30-tooth rear cog, and the front shifter cage has almost constant contact with the inside of the chain to keep it from coming off the outside chainwheel.
>
> Conversely, when running on the 32-tooth inside chainwheel to the 13-tooth rear sprocket, the chain will have too much slack and might also rub on the inside of the 46-tooth chainwheel, or on the lower part of the front shifter cage.

HANDLEBARS

Although there are at least three distinct styles of handlebars (see pages 88-90), and the type you use should be that which gives you the most comfort over a long distance, you may want to consider one special type for touring. Most downturned handlebars are relatively flat on the top, so you have fewer places to hold onto. On a long trip, it helps if you can vary the position of your hands, because you space out the use of different muscles.

For women, in particular, Dr. Graves recommends a dropped handlebar with a slight upswing, called a *randonneur*. A variation of this type of bar is sold by Cyclo-Pedia (see Appendix) for $8.50, complete with stem, levers, and rubber sleeves on the bars. The brake levers are positioned just under the top section of the bar, instead of on the foremost section, so that you can grasp the brake levers with the fingertips instead of having to lean forward.

THE SADDLE

Your bicycle saddle, for a long trip, should be made of leather and be well broken-in to your particular contour. This means that the saddle should have been ridden for at least 500 miles for the required shaping and resilience. A hard new leather saddle is as unaccommodating as a new pair of leather shoes.

TIRES—TUBULARS OR CLINCHERS?

There are skilled cyclists who wouldn't think of touring on anything but tubular tires. (You might want to review the chapter on tires at this point.) There is no question that tubulars are more resilient and offer a livelier, more enjoyable ride and easier pedaling. But tubulars are more prone to puncture than the heavier-built clincher tires. Tubulars are also a good deal more difficult to repair because they are sewn up all the way around, inside, and a leak is sometimes difficult to find.

Therefore, if you are not a skilled cyclist or are not willing to spend extra time fixing flats, you should use clincher tires. I would especially recommend them if you intend to travel off the beaten path, on gravel roads, or other rough surfaces.

If you insist on using tubulars, be sure to ease your weight forward and rise up off the saddle as you pass over rough spots, to equalize the weight over both wheels. This is particularly important if you're carrying well-filled rear panniers, and is good advice even with clinchers.

Another advantage of clinchers is that replacement tires are more readily available; for example, you can buy them in most Sears Roebuck stores, whereas only special cycle shops carry tubulars.

FENDING OFF RAIN

You never know when you will be caught in a rain shower on a tour, so I recommend using lightweight plastic fenders. These are easy to attach and remove, and they will keep mud and water from splashing onto the brakes, panniers, and your legs. Some tourists carry clip-on spring-held "spats" which shield both sides of both wheels and keep water from splashing off the inside of the fenders onto the rider. You can't buy these in this country, to my knowledge, but you could make your own.

OTHER ACCOUTREMENTS

You'll get thirsty from time to time during the day, so I recommend that you carry at least one, preferably two, plastic bottles in carriers. Carriers can be mounted on the handlebars so that you can reach for a swig from the saddle. Or a single bottle can be affixed to the seat tube, which will not interfere with leg or thigh muscles, or the heel of your shoe as you reach the top of the pedal stroke.

Rattrap pedals and cleat-equipped shoes (see pages 97-98) are a "must" for cycle touring, in my opinion. If you learn to ankle properly (pages 105-06), you will find that on hills particularly, your feet will slip off even rattrap pedals as you apply pressure, especially in the four- and seven-o'clock positions. Pedal straps should be tight enough to keep the shoe cleats in position. If you pedal in city traffic, or as you approach a rest-stop, you can bend over from the saddle and loosen the straps slightly so that you can lift your heel up and pull your feet out of the pedals quickly. Cycling shoes, built with steel shanks and shaped for this special use, are ideal for touring. You can carry a pair of slip-ons for off-bicycle use; cleat shoes aren't practical for walking about. I especially want to warn you against cycling with sneakers—they don't offer much protection against the surface or rattrap pedals. If you don't use cycling shoes, at least use flexible leather loafers. But cleats are preferable because they will keep your feet from sliding off the pedals.

Finally, if you want to get yourself in the picture, carry a 35-millimeter camera with a time-delay shutter or attachment. You can also use a small "C" clamp to tie the camera down to a fence, sign, or tree limb.

WHERE TO TOUR

Whether East, West, North, or South, the United States offers much in the way of enjoyable scenery and terrain. For the most part, however, the

Middle West is rather monotonous. Though parts of Wisconsin, Michigan, Indiana, and even Illinois are of interest to the cycle tourist, New England, the West Coast, and the South offer a good deal more variety. The Plains states, according to Dr. Graves, are best traversed by commercial carrier.

I won't go into a great deal of detail about specific tours, because Asa Warren's guide gives so much, but I will quote Dr. Graves with some general guidelines:

> If you want to tour in the East, you can choose almost any point along the Appalachians, between the Canadian border and northern Georgia. In the West, there is territory comparable to this along the coastal range as far south as Santa Barbara. Southern California is so overrun with freeways now that you have to pick and choose your areas there.
>
> In the vast region between the Great Plains and the Pacific coastal range there are magnificent mountains and canyons and beautiful valleys, but all are on a grand scale—not on the small scale a cyclist needs. Because he travels slowly, a cyclist has to have his scenery in a highly concentrated form. In the Great Plains area, most of the roads are high, wide and handsome instead of modest, gentle and intimate.

If you prefer to plan your own trip, or if you want to go no farther than a Sunday afternoon ride will take you, follow these tips: Use a local area map, preferably a county map. The Department of Interior publishes county maps at a scale of a quarter-inch to the mile. The United States Coast and Geodetic Survey publishes topographic maps that will give you an idea of how hilly a route is. For a specific route, select secondary paved roads that bisect as few main arteries as possible. Stick to county roads, if possible. Avoid state and federal highways at all costs. The back county roads generally go over more scenic, winding routes, while state and federal roads are designed for high-speed, straight-line travel. And, of course, superhighways and toll roads are not only dangerous but illegal for cycling use.

As for time of year, I recommend the spring and autumn. Try to avoid the hot season.

A WORD ABOUT TANDEMS

The ultimate in togetherness is a tandem. On a cycle tour, a husband-and-wife team can travel at a pace suitable to the weaker sex, and chat about the scenery as they pedal. Many cycle tourists, including Dr. Graves, have found that tandems are easier to pedal because they are mechanically more efficient (provided the rear rider is not just a passenger).

Some people love to tour on tandem; other couples have tried them and prefer a single bicycle. I can make no hard-and-fast rules except to suggest that if you and your partner have equable dispositions and matching physical endurance, perhaps a tandem is for you. But if you are considerably stronger than your mate, and tend to be a bit impatient, you might prefer to ride singly. If you can borrow a tandem for a short trip, to try it out, by all means do so. Tandems are expensive; at least the good ones are. Schwinn has just introduced a fine tandem, but it costs upward of $400.00. Do not confuse this Schwinn tandem with its less expensive model. The inexpensive bicycle is best suited to resorts for use as a rental; it's far too heavy and cumbersome for long trips. I would also recommend the Jack Taylor tandem, mentioned in an earlier chapter, for touring. This is a first-class, high-quality machine that can be bought from Wheel Goods, Inc. (see Appendix).

CAMPING VERSUS TOURING

As I said earlier, cycle touring usually means a deluxe trip which involves restaurant meals and hotel accommodations. Personally, I prefer cycle camping, which permits you to stop where and when you want. A small folding rod and reel enables you to catch your own dinner, and with a bicycle, you can be more selective in the choice of campsite than if you are traveling by car.

WHERE TO PITCH CAMP

Try to plan your stops at public campsites. You will feel much happier camping with people around you and with the protection of a state or federal ranger than you will off alone in the woods or in a roadside park.

One young woman cyclist I heard about had a novel approach to camping. She had no trouble traveling alone coast to coast, although she made absolutely no plans for her nightly camp stops. She was a very personable young woman, yet no one ever bothered her. It seems she camped every night in the local graveyard, pitching her tent behind the largest mauso-leum she could find, on the side away from the road!

If you carry your own foodstuffs, select a campsite about twenty-five miles away from the nearest small town or source of food and load up with what you will need for the next two or three meals at about 4:00 P.M.

EMERGENCY QUARTERS

If you can't find a youth hostel, camp ground, or motel for the evening, and it's getting dark, perhaps even raining, the flexibility of cycle camp-ing and touring really comes to your aid. Cycle campers have found emer-gency quarters in jails (from kindly police), caves, under a Sherman tank in a small town park, barns (ask the farmer first and offer him your matches), and even under haystacks.

If it's raining, avoid the temptation to pitch a tent under a tree; you are more vulnerable to lightning under one than you would be out in the open.

RIDING A LOADED BICYCLE

If you've never ridden a bicycle loaded with camping gear, take it easy the first day out until you get the feel of things. You'll find you can't bank steeply around sharp corners at high speed without risking a spill. Also, you must shift down sooner going uphill, and you must use brakes sooner to avoid speed build-up, unless the downgrade is straight, smooth, and relatively free of traffic.

CYCLE TOURING GEAR

If you tour the deluxe route, stopping at motels each night and, for the most part, eating in restaurants, you can get by with very little gear and equipment. And you certainly won't need to burden yourself with pan-niers—those large canvas carry-alls which hang over rear wheels.

For the deluxe tourist, a front and rear bag will provide a balanced load condition. (See Fig. 46 for correct way to distribute load.) These are the bags I recommend for deluxe touring:

Fig. 46: *The correct way to distribute load when cycle touring or camping. Note that bags are securely fastened, with carriers permanently fastened to frame.*

- *Handlebar bag:* T. A. Tourist Bag No. 272. 8 in. x 10½ in. x 5 in. Top of bag has pocket with transparent window for map reading. Also, two open side pockets and two rear pockets. This is the only bag I have found that opens from the rear, so you can get at bag contents without dismounting from the bicycle. Weight: 1 lb., 4 oz. Cost: $10.50. From Cyclo-Pedia (see Appendix for address).
- *Handlebar bag carrier:* T. A. Carrier No. 218. Fits on Mafac center-pull brakes. Weight: 4½ ounces. Cost: $4.00. Alternate carrier, if you don't have Mafac center-pull brakes, is the front alloy carrier. Weight: 1 lb., 4 oz. Both from Cyclo-Pedia.
- *Rear bag carrier:* Alloy rear spring-clip carrier. Weight: 1 lb., 6 oz. Cost: $3.50. From Cyclo-Pedia or your bike store.
- *Rear bag:* "Camper." 14 in. x 9 in. x 7½ in. 950 cu. in. capacity. Weight: 32 oz. Aluminum strap hardware. Cost: $7.80. From Carradice (see Appendix for address).

CYCLE CAMPING GEAR

If you plan to travel long distances and/or cycle camp, you will need more carrying capacity. For the ultimate in this regard, I recommend the front and rear bags mentioned above, plus:

- *Front wheel panniers:* 8½ in. x 8½ in. x 4½ in. 631 cu. in. Weight: 28 oz. Cost: about $7.20.
- *Front wheel pannier carrier:* Steel rod type with lamp bracket. Cost: about $3.50.
- *Rear panniers:* "Limit" carrier panniers. 12 in. x 11 in. x 7 in. Total capacity, 1,925 cu. in. Weight: about 3½ lbs. Cost: about $13.50. Aluminum loops on top of each bag will carry tent poles, capes, etc., outside of bag.
- *Rear pannier carrier:* Steel rod type. Cost: about $4.50.

All the panniers and pannier carriers noted above are made by H. W. Carradice in England, and are available from one of their dealers in the United States or England.

An alternate source for panniers and carriers is the American Youth Hostels, Metropolitan New York Council store (see Appendix for address). They supply:

- *Pannier bag* made for AYH by Bergen of Norway. Made of heavy gray canvas with chrome tanned leather straps and binding. Cut away at the heel to eliminate interference with pedaling. Cost: $11.50.
- *A better pannier bag,* also by Bergen. A removable model that can be hooked on and off the rear carrier and used as a handbag. 15 in. x 12 in. x 4 in. gives 720 cu in. Cost: $12.90.
- *A good set of rear pannier bags* (Fig. 46) and front (or rear) bags is made in the United States by the Colorado Outdoor Sports Corporation (see Appendix). Although they are more expensive ($33.00 per set), the price is well worth the added investment. The bags are very light. The rear pannier weighs about twenty ounces compared to the 2½ to 3 lbs. or so of other comparable capacity panniers. The bags are made of ultralight and extra-strong tent nylon—colored fire-engine red for visibility—are waterproof, and have a capacity of about 1,500 cu. in. The rear panniers have five *zippered,* controlled-weight distribution pockets which give you a balanced load and, most

important, convenient access to your gear. Molded plastic stiffeners hold the bags in shape under all conditions. The front bag (also usable in the rear) is of the same nylon material and color as the rear pannier. It's about time some domestic manufacturer realized that cycle camping calls for well-made and scientifically designed panniers that are extremely durable, very light, and really waterproof.

OTHER CYCLE CAMPING GEAR

I have pored over literally hundreds of pages of dozens of catalogs of camping gear and have come up with the following recommendations as to tents and a sleeping bag which offer the most in quality for the least in weight and bulk, regardless of price.

Tents

The one-man tent I recommend is the "Gerry Pioneer Tent" (Fig. 47), which has a sewn-in waterproof floor with mosquito netting at both ends. It weighs only 1 lb., 9 oz., folds up to a very small package, and measures 106 in. x 102 in. spread out. From Colorado Outdoor Sports Corporation.

A fine, lightweight two-man tent is Gerry's "Year-Around" unit, weighing only 4 lbs., 12 oz., with take-down aluminum poles. The sides are of breathable tight-woven nylon, and the floor is waterproof six inches up the sides to protect sleeping bags. Coated nylon rainfly sheds water away from the tent proper, and completely covers the inner tent. This tent costs $85.00 but is worth the price if you intend to do a lot of cycle camping. Size: 82 in x 48 in. x 43 in. high. From Colorado Outdoor Sports Corporation.

Sleeping Bag

For a sleeping bag, I recommend the "Hosteler," made of water repellent balloon cloth and filled with 100 percent goose down. Weighs only 2½ lbs. and, when packed, rolls into a bag about 14 in. x 7 in. Can be zipped with a second bag or zipped completely open for use as a bed quilt. Cost: $41.95. If you are over 5 ft. 10 in. tall, you should order the

Fig. 47: *This one-man tent with floor can be unzipped to make a two-man tent. Your author lived in this tent for two weeks very comfortably. It has netting with zipper flies at both ends, which close up to a small hole in bad weather. A very fine tent indeed for the cycle camper. Waterproof throughout.*

extra-long model of this bag, which costs $46.15. Temperature range for this bag is down to 30°F. Available from the Outdoor Shop, American Youth Hostels, Metropolitan New York Council.

Air Mattress

Go-Lite Air Bed. Lightweight, rubberized fabric, three-quarter size. Weight: 1 lb., 14 oz. Cost: $9.00. American Youth Hostels, Metropolitan New York Council.

Cooking Gear

The ardent cycle camper will pitch in for the evening not too far from a source of provisions and will take care to stock up at that time with the food items he will consume for dinner and the following day's breakfast and possibly lunch. To cook provisions (a hot meal is always desirable), I recommend the Hiker camp stove made in Sweden, the SVEA No. 123 (Fig. 48) which burns for forty-five minutes on one fueling of a third of a pint of white or leaded gasoline, boils one and a half pints of water in five to six minutes. Size: 5 in. high x 3¾ in.

Fig. 48. By stacking, you can even cook a three-course meal with this compact, gasoline-burning Swedish stove. Your author has cooked hundreds of meals with his stove and it's still going strong. Be sure to buy the fitted, nesting pots and pans and fuel bottle to go with the stove.

Rainwear

A cycling cape comes in handy, costs only $4.75 with hat, fits over an entire bicycle as well as yourself, folds up into a very small package, and weighs practically nothing. From American Youth Hostels, Metropolitan New York Council, by mail order.

Poly Bags

Polyethylene bags are inexpensive and absolutely indispensable for wrapping clothing and other gear that could be harmed by rain. You can get five 18-in. x 30-in. bags for $1.00 from the Colorado Outdoor Sports Corporation (No. A703).

A few items complete the list of what the well-equipped cycle camper should take along, in terms of basic equipment:

- *Cyclist's canteen:* Pure aluminum. Drinking spout on side. Weight: 7 oz. Cost: $1.98.
- *Cutlery Set No. 9147:* Solid aluminum with stainless steel knife blade. For one. Weight: 3 oz. Cost, per set: $.95.
- *Wood-Pal folding saw:* Polished blued blade of Swedish steel in raker-tooth style. Unfolded length, 27 in. Folded, 15 in. Weight: 10 oz. Cost: $3.95.
- *Map measurer and compass:* Just roll the measurer along the route on the map and discover the distance you will travel. With carrying case. Weight: 1 oz. Cost: $2.00.

All of the above items are available from Cyclo-Pedia.

- *Sleep sheet:* If you plan to stop at any AYH hostel, a sleep sheet is required. Order the SB-7 nylon sleep sheet for $5.95 from the Outdoor Shop, American Youth Hostels, Metropolitan New York Council.

Miscellaneous Clothing Items

- *Cold weather T-shirt:* Worsted and nylon outside, soft absorbent cotton inside . Weight: 7 oz. Cost: $3.95.
- *Money belt:* Zipper compartment. Dark brown with brass finish buckle. Cost: $6.00.

- *Men's lined boot pant:* Ideal for winter cycling. Outer shell of Appalachian cotton poplin, windproof and water repellent, lined with scarlet, 100 percent pure wool. With belt loops and suspender buttons, zipper fly, two slash front pockets, watch pocket, and two rear button-flap pockets. Eliminates need of heavy, bulky underwear. Weight: 31 oz. Cost: $21.85.
- *Men's nylon windshirt:* Featherweight, offers excellent protection against wind. Navy, red, or orange (orange best for visibility). I suggest you carry two, for use when it's extra cold out at any time of the year. Small, medium, large, and extra large sizes. Cost: $5.00.

All of these items are available from L. L. Bean (see Appendix).

Miscellaneous Cycling Camping Items

- *Rescue blanket:* An emergency blanket (Fig. 49) that comes in a plastic container small enough to fit in your shirt pocket, yet unfolds to 56 in. x 84 in. and reflects more than 90 percent of your body heat. If you might be stranded by cold weather on tour, and you are not equipped for camping-out, carry this blanket. Orange on one side for high visibility, silver on the inside for maximum reflectivity. Weight: 2 oz. Cost: $3.00. From L. L. Bean.

Fig. 49: Small enough to put in your hip pocket, yet big enough to offer emergency protection should you be caught out in cold weather without other covering, this emergency blanket should be in every cyclist's touring kit.

- *Trail axe:* 10-in length, with leather shield. Weight: 10 oz. Cost: $3.50. From L. L. Bean.
- *Chrome mirror:* High-chrome reflector on steel. Unbreakable. Folding easel back permits standing on table, or can be hung from wall or tree. In protective leatherette pouch. Weight: 4 oz. Cost: $1.50. From Cyclo-Pedia.
- *Bausch & Lomb 10X telescope:* In padded carrying case, 10 in. long. Weight: 9 oz. Cost: $8.75. From I. Goldberg & Sons.
- *Or mini-binoculars* (6X). Weight: 8 oz. Cost: $32.50. From I. Goldberg & Sons (see Appendix).

All prices quoted above reflect list prices current at the time this book was being written, which, of course, may be changed at a later date.

CYCLE CAMPING CHECK LIST

For cycle camping or cycle touring, the aim should be to carry the minimum amount of gear, all carefully selected for light weight and utility. The list below is for the complete cycle tourist-camper. If you plan to stop each evening in a motel and eat most of your meals out, you can eliminate such items as tent, sleeping bag, and cooking equipment. All gear listed, however, weighs only about thirty-five pounds, including tent, sleeping bag, stove, and utensils.

Camping Equipment

Sleeping bag—2 lbs., 8 oz.
Tent, one-man—1 lb., 9 oz.
Tent, two-man—4 lbs., 12 oz.
Stove—2 lbs., 4 oz.
Fuel bottle—1 lb. (full)
Air mattress—1 lb., 14 oz.
Handlebar light—8 oz. with batteries
Waterproof match box—2 oz.
1 dish towel—1 oz.
50-ft nylon cord—6 oz.
4 Brillo pads—4 oz.
1 inner sheet sleeping sack—2 oz.

First aid kit—6 oz.

Sewing kit—3 oz.

Insect repellent—2 oz.

DDT bomb—3 oz.

Dog spray—2 oz.

Toilet tissue—4 oz.

Tube of Fire Ribbon (to squeeze on wood or bottom of can)—5 oz. (2 for $1.50, from Colorado Outdoor Sports Corporation)

Camper knife, spoon, fork set—3 oz.

Trail axe with shield—10 oz.

Canteen—7 oz.

Map measurer and compass—1 oz.

Can opener—2 oz.

Personal Gear for Cycle Camping or Touring

2 pair socks

2 underwear changes

1 pair dress shoes (slip-on)

1 pair dress slacks

2 long-sleeved nylon sport shirts

1 light wool or loose knit shirt

Sunglasses

Cap with visor

1 pair wool mitts

1 three-quarter windbreaker with hood

1 cycling cape or poncho, for rain

4 handkerchiefs

1 pair sweat pants and sweat shirt

1 pair cycling shorts (doubles as swim trunks)

4 polyethylene bags (to keep clothes dry)

1 polyethylene 5-gal. water jug (8 oz. empty)

1 pair cycling gloves

1 pair cycling shoes

Toilet Articles for Cycle Camping or Touring

Tooth brush

Tooth paste

Soap and soap box
Washcloth
Towel
Razor and blades
Comb
Stainless steel mirror

Optional Items for Cycle Touring

Camera and film
Telescope or mini-binoculars
Two feeder bottles (mounted on handlebars, down tube, or seat tube)
Rescue blanket—2 oz.

TOOLS FOR TRIPS

Never leave for an extended bicycle tour without tools and equipment to make emergency repairs. Only major cities have competent bicycle repairmen, so you should at least be able to make those repairs and adjustments that will keep you on the road. Here is a list of tools and spare parts I recommend you carry:

- Tire patch kit (with ultrathin patches, needle, and thread if you use tubular tires)
- Extra tubular tires (two should do)
- Mafac tool kit (contains all the metric tools you'll need for most adjustments, including spoke wrench)
- 6-in. crescent wrench
- Small screwdriver
- 6 spokes
- 4 brake blocks
- 1 derailleur cable
- 1 rear brake cable
- 1 plastic bike protector (covers bicycle like a cape)
- 2 16-in. bicycle elastic straps with hook ends
- 1 spare pedal strap
- 1 bike lock
- 1 chain rivet extractor

- Spare chain
- 2 tire irons (for clincher tires only)
- 1 spare tube (for clincher tires)
- 1 pair small offset pliers
- Tube bike grease
- Freewheel remover
- *Don't forget the tire pump!*

AIRLINE AND RAILROAD BICYCLE SHIPMENT

You may want to start your tour hundreds of miles from home, and you *can* take your bicycle with you on a plane or train. But common carriers differ as to handling and have certain regulations and restrictions which you should know about.

My usual procedure when taking a plane is to simply wheel my bike up to the ticket desk, get a luggage tag put on, then wheel it down to the baggage room where I hand it over to a baggage handler. The bicycle will not fit down a luggage chute, which is why you yourself should always take it to the baggage room. The luggage checker will show you where the room is.

Although most major airline carriers have definite regulations about carrying such things as bicycles, their enforcement seems spotty at best, and often seems to depend on the mood or whim of the agent you confront with the bicycle. I have wheeled my fully assembled bicycle up to the baggage check-in desk and had the agent accept it for shipment at no charge. Yet, in this same airline, on the return trip, another agent charged the prevailing rate for air freight, which for a trip between New York and Chicago, for example, would cost more than $7.00, depending on the weight of the bicycle.

Airline people tell me that if it were merely a matter of accepting an uncrated bicycle, there would be no problem. But the sharp projections on a bicycle could damage luggage and, in rough weather, could also damage the aircraft itself.

The Trans World Airlines people state that they are going to stock a number of cardboard containers for various objects, and that their container for garment bags may well be suitable for bicycles—if the handlebars are turned parallel to the frame, the pedals are removed and inserted from the inside of the crank, and the wheels are removed and tied to the frame. If this were done, there would be no charge, as far as TWA is concerned, for the bicycle.

If you use rear panniers to carry your gear, and you intend to do much traveling by airline, buy the type of pannier that can be quickly slipped off the carrier and carried by a built-in handle, such as the Bergen pannier bags sold by American Youth Hostels, Metropolitan New York Council, for $12.90 a pair.

In general, Civil Aeronautics Board Provision No. 43 permits you to carry three pieces of baggage on major airlines. The largest of the three must not exceed sixty-two inches, computed by measuring the sum of width, length, and height. A disassembled bicycle will easily meet this size requirement.

On overseas flights, however, the rules change and there is a definite weight restriction on baggage. Check with your airline carrier for specific costs.

If you are using small feeder airlines, you will probably have to ship your bicycle air freight, because smaller lines are much more restrictive in the amount of baggage they will carry free.

In Germany, incidentally, you can hire a bicycle from the railroads in Bavaria, upon presentation of your passport and payment of sixty-five cents. You may ride off to local scenic areas and return the bicycle to any railroad station in Bavaria. The railroad will suggest itineraries.

Railroad charges for carrying bicycles are a bit steep in the United States. For example, according to Jerry Lambert, Travel Coordinator for the AYH Metropolitan New York Council,[1] eastern railroads charge about seventy-five cents per bicycle, but western railroads charge on a basis of excess baggage, and if total baggage is over this weight, excess baggage charges for a bicycle can be as high as $10.00 to $12.00 per bicycle for a long trip. Before traveling by rail, check your carrier to confirm baggage charges.

Railroads are notorious, at least in the United States, for their cavalier treatment of bicycles, and many a cyclist has sadly rescued his bicycle from the tender ministrations of baggage-car personnel too late to prevent twisted wheels, bent derailleurs, and various other kinds of damage. My advice is that you personally supervise the loading of your bicycle on the

---

[1] *American Cycling* (now *Bicycling!*), June, 1967, p. 22.

baggage car, making sure that it is out of the way of heavy items that may be loaded later on. If it is possible, hang your bicycle from the ceiling or the side of the baggage car.

IN CONCLUSION

I consider this chapter on cycle touring and camping the most important section of this book, because, until you start using your bicycle on trips, you will never really know how much fun cycling can be.

My objective in writing this chapter was to help you with planning details, using the experience of others, so that when you step off on your own, your trip will be as enjoyable as possible, with minimum problems caused by unsuitable and insufficient gear and lack of route planning.

The data in this chapter are complete enough to permit you to do any kind of cycle touring or camping that appeals to you. You can select gear and equipment for short weekend trips, a more complete lash-up for extended trips, or cut gear to the bone and go deluxe by stopping at restaurants and motels.

How you go is up to you. But do go, and enjoy yourself!

8

BICYCLE RACING—A NEW LOOK AT AN OLD SPORT

This chapter is about all aspects of bicycle racing. It will acquaint you with the types of races, and help you follow and understand, and therefore enjoy, bicycle races. If, after reading this chapter, you want to race, you should get in touch with the national headquarters of the Amateur Bicycle League of America (see Appendix for address), which is the governing body of racing in the United States. The ABL will be happy to refer you to the ABL official nearest you, and he, in turn, will help you get started in racing, if you meet the League's basic qualifications of health, stamina, and equipment.

I find bicycle racing a fascinating sport, which combines courage, speed, physical stamina, and skill with the mental agility and bluffing ability of a poker champion. Let me tell you why. In my opinion, as far as auto racing goes, I feel that after the first fifteen minutes, the Indianapolis 500 and similar races are just so much noisy, automaton-like movement around an oval track. You can't see the drivers, and the cars zoom past so fast that they make you dizzy or practically put you to sleep.

A bicycle race, on the other hand, takes place right in front of you. The riders are easy to see, and the physical agility and ability that goes into planning a race to outfox the other fellow is plain for all to see. Then, on the last lap, when the cyclists sprint, at thirty miles an hour or more, the excitement at the track is tremendous.

In France, Belgium, Italy, Holland, and England, where bicycle racing is understood and avidly followed as a national sport, winners of famous races, such as the Tour de France, are truly international heroes. They are covered with glory by the press, their national governments, and, if they are professionals, with a good deal of money.

An interesting fact about bicycle racing is that, as a rule, the dedicated racing cyclist has almost no interest in cycle touring, any more than you'd

RAY BOLDT

Fig. 50: Here's a typical road race. Notice haw the group is "bunched up." In particular, you will see that the man in the foreground, at left, is closely followed by another cyclist. In this way the cyclist to the rear forces the front rider to "break the wind" for him. This technique saves the rear rider's strength until a strategic moment arrives when he can "jump" the pack at high speed and take off to win.

Fig. 51: *At the track in Northbrook, Illinois, the three leaders in a 1968 ten-mile track race are, left to right, Eddie Van Guyse, Dennis Ellerton, and John Van De Velde. The three are in the middle of a sprint.*

expect auto racers to be interested in automobile touring. However, if you're far from home and something goes wrong with your bicycle, and you can't find a good bicycle shop, you'll find any ABL member in the area willing and able to help you. Incidentally, because the bicycle is so important in racing, the best bicycle stores are run by former champion racers. For example, Al Stiller, a champion and descendant of a family of Belgian racers, runs a store on Chicago's northwest side. Gene Portuesi, a Midwest champ and former United States Olympic Cycling Team coach runs a bicycle store and bicycle mail-order business in Cadillac, Michigan. And Tom Avenia, of New York City, one of the best bicycle mechanics in the East, still races on weekends.

In the limited space that we have to devote to racing in this book, it is not practical to do any more than discuss the various types of races. For tips and hints on racing techniques, I recommend the book *Cycle Racing* by Bowden and Matthews (see Bibliography). Incidentally, each racing champion has his own techniques, methods, and particular way of physical training, all of which, in most cases, he'd rather keep to himself.

TIME TRIAL RACING

In general, a time trial race is a race against time. A rider starts out alone, with a minute's space between him and the next man, so that no matter how many participate in any given race, the man with the best elapsed time wins. Because time trials need open roads, you'll find them starting very early in the morning, such as at 7:00 A.M. on a Sunday.

There are four types of time trials:

- 10, 25, and 30 miles
- 50 and 100 miles
- 12 and 24 hours
- Hill climbs, between 300 yards and 3 miles, depending on hill gradient

At the time of writing, the record for a 25-mile time trial is near 50 minutes, which means an average sustained speed of around 27 miles an hour for one hour!

MASSED-START RACING

A massed-start race is one in which riders start together, with the first man over the finish line declared the winner. As compared with time-trialing, mass-start racing pits one rider against the other in a personal contest of strength, technique, and skill.

Massed-start racing may be held on a public highway (at daybreak), in which case it is called a "road race," or on a circular park road, which is closed off to traffic for the duration of the race.

The famous Tour de France is a massed-start race. It takes the riders 2,600 miles in 22 days, over some of the most grueling ground in the world, including the Pyrenees Mountains, from Lille to Paris.

CYCLO-CROSS RACING

A variation of massed-start racing is real he-man stuff—cyclo-cross racing. Cyclo-cross is a combination of road racing and cross-country running,

Fig. 52: In high-speed cycling, racers sometimes stay absolutely still. "Jockeying" is the technical term for this maneuver. In Denmark, in 1966, from left to right, Preston Handy, Gordon Johnson, and John Chapman, at the start of a heat in the Grand Prix of Arhus.

using special bicycles with high brackets, chainwheel guards to keep the mud out, and special knobbed tires for high traction.

Most events are one or two miles long, but some are as long as eight miles, over open fields and streams, through bogs of mud and sand and even wooded areas. Part of the time the cyclist is riding, other times he is running, and sometimes he is carrying his bicycle.

If you like to wallow in mud, slither through grass, grope your way through dense woods with a bicycle on your back, ford streams, climb cliffs, and do all this at maximum physical effort, then cyclo-cross racing is for you.

TRACK RACING

Tracks for bicycle racing are built to very rigid specifications, and few cities have them because they are so costly. There are fine tracks in the United States, however, in Encino, California (near Los Angeles); San Jose, California; Portland, Oregon; Northbrook, Illinois (near Chicago); St. Louis, Missouri; New York City, at the old World's Fair Grounds; and Kenosha and Milwaukee, Wisconsin.

Track racing is unquestionably the most complex of all the forms of bicycle racing; to understand it takes some study and real dedication on the part of the spectator. But it is an exciting sport and well worth learning. There are various types of track racing.

Handicaps

These are short distance races, from a quarter-mile to a half-mile. Riders are handicapped by ability, with space between riders at the start according to the handicap.

Sprint

One of the most exciting types of racing, the sprint, takes two forms. Match-racing, used in the Olympic Games, involves only two or three racers per race. Usually sprint races are over 800 or 1,000 meter courses, or two or three lengths of a specific track. The last 220 yards or 200 meters only are timed, with the rest of the race used for tactical maneuvering.

Bicycling! (FORMERLY *American Cycling*)

Fig. 53: Jack Disney, left, and Sam Zeitland sprint for first place during a National Championship sprint race at the track in Northbrook, Illinois. This photo gives a good view, incidentally, of a track bike, without brakes, with fixed gears (no freewheel or derailleur), front fork nearly straight, short wheelbase frame.

In major championship races, most of the riders will be evenly matched physically, so that the only way to win is by outsmarting the opponent. One tactic is to jump to speed before the other rider is aware that you are sprinting to speed and before he can ready himself to keep up.

Another method is for one rider to give the impression that he is going all out, when actually he has considerable reserve power. This involves going around the track at a fast but comfortable pace, luring the opponent into following you closely and, at the last stretch, jumping to speed before the rearward rider can recover and try to catch up.

Another tactic is the attack from the rear. The attacker comes from behind and reaches the last banked turn before his opponent. Then he boxes him in until, in desperation, the trapped man eases back to try to pass, at which point the leading rider jumps to sprint speed.

Pursuit Track Racing

A pursuit track race is one in which two riders start on opposite sides of the track and try to catch each other over a standard distance, usually 4,000 meters. Because riders are usually evenly matched, they rarely do catch each other, so the race is decided on time, with the winner having covered the distance in the least amount of time.

Team pursuit races involve teams of four men, starting on opposite sides of the track. Each rider takes a turn at the lead, sheltering the others behind him. Smooth change of pace is essential to keep the pace and avoid breaking the chain of closely spaced riders. Time is called on the third member of each team as he passes the finish line.

An Australian pursuit involves teams of up to eight riders spaced out at equal distances, with any riders who are caught eliminated. An Italian pursuit involves two or more teams of three, four, or five riders, in which teams are equally spaced around the track and each team drops off one rider from the race each lap of the track. The last man in each team with the best time wins the race.

OTHER TYPES OF TRACK RACES

Scratch races are any races where all competitors start together, usually over a three-, five-, or ten-mile course.

Bicycling! (FORMERLY *American Cycling*)

Fig. 54: A sprint during the ten-mile point race at a National Championship match in St. Louis, 1967. At far left is six-time U.S. Champion Jim Rossi, who, at the time this photo was taken, was at the point of coming from twelfth to second place. Leading the pack at far right is Allen Bell, who won, and immediately behind him is the one-time Junior National Champ, Perry Metzler.

Devil-take-the-hindmost eliminates the last rider over each lap until at the last lap the remaining racers sprint to the finish line.

Unknown distance is a race in which the riders go on until a gong signals the last lap, at which point they sprint to the finish. If the field is solidly packed, the best attacker will usually win.

Point-to-point involves any number of competitors up to the capacity of the track for a specific distance or number of laps, with sprints at each lap or half-lap for points. Points are given to the first man over the line, or to the first two or three men over the line. The winner is the racer with the most points at the end of the race.

Madison takes its name from the old Madison Square Garden (New York City) six-day bicycle races. The original version was a fairly bloody, barbarous event, in which riders staggered around the track for six days, frequently falling. Although the race was finally banned, a version of it, in which teams of two riders pair up in a race, one rider racing while the other rests, is popular today. In Europe, the Madison is a very popular six-day race, although it can be any length, from thirty minutes to six days, or any distance. An exciting aspect of this race is the entry of a relieving rider into the melee, in which he is thrown by a grasp of the hand and a push on the bottom as a tired rider leaves the group. Variations of Madisons are point-to-point competitions, where the disadvantage for the spectator is that in order to make sense out of the race, he has to keep count on all points made by all riders as they are accumulated.

Paced riding is usually done behind a motorcycle, attaining speeds of fifty miles an hour tearing around a small track, with the cyclist staying glued behind the motorcycle as it breaks the wind. This type of racing is rarely seen in the United States, because it requires a specially made track that is properly banked and very smooth. The motorcycles used for these events have a small roller projecting from the rear to make sure the cyclist behind can't touch the motorcycle wheel and cause a wreck. If he catches up and contacts the motorcycle, the cyclist's front wheel merely spins against the roller without effect.

A "repechage" in track racing means, literally, a "second chance." This is a race in which riders who are eliminated in an earlier event get a chance to qualify in another one.

Fig. 55: A sprint for the 1964 National Championship at Kasina Bike Track in Flushing, New York. From left, Jim Rossi, Preston Handy, and Bob Binetti.

Fig. 56: At the 1968 Olympic Time Trials in Encino, California, Dave Brink shows top form in this 4,000-meter individual event.

TIPS FOR ASPIRING RACERS

The following tips for would-be racers were taken from a tape recording made by Gene Portuesi of Cadillac, Michigan some years ago, which he sent to members of his team before the Olympic Games in Tokyo:

If you're in training, keep a day-to-day record of track and wind conditions, how you feel, your times, hours of sleep per night, everything and anything that bears on your performance. At the end of the year you'll have a vivid picture of your performance and what affected it.

Proper rest and diet are extremely important. Use general good sense and stick to a basic diet of good meat, lots of vegetables, and milk.

In selecting gears, the mistake most novices make is to find out what the champions are using, and then strain on these gears. This makes about as much sense as to enter a weight-lifting contest and strain to lift a weight just because this is what the champ can lift. To select your gears, use a stopwatch and a little arithmetic. Trial and error will teach you what is possible with

Fig. 57: Cyclists in the Tour of Sardinia wheel past the impressive backdrop of the Colosseum at the beginning of the first lap of the event.

different gear ratios in terms of your own physical conditioning, and how to apply these ratios to a race of any kind, be it a hill-climb, sprint, time trial, or break-away. For example, a top-notch sprinter who covers the last 200 meters of a race in 12 seconds, using a 24 x 7 or a 92.6 gear [see page 118 for a complete explanation of gear ratios], would spin his cranks an average of 135 revolutions per minute.

Check your own cadence at the gear you can sprint best. For example, if if you ride a 25 x 8 gear, in the last 200 meters of a race your crank revolutions per minute will revolve 31 times; with 23 x 7 gears, cranks will revolve 29.5 times; with 24 x 7, 28.2 times and 25 x 7, 27 revolutions. The factor determining gear selection, as stated before, has to involve a combination of your physical condition with the mechanical factors of gear selections. It makes no sense to ride a big gear like the champions, if you're not ready for it.

About Training

Many cyclists start their training in the spring, but for those of us who live in cold northern climates, this is not soon enough. The power you can get into your muscles is directly related to your heart and respiratory system.

To begin training in April after a four-month lay-off and expect to get in championship condition in ten to twelve weeks is not practical. A winter program is essential. Many cyclists take up speed skating, or some indoor athletic program. Anything that makes the heart and lungs work hard will keep these organs in superior condition and permit you to enter racing training in reasonably good condition.

Weight lifting is a good winter training activity. Weight lifting, or weight training, keeps the heart and lungs in top condition, and increases muscle power, in particular, conditioning the muscles of the upper torso to a far greater degree than is possible by cycling alone.

Let me give you an example of the importance of winter training. When Nancy Neimann of Detroit was National Women's Champion, and rode for the first time on the famous Herne Hill Track in London, England, she used a gear that had won her the national championship. [Mr. Portuesi was Nancy's coach.] In what was then the fastest field of girl track riders, she spun her gear wide open. In trying to use the bigger ratios, Nancy found that she was not able to open up to top speed because the power required from her back and shoulder muscles to equalize the thrust from her legs simply wasn't there.

We instituted a winter training program for Nancy designed to improve the muscles in her upper torso, and as a result, she was able to improve her time by a half-second in the critical last 200 meters, and was able to beat the top women sprinters of England and Europe, and officially equal the then women's world record. The following year she beat the world record many times in the flats while training at home. What I am saying is that powerful legs will not give full thrust into the pedals unaided by equally powerful back, arm, and shoulder, muscles.

What do I mean by weight lifting? For women, try 10 repetitions of fifty pounds in arm exercises and 100 pounds in squats. For men, some variation is permissible according to build. For example, a man of 150 pounds should stay to a maximum of 100 pounds in arm exercises and 160 to 180 pounds for squats, ten repetitions of each. Do all exercises quickly, with rapid motion and deep breathing. Work out every third day or twice weekly. Start the program in the late fall and gradually build up the weights lifted. Put emphasis on the areas of your greatest weakness, then as soon as the good weather rolls around, forget the indoor training and hop on your bicycle.

Spring Training

For your first ride in the spring, go about 25 miles, and keep in low gear (23 x 10 will do). Dress, warmly, keep your legs covered with skating tights and seat pants, and use light layers of warm clothing for your upper torso. Put a sheet of newspaper between your last two outer garments to keep your chest warm against the cold wind.

Don't loaf along in low gear. Once you get warmed up, try to keep your cadence up over 100 revolutions per minutes. Use your stop-watch and count your pedal action over a 30-second period. In other words, do something with your miles and time besides sitting in the saddle and just pedaling.

After you are well warmed up, try a couple of one-mile time trials, with a slight rest in between. Then try a few jumps from almost a dead stop. First take off with the right foot, next take off with the left foot, and so on. Keep your action smooth. You will find this is very hard with a low gear, but the better you can coordinate yourself with a low gear, the more you will get out of a big one.

After about two weeks or 300 miles of low-gear riding, move up about 7 or 8 points on your gear. Pick a 5-mile course and see how much faster you are with the 69 than with a 62. Keep practicing your jumps from almost a dead stop. The gear is too small to go into it from a rolling start. Concentrate on using your straps. The top of your arch should hurt from having pulled up after a good workout. Stay smooth. Stay in a 69 for about 200 miles, then move up, just like your weight-training program. Keep a record of how fast you time-trial with each gear before you move up. Put it in the book. It will be something for you to improve next year. After the girls get into a 76 and the men into an 80 gear, go back to using your 62 a couple of times a week for a 25-mile workout. It's a good idea to work out on your low gears the day after a specially hard ride. Get at least two days of rest per week. Try to vary your riding so it's hard, but not fatiguing. Work out hard, but don't run yourself into the ground.

Now, with girls on a 76 and men on an 80, start timing yourself over a 200-meter, marked flying start. Try for five or six good times over a period of a week. Then move up two points on your gear and repeat. This is one reason I prefer the use of a half-inch pitch chain. You'll find that fewer changes in sprockets are required, and gears can be moved up in smaller graduations.

When the men and boys start getting into the 86 and 88 gears, some will find that a 4-point jump is too much. As you can see, this system allows you to feel your way up into your racing ratios as your physical condition improves. And, as the gears get higher, the graduations are smaller. Also, you will find that when you start using those speeds on your road-racing bike, you will know what to expect from every ratio on your bicycle.

Keep a weekly check on your body weight. Loss of weight can mean not enough rest, improper diet, or too many hard miles. Use a little common sense and try to correct what you think is wrong. If you must make changes in your routine, don't make too many at a time, because then you will not be able to attribute any change in performance to that which was directly responsible.

Gene Portuesi should know what he's talking about. Twice Michigan state champion himself, he coached Doris Travani, four times national champion woman cyclist; Robert Travani, formerly on America's Olympic team; Nancy Neimann, four times national champion, who tied the world's record; and Joanni Specken, national champion. He served as coach of the 1964 United States Olympic Cycling Team, and runs a national bicycle and parts business from his Cadillac, Michigan headquarters (see Appendix, page 317).

TRACK VERSUS ROAD-TRAINING TECHNIQUES

Bill Kund, a racing cyclist, offers some practical advice to track and racing cyclists as to the different types and methods of conditioning each should engage in.[1]

I have found that the best way to gain endurance is to ride. I spend from two and a half to three hours on the road daily, usually riding in a small gear,

---

[1] Bill Kund, "Speed + Endurance = Victory," *American Cycling* (now *Bicycling!*), April, 1966. Page 17.

Fig. 58: *Riding in the rain in the eighth lap of the 1968 Tour de France, these racers are on their way to Royan in western France.*

62 to 70 inches (46 x 20 to 47 x 18), at a fairly comfortable pace. If I am feeling good I will include some hills in the ride, or go into higher gear, 88 to 94 inches, and ride hard for five to ten miles. If I am feeling especially weak or stiff I will still ride for three hours, but at an easy pace in a small gear.

I also do speed work three times a week, and on Tuesday evenings, I go to the track and do interval training. This consists of about ten repetitions of 500-meter sprints at seven-eighths speed, with a one-mile rest between each one. The whole work-out, including fifteen minutes of pacing to warm up, lasts about an hour. This is a very tiring work-out, and I would not advise doing it more than once a week. On Thursday evenings I do four to six 300-meter sprints with long rests between. The emphasis on these sprints is speed, not fatigue. I usually get together with one or two other riders when doing this, and we take turns leading out the sprints. On Fridays, I incorporate at least one hour of hard motor pacing (30 to 35 miles per hour) into my three-hour stint on the road.

It is only through balanced training of this type that a rider can develop to his fullest capacity. Races are won with both speed and endurance, not with only one or the other. A sprinter who is unable to sustain his speed to the line is as worthless as a roadman in a bunch sprint who is consistently last.

ABOUT THE RACING BICYCLE

The kind of bicycle you use for racing depends on the type of racing you want to do. If your budget restricts you to one bicycle, you can strip it down for track racing by removing fenders, brakes, and freewheel, and converting the rear wheel to a fixed gear. You will be handicapped, though, for a road-racing bicycle simply isn't suitable for track use.

For road racing, a conventional touring frame will do, equipped with ten-speed derailleurs and tubular tires weighing from eight to twelve and a half ounces.

For track racing, rear fork slots open to the rear, instead of to the front as with conventional road-racing frames. The track frame has a shorter wheelbase, with minimum clearance for wheels under the fork crown and chain and seat stay bridges. The crown and bridge are not drilled for brakes and there's no room for fenders. Rear fork slot plates are heavier to take the strain of very firm axle-nut tightening done with a wrench.

Tires are very lightweight and rims are ultrathin, even more so than road-racing tubular rims. The track rims have no braking flats on the sides, and the concavity for tires is shallower and narrower. Track tires weigh from five to eight ounces and have a smooth or very fine tread.

DIET AND GENERAL HINTS

Every champion bike racer has his own favorite dietary rules which he firmly believes constitute one of the main ingredients of his success. Champs usually are loath to part with these secrets, which is understandable; but with some persuasion, we were able to pry some general rules, at least, out of a few of them.

Jim Rossi of Chicago, a United States national champion (from 1959 to 1963, and winner of the United States ten-mile race in 1965), a silver medal winner in the 1963 Pan American games in Brazil, and a gold medal winner in the 1959 Pan American games, began his dissertation on diet and training by pointing out that as far as he is concerned diet is very much an individual matter, depending on physical and emotional makeup. He pointed out that trainers often use placebo psychology, when they prescribe for a racer a prerace conditioning diet in which a sugar pill is included. Near-magical powers can be attributed to the sugar pill, and with this mental boost the racer can often win. The rider, of course, does not know what is in the pill. Incidentally, American bicycle racers are strictly forbidden to take dope, although barbiturates and stronger drugs are regularly, though surreptitiously, used by European cyclists. More about the drug problem later in this chapter.

To continue about diet: Cycle champs, including Jim Rossi, start off the spring training season by abstaining from all greasy fried foods and high-starch foods such as potatoes. Diet for a racing cyclist is very much a matter of meat and vegetables, with steak a favorite, accompanied by fresh vegetables cooked with a minimum of water to preserve the natural vitamin content. He drinks lots of fresh fruit juices (without sugar) and keeps on this diet until winter-accumulated body fat is replaced by muscle tissue, and he is down to his racing weight. Bread, if eaten, is either rye or whole wheat.

Although physicians say that additional vitamins are not needed with a proper diet, many racing cyclists take them anyway. Any good daily vitamin tablet or pill will do, such as Upjohn's Unicaps.

Whether you are setting off on a tour of a couple of hundred miles or

Fig. 59: Danish cycling ace Ole Ritter puts the power on during the fourth lap of the fifty-second Tour of Italy cycle race in May, 1969. This photograph illustrates how some racers drill out their brake levers, and the side-pull brake itself, for lightness. Notice also the small flange hubs on this bicycle; these make wheels more flexible and comfortable on bumpy Continental roads.

Fig. 60: *Felice Gimondi gives a drink of water to Belgium's cycling champ Eddy Merckx during the twelfth lap of the 1969 Tour of Italy.*

getting into shape for the bicycle-racing season, you must remember that cycling, more than most other sports, uses most of the muscles of the body and works them hard. Therefore, to keep in shape, a simple diet of fresh vegetables and meat, with a salad and lots of milk, is the best energy source you can provide your body.

Much about cycle training and racing diet is applicable also to other forms of athletic activity. For example, you should never gulp down large quantities of cold water right after a hard ride. If you do, you court stomach cramps that can slow you up. Instead, drink warm water laced with sugar, until your body temperature returns to normal.

Although personal habits differ, and some cyclists do not eat anything the morning of their race, Jim Rossi takes aboard a hearty breakfast consisting of steak and eggs, with coffee or tea, one hour before setting off for a long ride or race. Rossi also recommends raw eggs as an easily digested source of quick energy just before a race.

Diet in road racing, particularly a century (100-mile) run, is a little complicated, because no feeding stops are allowed for the first 50 miles. Yet Rossi and other champs assert that it's very important to replace energy lost through exertion *at the time* it's lost, rather than to wait until hunger signals appear. For by the time your stomach tells you when to eat, the time has passed when immediate muscle energy demands can be satisfied. This is why long-distance racers carry a small feedbag slung over their chest or back, filled with such sources of quick energy as sliced oranges, grapes, peaches, bananas, and meat sandwiches. If you watch these cyclists, you'll see that they eat small amounts of these foods frequently. And they take small sips, *not* huge gulps, of water, weak tea, or water laced with a sugar cube or two from feeder bottles mounted on their handlebars.

Cycle tourists would do well to take a tip from racing champions and instead of waiting for the conventional three meals on a long trip, avoid starving their muscle tissue by snacking once or twice an hour. The best schedule would be to eat a hearty breakfast one hour before departure (cycling right after a *full* meal is not recommended), snack during the morning ride, eat a light lunch, snack during the afternoon, then settle down to a nutritious dinner in the evening. Tea and coffee are not recommended with the evening meal because the stimulants they contain tend to keep you awake, when you should be resting up for the next day's ride.

Besides fruits and sandwiches for snacks en route, Rossi suggests candy

Fig. 61: *Italian rider Marino Basso crosses the finish line, winning the half-lap of the eighteenth stage of the 1969 Tour of Italy. Basso won the 115-kilometer stage in 2 hours, 51 minutes, and 28 seconds, at an average speed of 40.240 kilometers per hour (or 24.98 miles per hour).*

bars that won't melt or stick to your throat and gag you. Fresh figs or fig bars and dextrose tablets are also excellent. Stay away from honey and similar sticky liquids because they can clog your throat.

Following these general rules, you can alter what you eat to suit your own tastes and preferences. If you don't like fresh calf's liver, for example, try steak, chops, or broiled (not fried) chicken. For sandwiches, try roast beef, sliced chicken, or turkey on rye or whole wheat bread. Stay away from sandwiches that come apart easily, make a mess, and are hard to hold onto, such as salad ingredients (chicken or egg salad, for example), unless you are prepared to stop while you snack. Most racers eat on the go.

THE QUESTION OF DRUGS

As I have already stated, it is virtually unheard of for anyone on the United States cycle-racing teams to take drugs. In the first place, in this country the sport comes under rules governing amateur athletics. There are no professional bicycle racers. In Europe, however, where bicycle racing is a national obsession akin to baseball or football here, professional bicycle racers can earn from $50,000 to $100,000 a year. Pro racing competition is keen, and most racing athletes are fairly evenly matched physically, thus leaving only technique or drugs to decide who wins. The taking of drugs, either by injection into the bloodstream or orally, has long been a real problem in bicycle-racing circles abroad. Authorities prohibited all forms of stimulants long ago, and athletes are tested for drugs either by a spot check or by a careful physical checkup.

Taking drugs is a dangerous practice for athletes because it masks true symptoms of fatigue that, when ignored, can cause heart failure. Drugs have killed more than one racing cyclist, and have "burned out" many more athletes before their time. In fact, during a recent Tour de France road race, a world-famous cycling champion died shortly after toppling off his bicycle. At first, death was attributed to sunstroke, but a later examination showed that he had taken a stimulant which permitted exertion to the point of heart failure.

European cycling pros who take drugs follow a typical cycle of racing success, says Rossi. Generally, a cyclist who takes drugs can remain in peak form and condition from eighteen to twenty-four years of age, but during this period he will build up a tolerance for the drug, which will require progressively larger doses. After the age of twenty-four, he cannot continue taking drugs without becoming addicted and endangering his life. A racer will drop out of active competition for from two to four years until his body throws off the effects of the drugs he has been taking. And, at twenty-six or twenty-eight, he will be found again in the championship ranks until, after an even shorter period of drug-stimulated racing, he either drops out for good, goes through another "cure," or becomes permanently addicted.

I asked Rossi why cyclists don't carry small containers of pressurized oxygen which they could sniff from time to time to make up the oxygen deficiency caused by physical stress. His answer was that pure oxygen isn't much help because racing cyclists undergo physical stress that is sustained longer than in most other sports, and their training is rigorous enough that they should be able to oxygenize blood by means of normal respiration. Also, says Rossi, the few times a racing cyclist would be able to inhale a fractional cubic foot of oxygen during the heat and intense mental and physical strain of a race makes oxygen-sniffing impractical.

A WORD ABOUT CONDITIONING

There are a few special rules that apply to a cyclist who wants to keep in shape all year round that may not apply to other sports.

For example, swimming and bicycling simply don't mix, because leg muscles are stretched in different ways by these activities. Don't be surprised if, after a long, hard, and hot ride, your leg muscles cramp up if you jump in the lake for a swim. For safety's sake, if you tour, wait until you have at least cooled down before going in for a swim. For the cycle-racing enthusiast, swimming is strictly taboo, according to Rossi, who at one point in his career had to choose between water polo and cycle racing for this very reason.

At the beginning of this chapter, I pointed out that bicycle racers are strictly uninterested in touring. The major reason for this, Jim Rossi points out, is that a racer is not interested in anything that will not contribute to his physical conditioning, and touring is useless in this respect. Most tourists, even those who are in prime condition, go far too slowly to permit a racing cyclist to stay in peak shape. Racing cyclists on hard training rides frequently roll up 100 miles in well under four hours, which is impractical, to say the least, for a touring cyclist riding a heavy touring or road bicycle laden with gear. I know of at least one racer turned tourist, though. At the age of fifty-five he went 600 miles in three days, from Chicago to his lakeside cabin in upper Minnesota. One hundred miles a day is plenty for me; for the average tourist, fifty to seventy-five miles daily is enough. This amount of mileage is child's play to the racing cyclist. Rossi says that he would rather run around the block a hundred times than go on a cycling tour, at least where physical conditioning is concerned. Rossi is in the air-conditioning business, and on his trips to office buildings he spurns the elevator and *runs* up and down stairs, carrying his tools. I don't recommend this strenuous an activity for the average desk jockey, although I do feel that it is a good idea for anyone to climb at least the first twenty-five flights slowly, with pauses for rest every five or six flights. Certainly there's no excuse for taking an elevator *down* any number of flights. Exercise works the body to its maximum capacity in terms of output and time, and your heart should be forced to work up to 120 beats per minute, assuming you're in good shape.

An athlete in prime condition typically has a heartbeat that is rather low at rest, but one that goes to top cardiac output quickly under stress and returns quickly to the rest beat when stress stops. For example, Rossi's heartbeat when he was twenty-eight years old and in training was from sixty-five to sixty-eight per minute. After two minutes of squats, his beat would rise to 128 and after two minutes of rest return to sixty-five. If you can establish this, consider yourself ready for the Olympics.

IMPORTANCE OF WARM-UP

Your body cannot be expected to perform at maximum work output from a cold start, any more than the motor of your car can. Not, at least, without damage. In the case of the body, it's nearly physiologically impossible. When the body is at rest, the blood vessels are not dilated, which means that they will handle a minimum amount of blood volume flow. This is why the first two or three miles of cycling, from a resting state start, is a strain for most of us. Once the muscles begin to demand more oxygen and nutrients, the blood vessels dilate wide open, the heart speeds up, and the muscles' needs are satisfied. The body performs more smoothly and you feel much more comfortable and ready to go a hundred miles. But until the muscles get fed, the first couple of miles are tough.

WINTER TRAINING

Few racing cyclists make much of an effort to ride outdoors during very cold weather. Roads are frequently clogged with ice and snow, so that the regular riding mileage at the speed demanded by effective training techniques is not possible.

Instead, cyclists turn to other forms of *regular* exercise, such as basketball, speed skating, handball, weight lifting, or simply running around the block. The importance of frequent regular (at least three times a week) exercise cannot be stressed enough, because, as Gene Portuesi stated earlier in this chapter, once out of condition an athlete cannot be expected to get back in shape soon enough during the spring to compete in major cycling events. As for the rest of us, we too need regular winter exercise. If you can't fit into last summer's clothes, and if a ten-mile bike ride exhausts you, your winter exercise program needs a closer look.

Winter or summer, at least eight hours of sleep is indicated, and cycle champs in training often go to bed around 10:00 P.M. This makes for a dull life, as far as parties are concerned, but that's the stuff champions are made of. Speaking of parties, a champion in training should not drink alcoholic beverages, certainly nothing stronger than beer and not much of that. Alcohol is fattening, and there is also a strong temptation to snack while drinking.

If you do ride in cold weather, remember that it's best to dress for the weather as though you were not exercising, and peel off layers of clothir.g as your body warms up. I cycle to work frequently during the winter months, and on cold days I start out with thermal underwear, pants, thermal socks, a heavy long-sleeved shirt, a sweater or two, and a thermal nylon jacket. After three miles or so I stop, take off the jacket, peel off the sweater and possibly the shirt, put the jacket back on, and continue cycling.

I must admit that I have never raced myself, although I thoroughly enjoy the sport as a spectator. I hope that, along with the increased popularity of cycling as a healthful hobby, we will see the spread of cycle-racing tracks to all parts of the country, and that this truly exciting spectator spcit will get the audience it deserves.

9

THE FAD THAT LASTED—
A SHORT HISTORY OF BICYCLING

When Baron Karl von Drais introduced his "Hobby-Horse" to the citizens of Karlsruhe, Germany, in 1816, he started a love affair with man-propelled wheels that has persisted to this day.

The Hobby-Horse, or "Draisene," (Fig. 62) was a monstrously heavy affair, consisting of a wooden frame, wooden wheels, and a most uncomfortable-looking saddle. The rider straddled the Draisene and propelled himself forward by pushing with his feet—the result was something like riding a kiddie-car.

Costly and cumbersome though it was, the Draisene was immediately accepted by the wealthy and the more enterprising middle class of the day. Within a few years, playboys of western Europe were pushing their way up and down the boulevards of major cities on the hobby-horse. Draisene owners formed clubs and held races and sporting events.

Obviously, the Draisene was only suitable for the young and sturdy. Also, since it was so heavy and cumbersome, it could not be pushed very far or fast. Therefore, there was great incentive to find a way to make this form of propulsion more efficient.

Fig. 62: *The original Hobby-Horse, invented by Baron von Drais, in the Museum at Breslau.*

One of the earliest attempts at mechanizing the hobby-horse was made by an Englishman, Lewis Gompertz, who in 1821 devised a rack-and-pinion arrangement that enabled the rider to pull the handlebars back and forth. By pushing with his feet and pulling with his arms, he could presumably go faster and farther. How he steered this contraption at the same time has not been recorded, but most likely it was inaccurate.

Bicycling really began to take over the streets and countryside when an enterprising Englishman named Kirkpatrick MacMillan put foot pedals on the front wheel of the hobby-horse in 1835. By the mid-1800s, it was truly the fad of the century. Young people found bicycling a good way to get out from under the stern eye of their parents; society saw the bicycle as an expensive and exclusive toy and pastime; and sporting enthusiasts of all ages adopted one of the thousands of variations of the two-wheeler for their activities.

As the bicycle improved, more and more people began to ride and even to go on picnics in the country and take short tours. At last man was free from the horse and wagon. A bicycle never needed daily cleaning and currying; it didn't eat, and it did not use an expensive harness that took time to put on and take off. One could just jump on his bicycle and quickly be away from his house. The impact of the bicycle was almost as great, in fact, as the advent of the Model T Ford. Much to the indignation and consternation of their elders and the ministers of the day, young boys and girls could ride out into the country together. Women's fashions changed to suit the bicycle. Clothes became less confining; the Gibson Girl on her bicycle, with her voluminous bloomers and leg-of-mutton sleeves, set a new style (Fig. 63).

Just as with the automobile, the first bicycles were costly, so in the beginning, they were the playthings of the wealthy only. Between 1890 and 1896, over $100 million was spent on bicycles. If you consider $250 too high a price for the best modern bicycle, what would you think about paying $800? The $100 price for bikes in 1896 is the equivalent of $800 today. There was a cheaper model available for $80. The earliest bicycles —those sold in the 1860s—cost upward of $300 (which would be $2,400 today). Complicated machines, such as tandems and two- and even three-seat side-by-side rigs, cost even more.

The exhilarating new freedom of mobility which the bicycle brought to the common man was undoubtedly the cause of what was truly a bicycle mania in the 1800s. An early form of this velocipede was intro-

Fig. 63: *This old photograph shows an early female bike enthusiast in the clothing fashion of the day.*

duced to the United States from England in 1869. This machine had iron-rimmed wooden wheels, for which it was nicknamed the "boneshaker." The front wheel was equipped with pedals.

The velocipede became so popular that riding academies with indoor rinks were established where would-be cyclists were taught, and where feats of riding skill were performed before enthralled audiences. Cycling clubs were formed in large cities across the nation by social sets, and were soon very exclusive indeed. The Michaux Cycle Club of New York (Fig. 64), for example, was housed in an elegant three-story brownstone mansion. Its riding rink was well lighted, and ladies and gentlemen could watch riders drill from balconies, while waiters brought them food and drinks.

The five-foot-high "Penny-Farthing," which emerged in England in 1872 (Fig. 66), was an outgrowth of the boneshaker, and an attempt at

Fig. 64: *The bicycle fad at its peak. New York's Michaux Cycle Club.*

achieving more speed. It wasn't long before an enterprising engineer figured out that the bigger the wheel with the pedals, the faster the bicycle would go (up to a point, that is). Eventually, the wheel diameter became too big for even the strongest human to push. It would seem that bicycles developed backward for awhile, until the Penny-Farthing or "ordinary," as it was called in the United States, eventually became a dangerous thing to ride, with its sixty-inch-diameter front wheel and tiny rear wheel. The ordinary was very unstable—if the rider hit a pothole, he could easily be thrown over the front wheel from a height of more than five feet, and possibly at a speed of six to ten miles an hour. There were a good many fatalities and cracked heads associated with it. Only the novelty of cycling and the freedom of movement it gave to riders accounted for the continued growth of the sport when this machine was in its heyday.

Fig. 65: *View of Oldreive's tricycle, or the new iron horse, with a lady inside.*

In 1876, Colonel Albert A. Pope of Massachusetts began to import these high-wheelers from England, and in 1878, he began to manufacture them in Boston. At this time the ordinary weighed over seventy pounds and cost $313, which would be about $2,400 today.

Prominent men of the day—one might call them the forerunners of our "jet set"—biked around the country on ordinarys. Well-known social figures made headlines by touring from coast to coast, from Chicago to New York, and New York to Boston. British nobility in the 1880s rode bikes around their estates, and even the Prince of Wales attended the bicycle races of the day. Bicycle clubs grew and became ritualized and institutionalized as the bicycle became improved mechanically.

In 1885 the high-wheeled ordinary gave way to the "safety bicycle," invented by an Englishman, J. K. Starley. This bicycle had a chain-driven rear wheel, and wheels about thirty inches in diameter, with solid rubber tires. Three years later, an Irish veterinary surgeon produced an invention without which the automobile could never have flourished. Dr. J. B. Dunlop of Belfast, Ireland, gave a hard-tired tricycle to his son, Johnny, who reported that his new present was quite uncomfortable and very hard to pedal. Dr. Dunlop liked to tinker in his spare time, and one of his hobbies was fabricating his own gloves out of canvas and rubber. From these he devised a set of "gloves" that could be filled with air for his son's tricycle. From rubber sheeting and strips of linen from one of his wife's old dresses, he built an air-filled tire, thus the first pneumatic bicycle tire.

Dr. Dunlop continued to make improvements on his tire until one day his friend, William Hume, president of the Belfast Cruiser's Cycling Club, persuaded him to make up a pair of tires for his racing machine. With his new tires, Mr. Hume easily beat the crack cyclists of the area in a race on May 18, 1889. After this, Dr. Dunlop was in business, and soon pneumatic tires were being manufactured by a number of firms in the United States. By 1891, the pneumatic tire was an accepted bicycle feature. The fad continued to flourish and spread.

During the 1890s, the bicycle population grew by leaps and bounds— by 1896, there were over 400 bicycle manufacturers in the United States alone. The bicycle craze even alarmed businessmen in major cities for a while. They thought the bicycle would bring the nation to economic collapse, and there were a number of compelling statistics to bear them out. The bicycle was not only a status symbol of major importance; it was the only way the average person could move about, unless he owned a horse and carriage. By 1896, the watch and jewelry business had fallen almost to zero, piano sales had been cut in half, and book sales had dropped disastrously. Apparently, no one stayed home and played the piano or read, and instead of buying jewelry, people bought bicycles.

Also, most people must have been too tired or too broke at night to go to the theatre, because attendance at theatrical performances also fell off drastically during the 1890s. The song that would have reached the top of the hit parade, had there been one in 1896, was about a girl named Daisy and her "bicycle built for two."

There were also plays written about bicycling. *The Bicyclers,* by John Kendrick Bangs, was a farce published by Harper & Brothers in 1896. It opens in the drawing room of Mr. and Mrs. Thaddeus Perkins, at their home in New York's Gramercy Square. It is early evening.

The bell rings and Mr. Perkins, attired in a cycling costume of knickers and socks, answers the door. His friend, Ed Barlow, is at the door, attired in evening dress. There follows much good-humored banter, during which Ed asks Thad if he might speak to his father. It seems that up until the bicycle craze only children wore knickers. Ed's wife, it is revealed, is en route by bicycle from the Barlow home in the upper Seventies, a distance of some eight miles from Gramercy Square.

While waiting for the arrival of Mrs. Barlow, Thad Perkins brags about his new "Czar" bicycle. He says, in answer to Ed Barlow's question about whether he's had any riding lessons:

"None yet. Fact is, just got my wheel. That's it, over by the door— pneumatic tires, tool-chest, cyclometer, lamp—all for a hun. The only thing they gave me extra was a Ki-Yi gun; it's filled with ammonia and it shoots dogs. You shoot it into the dog's face; it doesn't hurt him, but it gives him something to think of."

While Mr. and Mrs. Perkins and Ed Barlow await the arrival of Mrs. Barlow, the phone rings. It is Mrs. Barlow, in great agitation, phoning from a police station. She has been arrested for riding without a light. Ed Barlow, in his concern about his wife, forgets that he's had no riding experience, and jumps on Thad's bicycle. The play ends with Barlow's voice, off-stage, louder at times, then fainter, as he circles around and around the block, not knowing how to steer properly, or how to stop.

Much of the dialogue in the play is devoted to the merits and short-comings of various makes of bicycles. Certainly, bicyclists of the 1890s had a good many machines to talk about, just as car owners do today.

Among the bicycle manufacturers of the era were many famous names —Henry Ford, Wilbur and Orville Wright, Glenn Curtiss, and Charles Duryea. United States manufacturers alone produced 2 million bicycles in 1897, when the population was about 65 million. By contrast, the six or seven bicycle manufacturers in America today produced 7.5 million bicycles in 1968, when the population was over 200 million. That means that there was roughly one bicycle made for every 10 people in 1897 and one for every 350 people in 1968.

The following description of the bicycle business in the February, 1896, issue of *Outing* Magazine resembles an article in today's *Business Week*. Cycling in those days was a sport of the wealthy. *Outing* was devoted to the leisure time of the moneyed class, somewhat like today's *Holiday*.

The cycle trade is now one of the chief industries of the world. Its ramifications are beyond ordinary comprehension. Its prosperity contributes in no small degree to that of the steel, wire, rubber, and leather markets. Time was when the spider web monsters, now nearly extinct, were built in one story annexes to English and American machine shops; now a single patented type of a jointless wood rim, one of the minor parts of a modern bicycle, is the sole product of an English factory covering over two acres of ground. A decade ago the American steel tube industry was unprofitable. The production of this most essential part of cycle construction has, during the past two years, been unequal to the demand, and even now every high-grade tube mill in this country is working night and day on orders that will keep them busy throughout the year. Nearly every season since 1890 has witnessed a doubling of the number of our factories and a multiplication of the product of a large proportion of the older ones. Yet the supply from the opening of last season to mid-summer was unequal to the demand, and although preparations of astounding proportions have been and are being made to meet with a multiplicity of models of the most approved designs and best workmanship, the demands of '96, the prospects are that the field offers reasonable prosperity to all makers of high-grade products. The present prices are quite reasonable, considering the quality of material and workmanship involved. Prices will be very generally maintained, and the number of riders, of both sexes, will be at least doubled.

It might interest some of our readers to review the specifications of a few of the safety bicycles of the 1890s. For example, the new 1898 line of Columbia bicycles, made by Pope Manufacturing Company, had a split crank shaft. Model 40 Columbia "light roadster," selling for $100, had a "23-inch frame, 10-inch steering head, 28-inch wheels, 1⅝ pneumatic 'Hartford' tires, detachable sprockets, improved self-oiling chain, 6¾-inch patent round cranks, 5-inch tread, 3⅜-inch pedals, reversible handle-bars, tubular seat rod, 66-inch gear and weighed 24 lbs."

Reviewing the specifications of these early bicycles points up the fact that gearing was low, which was necessary because there were no gear-shift mechanisms in popular use at the time. In addition, the metallurgy of the bicycle frame and parts was far inferior to that of today's higher-quality bicycles. Gene Portuesi has told me that racing cyclists of the day could reach fantastic crank speeds. Zimmerman, a racing champion of the 1890s, could wind up to 140 crank revolutions per minute, which he had to do to get any speed out of the low gear ratios used even on the best racing bicycles of the day, A powerful modern racing cyclist would literally tear apart a racing bicycle of the 1890s, according to Portuesi.

Reviewing the names of the bicycle manufacturers of the 1890s, which seemed to be located in every major city, made me somewhat nostalgic. The Columbia line was popular up until the late 1920s or early 1930s. Some readers will remember the Spalding, Iver Johnson, Rambler, Remington, Waltham, and Singer bicycles.

Most of the better bicycles produced during this period had turned-down handlebars. One bicycle of 1896 even had an all-aluminum frame. It was manufactured by the Lu-mi-num Company of St. Louis, Missouri, and was successful enough to be licensed for production in England. You can buy all-aluminum bicycles today, which are made in Japan, but I don't recommend them. I found the frame weak, stiff, and unresponding. The slight saving in weight isn't worth these major shortcomings, in my opinion.

The introduction of the "safety" bicycle, complete with chain drive and twenty-eight-inch wheels and brakes, did not guarantee safe cycling, however. A review of early cycling hazards makes cycling today seem safe, despite the density of urban motor vehicle traffic.

There may have been no automobiles back in the 1890s, but the roads were full of potholes, except for main arteries in and near major cities. And dogs attacked cyclists just as they do now. In those days, they were not restrained as they are today in cities.

Also, the general populace resented cyclists, just as many people were against the early automobiles. Farmers took personal delight in blocking the narrow roads of the day with their wagons, and they went as slowly as possible just to aggravate cyclists behind them. Country bumpkins took great delight in thrusting sticks between the spokes of cyclists' wheels to knock them off their seats. When people were riding the "penny-farthing" in the early days of cycling, a stick between the spokes of the high wheel brought disaster to the cyclist and guffaws from pranksters. One of the reasons the early cycling clubs were formed, aside from social purposes, was to provide protection against wanton attacks on cyclists. Horse-drawn vehicles, in addition to blocking the roads, were often deliberately sent careening into groups of cyclists, which injured the riders as well as harmed their machines.

In England, at this time, restaurant and tea-shop owners refused to serve cyclists, particularly female riders who wore what the owner of one restaurant described as "outlandish and shocking costumes."

The world's first nationwide cycling club, the British Touring Club, organized for political as well as for social reasons, was formed in England in 1878. It was an amalgamation of a number of small regional cycling organizations, and soon began publishing its own magazine, *The Bicycling Times*. In 1883, the BTC's name was changed to its present title, the Cyclists' Touring Club. The publication became known as *The Gazette* and is now *Cycle Touring*.

The Gazette was an outspoken and fearless defender of cyclists and cycling in England. In fact, its early pronouncements must have been fairly vitriolic, because in 1898 the editor was denounced for his outspokenness at one of the Club's national meetings by some of the members, some of whom were the representatives of bicycle manufacturers. At the same meeting, George Bernard Shaw, who was an ardent cyclist and lifetime member of the Club, arose to defend *The Gazette:* "Do you want it to contain fact or fiction?" he said. "You already have plenty of fiction in the advertising pages . . . I want to raise a strong protest against what has been said as to raising the tone of *The Gazette.* What we want above all things is an abusive *Gazette.* If I wish to read a nice complimentary cycling paper, one that has a good word for everybody, for every dealer and seller, and every sort of kind of invention—I can easily buy one for a penny at any news shop. But we want something quite in the opposite direction and we get it in our *Gazette,* even if that publication does sometimes refer to a lady's article as piffle." (Roars of laughter.) "In my view the gentlemen who object to ladies having to stand the same treatment as is meted out to men are the same people who object to ladies cycling altogether, and therefore I do not think they need be taken very seriously."

The hostility of the noncycling public seemed to be universal, so throughout the Western world, Europe and America, cyclists banded together into clubs such as the CTC to protect their status. In England, the Highway and Railway (Amendment) Act of 1878 referred specifically to bicycles, and gave county authorities power to regulate their use. Many of the laws passed by local authorities were unreasonably restrictive. In some instances, cyclists were forbidden to use public highways, or had to pull over and stop whenever a horse-drawn vehicle appeared on the horizon. Within ten years, however, the CTC had grown enough in size and importance so that it was able to push through Parliament what became known as the Magna Carta of Bicyclists. The Local Government Act abolished the power given by the Highway and Railway Act to local county governments to regulate bicycling. This signaled further successes for the Club, which was able to push through other laws that provided for the improvement of highways, the safe carrying of bicycles on railroad baggage cars, and recourse against the antagonisms of the general public against cycling.

A landmark case occurred in 1899 in Surrey, England, when Lady

Harbeton, an influential member of the CTC, was refused service in the coffee room of the Hautboy Hotel. They offered to serve her in the bar parlor instead. The Club jumped to Lady Harbeton's defense, and the hotel's owner was indicted for "wilfully and unlawfully neglecting and refusing to supply a traveller with victuals." Lady Harbeton showed the court a picture of herself, which was described as portraying "an elderly lady, wearing a pair of exceedingly baggy knickerbockers reaching below the knee, and a jacket which came well over the hips and opened sufficiently to reveal the silk blouse underneath."

In the summer of 1880, a group of American cyclists visited the CTC's headquarters in Liverpool, and returned to the United States to form the League of American Wheelmen, in Newport, Rhode Island. By 1898, membership in the League of American Wheelmen had soared to its all-time high of 102,636. But thanks to the horseless carriage, it dwindled to 8,629 by 1902. The League struggled on, however, under its indefatigable secretary Abbott Bassett, until 1942, when it succumbed to massive public indifference.

In 1964, the League was reactivated, this time in Chicago, under the leadership of Joe Hart. With its membership exceeding 4,000, the LAW today, as it was before the turn of the century, is dedicated to the needs and interests of the ardent cyclist. To the tourist traveling across the land, an LAW membership roster is a sure guarantee of welcome in every community where the League has a chapter.

In the days before road maps, the LAW published its own maps, lists of accommodations, condition of roads, and other vital information which was otherwise unobtainable. To embark on an extended tour without an LAW touring bureau itinerary was unthinkable in those days. By 1890, the LAW had a chapter in virtually every town big enough to have a hotel.

During its heyday, many famous men and women were LAW members, among them Orville and Wilbur Wright, Commodore Vanderbilt, and even Diamond Jim Brady. The organization was a political force to be reckoned with, more because of the influence of its wealthy members than for the size of its membership. During the early days of its existence, the League faced many of the same problems as did its counterpart in Great Britain. Cyclists were denied the right of way in America, excluded from public parks, and horsemen and, later, early motorists deliberately crowded them off the highways. The LAW first flexed its political muscle

Fig. 66: *American wheelmen reposing in the woods, ca. 1890.*

around 1884, when it dealt with the Haddonfield (N.J.) Turnpike case.[1]
The turnpike authorities refused to permit cyclists on the turnpike. At
that time, turnpikes were simply cross-state roads used by horse-drawn
vehicles. There were no automobiles yet. The turnpike's ruling caused a
furor among cyclists. If this was allowed it would set a precedent, which
could restrict cyclists to cowpaths, or worse. With the backing of the
League, the Philadelphia chapter brought a test case, which resulted in
the turnpike authority's rescinding its no-cycling stricture.

Before this landmark decision in 1879, the New York Board of Com-
missioners had decided that bicycles in New York City's Central Park
were an eyesore and a menace to the citizenry. Shortly after the League
was formed, it took this case to the courts and, after an eight-year fight,
was successful in getting the governor of New York to revoke all restrictions against bicycles. After this ruling, cyclists were free to ride on any
public roadway in the state of New York, which set a precedent in other
states which granted cyclists the same privileges. Today, New York's
Central Park is the exclusive province of cyclists on weekends and Tuesday evenings during the summer, when no automobiles are allowed in
the park at all.

---

[1] *American Cycling* (now *Bicycling!*), August, 1965.

Under joint backing of the LAW and the Bicycle Institute of America (an organizaticn formed by United States bicycle manufacturers to promote cycling generally), bicycle paths are now being laid down by a number of cities and states throughout the country. Today there are a number of fine bicycle paths and trails. Chicago, for instance, has a cycle path that extends nearly the entire 20-mile length of the city, along Lake Michigan. Wisconsin has a trail across the state from LaCrosse to Kenosha (a distance of 350 miles). It traverses much of the state's most scenic spots. Fifty miles of it is over an abandoned, cinder-tracked railway that is restricted to bicycles, and far from any road. Milwaukee, Wisconsin; Clearwater, Florida; Arlington, Virginia; and many other cities also have good trails and paths now. There are also, or will be soon, bikeways in many of our national and state parks, including the Indiana Dunes National Lakeshore, Sleeping Bear Dunes National Park in Michigan, Cape Cod (Mass.) National Sea Shore, and Fire Island National Seashore in New York. I should point out that cross-state bicycle trails are also used by automobiles for much of the way, at least. However, these trails are carefully chosen back roads, which traverse scenic areas that bear little traffic and have a good black-top or concrete surface. Efforts are now being made to link cross-state trails so that cyclists can ride all the way across the nation.

These wonderful new bikeways might, and should, tempt you to take extended touring and cycle camping trips, but long-distance touring was a far different situation back before the automobile. The first man to cross the United States by bicycle was Thomas Stevens, who in 1884 rode a high-wheel "ordinary" from Oakland, California, to Boston. "Rode" is hardly accurate—Mr. Stevens carried, pushed, shoved, and dragged his seventy-five-pound steed across mountains, deserts, streams, and fields. His journey took him 103½ days. In comparison, in 1954, Richard Berg of Chicago cycled from Santa Monica, California, to New York City in just over 14 days.

Mr. Stevens had a horrendous task. He rode an ungainly high-wheeler over roads that were largely uncharted (where they existed at all), and public accommodations were chancy all the way. Also, the attitudes of the people he met ranged from scornful indifference to downright hostility.

Let's take a look at the kind of bicycle Stevens rode. It had a high front wheel, about fifty inches in diameter, and a small rear wheel, about seventeen inches in diameter. The frame was like a curved backbone, topped by a saddle just aft of a pair of flat handlebars. The machine weighed about seventy-five pounds.

The high wheel was not very maneuverable. Stevens was wedged right up against the handlebars, so steering way was limited and sharp turns nearly impossible to make. He had to sit almost over the centerline of the front wheel, which made even slight uphill runs a matter of hard pedaling. Coasting downhill was precarious, for a small chuckhole in the road, or even a pebble, could upset the delicate balance of the rider and send him toppling headfirst toward an unyielding roadway. In fact, Stevens used to practice taking headers, and his skill at it probably contributed as much to his survival as did his cycling proficiency.

It was quite an eventful trip. Much happened to Tom Stevens, including being made to perform for a bunch of rowdy cowpokes who shot bullets around him as he rode in and around pool tables, being pursued by packs of coyotes, crossing a railroad trestle in the Rockies and discovering halfway across that a train was coming (he hung onto the side of the trestle, seventy-five-pound bicycle and all), fording rivers swollen to flood stage, riding down the Rockies at breakneck speed, with his metal brake spoons heated red hot, and being cursed at by boatmen on the Erie Canal, whose mules reared and balked at the sight of him. He was feted from Chicago on, and in Boston received the magnificent reception he deserved.

If you are interested in reading the complete account of this unusual trip, you might try to find a copy of the two-volume story of his adventure, *First Across America by Bicycle,* which was published about 1888, in a secondhand bookstore, or buy a copy of an excellent summation of his ride, which was published in a limited edition by Dr. Irving Leonard. (Write to Bear Camp Press, South Tamworth, New Hampshire, enclosing your check for $5.95.) Professor Leonard also has an interesting collection of old bicycles in his barn at South Tamworth, which he will be happy to show you should you pass that way. There are other fine collections at the Smithsonian Institution in Washington, D.C., the Museum of Science and Industry in Chicago, and the Ford Museum (Greenfield Village) in Dearborn, Michigan.

There have been other cross-country and even around-the-world trips by bicycle, many of which make fascinating reading to the experienced cycle tourist who has been through similar adventures. In 1894, a young

Fig. 67: Bicycle racing in the 1890s—an unusual action shot.

American girl named Annie Londonberry set out one July morning to tour the world, which she succeeded in doing. She left without a penny, and earned over $2,000 en route from publicizing her cycling exploits. Another famous woman traveler was Fannie Bullock Workman, who spent ten years touring the world, accompanied by her husband William. Mrs. Workman was the wealthy daughter of a governor of Massachusetts, and her husband was a physician. Old photographs show Mrs. Workman mounted on her trusty Rover safety bicycle, clad always in a high-necked blouse, a voluminous skirt, and a pith helmet.

The Workmans made an unforgettable trip over the Atlas Mountains to the Sahara, in 1895. One can only marvel at their fortitude. They published at least three lengthy volumes of their trips, which, if you are lucky, you might find in your public library or an old bookstore.

Mr. Richard Berg's record-breaking fourteen-day trip across the United States in 1954, which we mentioned earlier, was not without incident. Berg, an experienced, twenty-three-year-old racing cyclist, rode a bicycle stripped down to the essentials, an eight-speed machine with tubular sew-up racing tires. He carried no luggage, not even a toothbrush or shaving kit. He made concessions to safety and comfort only; a rear light for night travel and a water bottle.

Berg left Santa Monica's City Hall, bound for New York, with speed his main concern. He crossed the Mohave Desert at night, as he had

planned, and rode twenty-four hours a day more than once during this trip. Coming down the eastern slopes of the Rockies he often hit better than sixty miles per hour, as he was told by incredulous motorists after he passed them.

Berg stayed at any motel he came to, when he was tired from the day's exertions. If he could not find a motel, he would pull off into the nearest field for the night. His biggest problem was flat tires. It seems that out West, where the cactus grows, there are two-sided pronged thorns waiting in ambush on all roads. He used to spend his evenings repairing his sew-ups, and reports having had as many as thirteen flats in one day until he hit the plains of Kansas. Incidentally, he told me he would still use tubular sew-ups if he were to make the trip again, because he believes that thorns will pierce any tire, and tubulars make cycling much easier.

RACING BEGAN AT ONCE

Starting with the Draisene, and as each improved version of the bicycle became popular, stripped-down models were used in racing events. The first bicycle race in America—at least the first officially sanctioned race—was held in 1878, over a one-mile course. It was won by Will R. Pitman in three minutes and fifty-seven seconds of what must have been arduous exertion indeed. His machine was heavy, crude, and even more cumbersome than the racing bicycles of the 1890s. In 1895, the fastest racing cyclist beat the fastest race horse for the first time, when E. F. Leonert pedaled one mile in one minute and thirty-five seconds. At this time, also, cycle racing turned professional. Six-day bicycle races held at Madison Square Garden in New York drew thousands to view this murderous and bloody spectacle. The first six-day race, held in 1891 at the Garden, was won by William "Plugger" Martin, who pedaled 1,466 miles and four laps during the six days. The six-day race has been outlawed as an inhuman spectacle, which, indeed, it was; however, a less gory version called the "Madison" is still run in Europe.

Perhaps the greatest bicycle racer of all time was A. A. Zimmerman. Zimmerman, a professional racer, was king of the wheel in both the United States and Europe, and is still talked about by racing cyclists today. In 1891, Zimmerman pedaled to a new world record for the half-mile—on the seventy-pound high-wheel "ordinary"—in one minute, 10¾ seconds.

Zimmerman violated all the laws and rules of training, going out with the boys and drinking and carousing, while his teammates slept. In one notable instance, he climbed on his trusty safety bicycle, after having attended an all-night party and pedaled a paced mile in one minute, 57⅘ seconds at the annual LAW meet in Asbury Park, New Jersey. But what seemed to gain Zimmerman the most notoriety was the fact that he never attempted to beat a record or win a race by any more effort or speed than was necessary. There is no record of how long he lived.

Until the advent of the automobile turned America's interest from bicycle to auto racing, many professional bicycle racers became wealthy from their winnings. In 1895, there were over 600 professional racing cyclists in the United States alone, and more than that in Europe. Today there are *no* professional racing cyclists in this country, although there are hundreds in Europe who have earned a lot of money from the sport. In Europe, bicycle racing has always been the principal national sport of many countries, such as Italy, France, Spain, and Belgium. The average low income of the European worker, plus the high price of gasoline, helped keep the bicycle popular, although, with the rising standard of living of the past few years, bicycling has decreased somewhat there. In the meantime, the sport has grown in popularity in America.

Early track records are mighty impressive today, when one considers the crude bicycles on which they were made. In 1895, the long-distance track record (made in Paris on September 8 and 9 by Constance Huret) was 529 miles, 585 yards, in twenty-four hours. This was a sustained average of about 22 miles per hour. By contrast, in 1968, Beryl Burton, England's current top female racer, made 100 miles in three hours and fifty-six minutes, at an average speed of 25.4 miles per hour. In 1899, Charles "Mile-a-Minute" Murphy pedaled a record mile in 57.8 seconds, following a train over a boarded-over section of the Long Island Railroad. It wasn't until 1909 that a car beat this record, when a Stanley Steamer, driven by F. W. Stanley, reached 59 miles per hour. And, in 1904, Barney Oldfield did a mile in 55.8 seconds in Henry Ford's "999."

Things got really fast later on. On May 17, 1941, Alfred Letourner zipped to 108.92 miles per hour behind a racing car at Bakersfield, California. Letourner rode a gear ratio of 252, combining a microscopic six-tooth rear gear with a fifty-seven-tooth chainwheel. On July 19, 1962, Jose Meiffet of France reached a fantastic 128 miles per hour behind a car on Germany's Autobahn.

ANSWERING THE COUNTRY'S CALL

There is one development on the history of bicycles we haven't mentioned so far. At one time, bicycling was threatened with incorporation into the army. The military mind of the 1890s clearly visualized the bicycle as an invaluable tool in advance scouting, for outpost duties, for patrols, and for convoys, and to enable officers to make quick observations.

Harper's Weekly's special bicycle issue of April 11, 1896, carried this notice: "It is in rapidly moving considerable bodies of infantry that the bicycle will find its highest function in time of war. Fancy a force of infantry, independent of roads and railroads, moving in any direction, forty or fifty miles in one morning, and appearing on a field not weary and exhausted as after a two-day's march, but fresh and prepared to fight . . ."

The Italian army was the first to adopt the bicycle. In 1870, four bicycles were furnished to each regiment of infantry, "grenadiers, sappers and miners, engineers and cavalry. The machines are provided with a brake, lantern, knapsack, rifle support and a leather pouch for orders." I suppose the first folding bicycle was made with a soldier in mind, for,

Fig. 68: *The use of bicycles by the military. In this photograph, two soldiers carry early collapsible bikes on their backs.*

in 1896, the French army had one with a hinged frame. This machine weighed only twenty-three pounds and could be carried slung over a soldier's back. In 1885, Austrian soldiers, carrying full field kit, made 100 miles per day with bicycles during field maneuvers, outdoing what the cavalry could do on horseback.

In America, the first branch of the military to use bicycles was the National Guard of Connecticut. Eventually, the U.S. Army Signal Corps and other divisions of the military used the bicycle as a direct weapon of war. The army bolted two bicycles side by side and mounted a "mountain-cannon" between them. A military tandem was equipped with rifles and revolvers as well as a field pack, and a duplex (tricycle) was rigged with a machine-gun. Another tricycle was equipped with a Colt rapid-firing machine-gun mounted on the headstay and handlebars.

Between 1890 and 1900, large numbers of soldiers learned how to ride, drill, and deploy on bicycles. New methods of using the bicycle were continually studied by an organization formed for this specific purpose. The United States Military Wheelmen, a volunteer auxiliary adjunct to the National Guard, trained soldiers in the use of the bicycle. Lieutenant

Whitney, of this association, stated in 1896: "The balance of power is so nicely adjusted that the chances in the coming conflict will be governed by efficiency in detailed preparation. The bicycle will weigh in the scale. We are told somewhere that for want of a horseshoe nail a battle was lost. In the next war, for want of a bicycle the independence of a nation may be forfeited."

Over the past 150 years, we have seen the bicycle evolve from a wealthy man's toy to a vehicle of precision and beauty, with an infinite variety of uses. There are faster ways of getting places but few more enjoyable than this ever-growing sport.

Fig. 69. *Some modern police forces have found the bicycle useful for patrolling suburban areas more quickly and silently. This photograph of a Hennepin County, Minneapolis, Minn., officer was taken in 1961.*

UNITED PRESS INTERNATIONAL

Fig. 70: *Bicycling is an ever-growing sport! New York City's Central Park is closed to traffic on weekends and Tuesday evenings during the summer to allow cyclists to*

pedal freely. Above, New Yorkers prepare for a "pedal-in" at Bethesda Fountain in the park.

10

ACCESSORIES, PLAIN AND FANCY

The gadgets that are available to be hung on bicycles and weigh them down number in the hundreds. The accessories you will find really useful, however, are fairly few. Unless you look long and hard, most of the accessories you will see will be of poor quality. The truth of the matter is that many bicycle accessory equipment manufacturers persist in thinking of a bicycle as a toy, rather than the serious hobby it is for many thousands of adults.

LIGHTS

If you do any night cycling at all, good front and rear lights are a life-saving necessity. You will seldom need a front light to see where you are going, particularly on moonlit nights or lighted city streets, but both front and rear light *will* let the motorist see *you,* and are therefore vital to your safety.

I will state categorically that there is no such thing as a really good bicycle light on the market. Most lights found throughout the United States in bicycle stores and bicycle-equipment sections of retail stores are pure junk and not worth wasting money on. They are flimsy, with faulty, unreliable switches and battery contacts.

The dynamo lighting sets found on British bicycles will provide dependable light brilliant enough at least to give you a glimmering of where you are going, and for a motorist to see from two blocks away. The trouble with generator lights is that the generator itself is quite a drag on the wheel, and if you have to cycle a good distance, you will find the drag quite a burden. Also, when you stop, for example, at a traffic light, you will have no light at all because the generator won't be operating.

A Japanese-made light combines a small fluorescent tube with an incandescent bulb, and is powered by a small dual voltage generator (ninety volts for the fluorescent tube and six volts for the incandescent bulb). This light is also inadequate, and I do not recommend it.

The so-called Dynahub used on Raleigh bicycles, usually on the front wheel, reduces generator drag considerably but, like the generator itself, it is heavy and will not work when the bicycle isn't moving.

Without going into more details, let me save you a lot of time and tell you about some lights that I have found to be as good a compromise as any. Of all the dozens of lights I have tried, I prefer the Hong Kong made Toplite for the front of a bicycle. This light uses two standard "D" flashlight cells and can be removed instantly from a handlebar-mounted bracket when it is not needed, or when you want to carry it about a camp-site at night. The Toplite costs about $1.75, without batteries. It has a good switch and throws a fair beam a fair distance, wide enough to see obstacles soon enough to avoid them (Fig. 71).

For a rear lamp I recommend the No. 805 Oxford tail-light, also made in Hong Kong and sold by Sears Roebuck, bicycle stores, and other outlets for about $1.20, without batteries. This is the only rear light that can be seen equally well from both the sides and the rear. It also takes two standard "D" size flashlight batteries. If you want to get fancy, you can substitute the standard 2.4-volt bulb in this light for a 2.4-volt blinking light bulb which you can find in larger hardware stores. The No. 805 light is really designed for mounting on the banana seats found on children's bicycles. However, I discarded the clamp and simply fastened the light to the rear of the carrier with electrician's tape. If you do not have a carrier, it can be fastened to the seat stays under the saddle.

A word of caution about the No. 805 rear light, however. Alkaline or

Fig. 71: *This is the best bicycle light on the market, throws a fair beam, has a reliable switch, can be clipped to handlebar stem or fork, or detached for other use. Duplicate with red lens is available for rear light which can be fastened to rear stay or carrier.*

mercury type batteries are heavier than ordinary batteries, and if you use them, they will press down heavily enough on the bottom contacts to keep them from touching the battery. After a few blocks you will have no rear light. I solved this problem by propping up the contacts on the bottom of the light with a small piece of coiled electrician's tape, so that they are held up where they must touch the bottom of the batteries firmly. The switch is not too reliable and takes a bit of fiddling with to get it to make contact. I recommend substituting this switch with a single-throw toggle switch which you can buy at any hardware store for about fifty cents.

Also, on the No. 805 rear light, the case has a tendency to pop open when you hit a bump, causing your batteries to spill out on the ground. This is costly if you use rechargeable or alkaline cells, and can be very dangerous at night if you are not aware of what has happened. You can solve this problem by taping a piece of electrician's plastic tape around the rim of the light to keep the case from opening.

I know that all this might seem a lot of bother just to get a reliable light, but as long as manufacturers persist in applying toy quality to an accessory as necessary as a rear light, you will have to make a few minor and inexpensive alternations for your safety or that of your child.

The two lights I have mentioned offer the advantage of light weight, compactness with visibility, and, with minor alterations, reliability.

There is one other light I recommend. This is a French-made light (Fig. 72) that can be strapped on an arm or leg. It costs only $1.50, without batteries, uses two "C" size flashlight cells, and weighs only five ounces with batteries. This light has a red light to the rear and a white light to the front, and, when strapped to a leg, the up-and-down motion of the leg adds extra visibility to it. On long night trips this light is an excellent back-up to main lights, if they fail. Detached, it can also be used to read maps, to signal with, and to make repairs by.

NAIL PULLERS

Nail pullers are available but can be used only on tubular tires of the smooth tread type. They attach to the front and rear handbrake center post and ride lightly on the tire. If a nail, piece of glass, or other foreign body becomes embedded in the tread (which can cause a flat if not removed), the nail-puller accessory will scrape it away automatically. Nail

Fig. 72: *Here's a real attention-getter. This French-made light can be strapped on arm or, better yet, leg, where it throws a red light to rear and white light to front. Can also be used to read maps and the like.*

pullers cost about $1.00 a pair and weigh about a half-ounce. They can be ordered from Cyclo-Pedia (see Appendix).

BABY SEATS

This popular accessory can be used to safely carry a small child up to three or four years of age. However, only the *rear* baby seat is safe. Balancing a child weighing up to thirty or forty pounds on a carrier mounted over the front wheel makes for a very unbalanced situation and is dangerous.

After examining and using a number of these carriers, I recommend a child-carrier design that is suitable for either twenty-six-inch or twenty-seven-inch wheels and which has leg shields to keep the child's feet out of the spokes. A child of two or three can easily get his foot tangled up in the spokes, and, if this happens, you are in for a nasty spill, at best, and, at worst, for both a spill and an injured foot for your child.

The seat should have an adjustable foot rest and a safety strap to tie the child in. One such design costs about $9.00, weighs two pounds, eight ounces, and is obtainable from your bicycle store or from Cyclo-Pedia. There are a number of other seats on the market, but this is the only one I have found with leg shields.

LOCKS

This is simple. I prefer the cable combination lock. It's light (six-and-a-half ounces), strong (made of quarter-inch steel cable), plastic-covered to protect your bicycle's finish, and costs only $1.50 in most bicycle stores.

KICKSTANDS

I think a kickstand is an utterly unnecessary piece of equipment. In the first place, it is unreliable. A good breeze or a slight shove from a passer-by can knock the bicycle over, and in doing so, damage the derailleur. It is much better, in my opinion, to lean the bicycle against a tree, store-front, or telephone post, where you can also put a chain around it. Kick-stands are heavy; they add at least a pound of dead weight. They can actually damage the chain stays, too, because it's easy to overtighten the kickstand when it becomes loose, as it will, and in so doing, you can bend and weaken the chains stays behind the bottom bracket.

ODOMETERS AND SPEEDOMETERS

An odometer is a good idea if you like to keep accurate track of your cycling mileage. The Lucas cyclometer, available to fit twenty-four-, twenty-six-, twenty-seven-, and twenty-eight-inch wheels, costs $2.50 and fits on the front fork. However, I find the tick of the cyclometer, as the metal striker on the spoke hits the counter wheel, annoying. I prefer the more natural sounds of the countryside.

As for speedometers, these are strictly in the gadget and toy category.

They all have a habit of going bad and causing trouble on trips, the most common complaint being jammed cables. There is considerable drag on the wheel striker—try moving the striker by hand and imagine this working against your pedaling. And the speedometer adds another unnecessary pound or so to your bicycle, which makes pedaling still more difficult. Since most of us who tour seldom, if ever, at least on a flat road, get above fifteen miles an hour for very long, the idea of carrying around a toy to check speed is ridiculous. A speedometer is fine for a child, who still equates a bicycle with a scaled-down automobile.

TIRE PUMPS

A pump that can be seat-tube mounted is a "must" if you tour or take trips very far from home. After having used a number of pumps, I find the Silca or the Campagnola plastic pump the best and easiest to use. These pumps can be obtained with either a Presta head for tubular tire valves, or Schraeder for American tube valves. They cost about $4.00 and are well worth it. Other pumps I have tried soon fell apart or became dented and were therefore useless.

FEEDER BOTTLES

Feeder bottles, to carry liquids for long tours, are available in either aluminum or plastic. They are kept in cages mounted on either the handlebars, seat, or down tube. Aluminum bottles are more elegant, but I prefer plastic ones, for lightness. A plastic feeder bottle, with its cage, weighs only six ounces and costs $1.50, complete.

HORNS

The loudest horn you can buy is a Freon-powered portable boat horn, which costs about $7.00. The Freon propellant, good for about 200 blasts, comes in a replaceable can slightly larger than a standard beer can and costs about $1.75. It can be mounted in a feeder bottle cage on the handlebars and makes a truly horrendous blast that can be heard for several city blocks. After using such a horn for a year, I can report that it serves only to frighten motorists and to reduce one's own feeling of anger and frustration. This horn never saved me from an accident. I find that if I have to warn a pedestrian that I am approaching, a shout serves just as well, and it also prevents him from suffering a heart attack as a result of the sudden blast of the Freon.

There *was* one occasion when my Freon horn came in very handy. I was in immediate danger of being jumped by hoodlums in a park one night. When the youngsters suddenly appeared from the bushes in my path, I waited until I was almost upon them before blasting my horn. They fled with satisfying alacrity. The lesson of this story, however, is not to buy this horn but to avoid riding in lonely places at night.

For sidewalk riding, for children, a simple handlebar, bell-type, lever-actuated tinkle horn is pleasant sounding and unmistakably warns a pedestrian that a bicycle is approaching. All other horns are either junk that soon stops working, such as the bulb-bugle horn, or too heavy, too expensive, or easily damaged. There's nothing, in my opinion, like one's own vocal cords to sound an alarm. They're free, automatically installed, and add no extra weight.

BICYCLE CARRIERS

Most of us live in big cities or major metropolitan areas, where opportunities for enjoyable, leisurely, and scenic cycling are almost nonexistent. For this reason, many cyclists prefer to get a head start on a weekend of cycling by carrying their bicycles on cars the fifteen to twenty-five miles necessary to get out into the country.

The problem is that even disassembled bicycles are ungainly things that take up a lot of room in a car. Without some sort of carrier, transporting more than two assembled bicycles at a time is well beyond the space capacity of the average car. A good deal of attention has been given to the problem of car bicycle carriers. The best results have been the homemade contraptions. All the commercially made carriers are limited to two bicycles, some are junky, all are costly. You would be much better off making your own.

How to Make Your Own Carrier

Anyone can easily make his own rooftop bicycle carrier with a little ingenuity and effort. Start with any ordinary pair of metal bar roof carriers, the kind that clamp to rain gutters or bolt to the roof, *not* the suction cup type, which can come loose.

L. L. Bean (see Appendix) carries an aluminum alloy load bracket with drip eave clamps and carriage bolts for your own wood crossbar, costing $12.60 for a set of four (Fig. 73). These are made by Quik-n-Easy Products, Monrovia, California.

"Chick" Mead, a bicycle dealer in Marion, Massachusetts, has designed a fine homemade carrier. His instructions, which follow, are simple (Fig. 74). They call for:

1. Two wood pieces, 2 in. x 4 in. x 53 in.
2. Two solid aluminum ⅜-in. x 6-in.-long rods (from any hardware store) to cut up for dowels.
3. One pint of wood sealer.
4. One quart of flat white paint.
5. Rubber rings to hold bicycles down. These may be cut up from old auto tubes or truck tire inner tubes, an inch or so wide. You can also use leather straps or old toe straps.
6. Four rooftop aluminum alloy gutter brackets (as described above, available from L. L. Bean for $12.60).

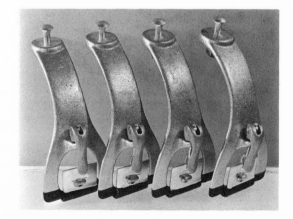

Fig. 73: You can carry up to five or even six bicycles on the roof of even the smallest European car with the "Chick Mead" carrier illustrated in Figures 74 to 76. These cast aluminum brackets are sturdy, reliable, and inexpensive.

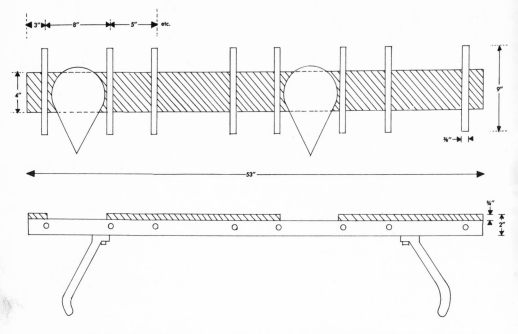

Fig. 74: From these plans you can make a four- or five-bicycle carrier for around $15.00. The plans are simple and speak for themselves to any home handyman.

The nine-inch dowels of the ⅜-inch aluminum rod should stick out about two inches from the two-by-fours. Press them carefully into the holes, preferably with an arbor press, to avoid damaging the soft aluminum.

Allowing thirteen inches apart for each bicycle, you will be able to carry up to four bicycles on this carrier. Be sure to pad the two-by-fours liberally with old hose or other soft but durable material, to avoid marring the handlebar finish.

When ready to tie down the bicycle, use the rubber holders (or leather straps) to tie both sides of the handlebars and the seat to the carrier. Stagger bicycles on the carrier, as shown in Fig. 75. And make sure the carrier is securely fastened to the car roof!

I made one of these "Chick" Mead carriers myself, and I am able to carry four bikes on my Volkswagen (Fig. 76). My expenses totaled about $15.00 for everything, and the result is a very useful and practical carrier indeed.

With any bike carrier, remember that you must unload the bicycles

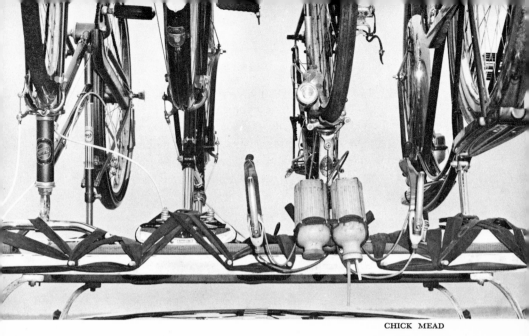

Fig. 75: Even on this compact car, you can carry four or five bicycles with ease on the "Chick Mead" carrier you can make yourself. Note how bicycles are staggered.

Fig. 76: This is how the "Chick Mead" carrier looks on a Volkswagen square-back. Elastic bands made from an old tire tube hold the bicycles firmly, even at high car speeds.

before driving into the garage. This seems obvious, but many people have been known to forget it with disastrous results.

Incidentally, the "Chick" Mead bike carrier is also very handy for transporting luggage and other miscellany. The aluminum rod tiedowns are very convenient for securing almost anything. My carrier is always fitted to my car, though it could be removed quickly and easily.

11

YOUR TIRES AND
HOW TO CARE FOR THEM

There is a lot more to bicycle tires than first meets the eye. With proper care they can last a lot longer than you think they can, and they need not go flat so often. But you should know that not even the knobby, balloon-tired monsters are immune to abuse. You simply cannot ride up and down curbs as though they weren't there, or ride on tires half-inflated, and not expect a bruised tire and a punctured tube, not to mention a ruined rim.

On the other hand, you can cross the continent on flimsy road-racing tires that weigh less than sixteen ounces including tire, tube, and valve, if you know how to take care of the tire, and ride properly.

All this is to introduce one of the least understood aspects of bicycle maintenance and use—tires and tubing.

BICYCLE TIRE CARE AND REPAIR

With a little care in use and maintenance, bicycle tires can last for thousands of miles. The scrap pile of cut and bruised tires that you can see in any bicycle store, however, is sad testimony to the fact that young cyclists, and some adults, need to learn more about tire care. Proper care will yield many more miles of life from tires than most cyclists seem to get today. When it comes to the more costly tubular-type tires used for touring and racing, careful maintenance is essential.

There are many different kinds of tires—tires for everyday use; for road, track, and cross-country racing; for rain and mud; for high speed; for touring; and for carrying loads. (See Table VI and Fig. 77.) But the tire is only part of the story; the entire bicycle must be considered in the light of the kind of riding you plan to do.

Table VI: *There are literally dozens of different types of tubular (sewn-up) tires. Table VI lists most of the popular applications and the tires available for these uses, ranging from racing of all kinds to touring. The "Clement Elvezia" is recommended for cycle touring, as are the D'Allesandro "Sport" and the Dunlop No. 9 and No. 10.*

MAKE	RECOMMENDED FOR	TREAD PATTERN	WEIGHT OZ.
Dunlop—			
No. 0 Cotton	Smooth Tracks	Matt	6
No. 0 Silk	Smooth Tracks	Matt	5¼
No. 1 Cotton	Smooth Tracks	Matt	8
No. 2 Cotton	Track, short distance road	Rib	9½
No. 2 Silk	Track, short distance road	Rib	8
No. 3 Cotton	Medium Road	File/Rib	10
No. 5 Cotton	Massed Start	File/Rib	12¼
No. 5 Silk	Massed Start	File/Rib	9½
No. 8 Cotton	Massed Start	File/Rib	12½
No. 9 Cotton	Training	Herringbone	15
No. 10 Cotton	Training	Herringbone	17½
Clement—			
No. 1 Silk	Smooth Tracks	Matt	4
Super 10	Track, short distance road	Fine rib	8
No. 50 Silk	Road, medium	Fine rib	11
No. 48 Silk	Massed Start Training	Rough file	12
Gran Sport	Massed Start	Fine rib/File	14
Elvezia	Training	Fine rib	14
Freebairn—			
Track	All tracks	Matt	8
Road	General Road	Rib	11
D'Allesandro—			
Imperforabile	Road	File or matt	9¾
Primo	Track/Short Road	Matt	7¼
Criterium	Distance Road	Matt	8¾
Imperial	Road		12½
Leone	Massed Start	File	13¼
Sport	Rough Road surfaces	File	14
Worthy	Training, Grass tracks	File	16
Constrictor—			
Viper	Road	File	12
Fifty	Road	File	11
Supalatti	Path/Short Distance Road	Centre File	10

   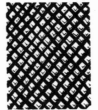 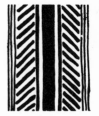

Multirib   Diagonal or   File (lot of lit-   Mesh (lot of   Mixed . . .
                  herringbone   tle pyramids)   little pits)   here consisting of
                                                                                      rib, diagonal and
                                                                                      rib

1. Everyday or training 12/   2. Vulcanized road racing
15 ozs. Mesh or file treads are   7/11 ozs. Tread according to
common   taste. Multirib shown here

3. Handmade road racing   4. Cyclo Cross. Very spe-
shown here with matt tread.   cialized tread to operate on
Range between 6 and 10 ozs.   loose or muddy surfaces. Weight
                                  10/16 ozs.

Fig. 77: *Just a few of the tire patterns of tubular tires. Note how these tires are sewn up all around, so that the tire and tube become virtually one unit. The heavier tires, shown at far left, used for training and weighing from 12 to 15 ounces, are also ideal for cycle touring.*

Tire Pressure

Probably the most neglected aspect of tire care is air pressure. Use this tire chart as a guide to correct minimum tire pressure, increasing pressure according to the weight of the rider and any extra load carried.

Table VII: *In general, these are the air pressures you should use with various types of tires. Remember that if you are a bit heavier than average, you should add about five pounds more pressure. If tire bulges markedly, you are too heavy for the pressure used. Tire should not bulge, or at most, bulge very slightly when ridden.*

TIRE SIZE	AIR PRESSURE (IN LBS. PER SQ. IN.)
12 in. x 1⅜ in.	30–40
16 in. x 1⅜ in.	30–40
18 in. x 1⅜ in.	35–45
20 in. x 1⅜ in.	45–50
24 in. x 2.125 in.	35–45
26 in. x 1¼ in.	45–50
26 in. x 1⅜ in.	45–50
26 in. x 1¾ in.	30–35
26 in. x 2.125 in.	35–45
27 in. x 1¼ in.	75–85
27-in. tubular tires	Tracks with very smooth surfaces: rear wheels, 90–120; front tires, 80–110 Tracks with uneven surfaces: rear tires, 80–100; front tires, 70–90 Road racing: rear tires, 75–100; front tires, 65–90, depending on road conditions Touring: rear tires, 85–100, depending on load and road conditions; front tires, 75–90

For tires used on tandem bicycles, increase above pressures from 10 to 20 pounds per square inch to handle the extra load safely.

Note: On cool days one can inflate tires to maximum pressures safely. However, on very hot days, with temperatures in the eighties and higher, it is safer to reduce pressures by 3 to 5 pounds under the maximum to avoid heat buildup. Air expands as it heats, and on a hot day, you could experience a blow-out.

How to Inflate

Most tires are inflated at gasoline service stations. Most tires are also overinflated and blown-out at service stations. Bicycle tires take so little air that with the automatic pressure gauges that provide air at upward of 200 pounds per square inch, it takes just seconds to fill a tire and a split second more to blow it out. If you don't have near you a service station with an air pump that you can dial to set the pressure you want, and not have to worry about overinflation, you should be very careful about using an air hose. The best procedure to follow is to push the air hose firmly down onto the tire valve for a second and release it immediately, then squeeze the tire between thumb and forefinger, continuing this process until the tire feels hard. This process won't guarantee your tire against a blow-out, however, so if you can, use a dial-type air outlet, a tire gauge, or a hand-operated tire pump, preferably with a built-in gauge.

Do not let a service station attendant fill your tires. If you're a good-looking woman, he'll probably rush to help you, and is likely to blow your tire off the rim. He's used to car tires, which need a lot of air.

Tubular tires (27 inches) come with Presta (Fig. 78) or Woods Continental-type valves. For service station air filling, you'll need to convert the Presta valve to an American Schraeder valve connection. The adapter that you buy for this screws right down over the valve. Presta valve stems must be screwed open (counterclockwise) before you can fill the tire with air, and screwed closed after filling to prevent leakage.

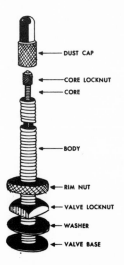

DUST CAP

CORE LOCKNUT

CORE

BODY

RIM NUT

VALVE LOCKNUT

WASHER

VALVE BASE

Fig. 78: *Tubular tires come with European "Presta" type valves, which American-made tire-pump air outlets won't fit. Use an adapter or a hand-pump with Presta fitting. Remember, Presta valves must be hand-opened counterclockwise when filling, closed clockwise by hand when tire has correct pressure.*

Underinflation Damage

Underinflated tires put more tire tread on the road and use up more energy by flexing and creating heat, which makes the bicycle considerably harder to pedal.

An underinflated tire cannot take bumps and stones, and ordinary contact with pavement roughness can be sufficient to force the tire casing inward far enough to pinch the tube against the metal wheel rim. This can cause a blow-out and might even bruise the tire casing beyond repair, causing a flat spot on the rim that cannot be pulled out. Here are some common types of tire damage and how to avoid them.

Glass damage causes knife-like cuts on the tread or the sidewall. To avoid running over glass and similar sharp objects, watch the road just in front of you as you ride. If you ride at night, ride only on roads with which you are familiar and know are not likely to have glass, and use a good light to detect glass as far in advance as possible to give you time to swing out of the way. (Watch out for passing cars—swing right instead of left if you can to avoid glass.)

Blow-outs can be caused by overinflation (Fig. 81), underinflation, and tire-casing damage such as glass cuts. A glass wound (Fig. 82) will open and close as the tire casing flexes and will eventually pinch a hole in the tire tube. This is why you should always look for the *cause* of a flat after a patch has been applied to the tube.

Nails and other sharp objects such as fine pieces of wire will cause a flat by piercing both tire and tube. Be sure to remove the nail before reinstalling the tire and tube. If the nail is still in the tire when you go to repair it, it will be a good guide to the location of the leak in the tube.

Ruptures (Fig. 79) are *always* a sign of abuse, barring accidents. Riding up and down curbs, into sharp stones and curbs, is a sure invitation to ruptures and a very short tire life.

Rim cuts (Fig. 80) are long, thin-looking cuts in the sidewalls and are caused by riding an underinflated tire, rusty rims, or an overloaded bicycle.

Uneven tread wear (Fig. 83) can be due to crooked rims, quick stops that grab and lock the wheel (otherwise known as skidding to a stop for kicks), or out-of-adjustment caliper brakes that grab the rim. Out-of-true rims also cause excessive tire wear because the caliper brake will grab at the out-of-true spot. It is a good idea to look far enough ahead to be

RUPTURE

Fig. 79: Jumping curbs and riding over sharp objects such as stones cause this type of tire rupture. Stop, dismount, and ease bike gently over curbs, if you ride on sidewalks.

RIM CUT

Fig. 80: Rim cuts like this one are caused by riding on underinflated tires, overloading the bicycle, or rusty rims.

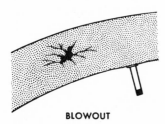

BLOWOUT

Fig. 81: Tube blow-outs are often caused by overinflation. If tire is not seated properly on the rim, tube may also blow out because pressure can force the tube out between tire and rim.

STAR BREAK

Fig. 82: Star breaks on tires are usually caused by riding over sharp objects such as stones. Such an injury may not be visible on tire's exterior. Always check for tire damage when repairing tube puncture.

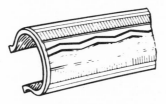

UNEVEN TREAD WEAR

Fig. 83: Uneven tire wear can be caused by improperly adjusted brakes that grab or lock the wheel, skidding stops (all too popular with youngsters), or crooked rims. (Figures 79 through 83 courtesy Schwinn Bicycle Company.)

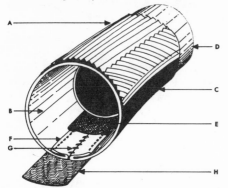

Fig. 84: *If you use tubular tires, you should know how they are made and the names of each part. This drawing dissects tubular tires, naming the parts.*

A. Tread.

B. Casing, made of fabric.

C. Outside of casing, between bottom of tread and base tape, is called the "wall."

D. Inner tube.

E. Chafing tape, to prevent inner tube from puncture by rubbing on tire stitching.

F. Hems of casing are made by gluing back the edges of fabric to the inside. In some tires, hems are folded to the outside.

G. Stitching. When repairing, use a simple hand-over-hand stitch.

H. Base tape protects stitching and provides seating for entire tire.

able to avoid sudden stops, for your own as well as for your tires' longevity.

How to Repair Tubular Tires

Tubular tires (Fig. 84) are the kind used by track- and road-racing cyclists. They come on the more expensive European bicycles and the one high-grade American-made racing bicycle (Schwinn Paramount). These tires come in a variety of weights, ranging from the very lightest track-racing types, which weigh in at six ounces or less, to heavier road-racing and touring tubulars at twelve to sixteen ounces or more. (These weights include tube and valve.) Tubulars give great strength with extreme lightness. The heavier types are quite suitable for even extended touring, although they are somewhat more prone to punctures than conventional wire-on types of tires, and considerably more difficult to mend. Personally, I prefer tubulars to more conventional tires, except for city cycling, where streets are more likely to be littered with glass shards and other puncture-causing debris. A plus for tubular tires is the fact that you can carry one or two complete tires and tubes rolled up and fastened to the seat strut on the back underside of the saddle. (A special strap can be bought for this purpose, or you can use an old toe strap.) In the event of a puncture, you can change these tires far more easily and quickly than you can the conventional wired-on types, without any tools.

The tube is sewn in place, so you don't have to worry about pinching it when you fit the tire to the rim.

However, because the tube is sewn in, these tires, as mentioned, are considerably more difficult to repair punctures on than conventional tires.

To repair tubular tires, you will have to cut a few stitches in the area where the puncture is located, repair the puncture, and restitch the tire. To repair tubulars, follow this procedure:

STEP ONE: You will need a patch set consisting of:

a. Special thin tube patches (such as the ones made by Dunlop)
b. A three-pointed hand-sewing needle
c. Tubular tire linen thread
d. Rubber cement
e. A small tube of talc powder
f. A small piece of yellow chalk
g. A small screwdriver
h. A sharp knife or razor blade
i. A small square of fine sandpaper

Most of the bicycle mail-order houses (pages 317-18) sell a tubular tire repair kit with most of the above items. The reason for the extra-thin tube patches is that tubular tires have a very thin tube. An ordinary bicycle tire patch is far too thick for this tube and would cause a lump inside the tire which would thump as you ride. Thin patches are especially needed for the six-ounce track-racing tires, which are generally handmade from silk cord and rubber latex.

STEP TWO: If you have an old rim, mount the tire on the rim, inflate it to sixty or seventy pounds of air pressure, and set the tire and rim in a half-filled washtub. Or simply remove the tire from the wheel, inflate as above, and put it, a bit at a time, into the washtub. If you can see no puncture, you could have a loose or torn valve or a puncture at the valve area.

STEP THREE: As you insert the tubular tire into the tub of water, you will notice that a lot of air seems to be bubbling up from around the valve stem first (Fig. 85). The tire is sewn and has a rubber-cemented strip over the sewing, so this is about the only place air *can* escape, except through the puncture itself.

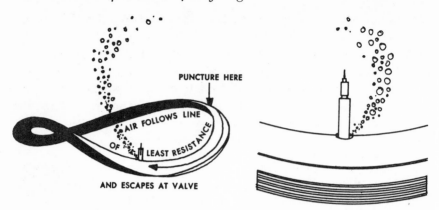

PUNCTURE HERE

AIR FOLLOWS LINE

OF LEAST RESISTANCE

AND ESCAPES AT VALVE

Fig. 85: When checking a tubular tire for leaks, don't be misled by air escaping from around valve because air will follow the line of least resistance. Always mount tire on old rim, or leave on rim, dip in vat of water, and note where air escapes from tire, to find exact spot of tube puncture before cutting stitching to get at tube.

Rotate the tire slowly until you come to the spot where air is seeping out through a small puncture in the tire casing. With a piece of yellow chalk, mark this area; it is also the location of the tube puncture. Deflate the tire and remove it from the rim.

STEP FOUR: With the small screwdriver or another flat (but not sharp!) tool, carefully pry about two-and-a-half inches of the tape on both sides of the puncture away from the inner circumference of the tire (Fig. 86).

STEP FIVE: With the razor or small sharp knife, carefully cut the stitching about two inches on either side of the puncture. Do not cut down *into* the tire, but insert the knife edge under the stitching and cut upward to avoid cutting into the tube, which lies just under the stitching.

STEP SIX: Pull about four inches of the tube out gently (Fig. 87), and with a hand pump, inflate the tube enough to find the puncture. With the yellow chalk, outline the puncture, centering it in a chalked circle about the size of a quarter. A simple way to find the puncture is to hold the tube near your lips and rotate it slowly. You should be able to feel the flow of air from the puncture. If you can't find the puncture this way, put a drop of liquid soap in a glass, fill it with warm water, and place this mixture on the tube until you find a bubble marking the location of the puncture.

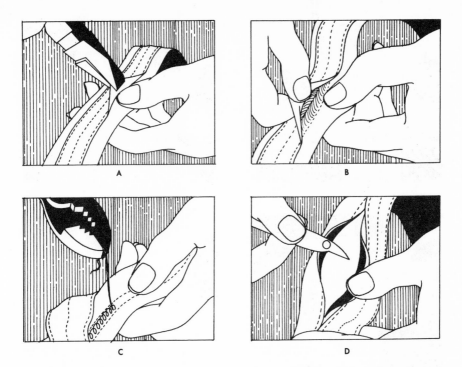

Fig. 86: *Follow these steps in repairing tubulars: (A) Lift base tape gently with pliers (after locating leak). (B) Finish lifting base tape with fingers. (C) Try to remove stitching without cutting it, so you won't have to pull out each little piece of cut-off thread; you will have to use same holes for rethreading. (D) Pull out chafing tape between tube and tire. If chafing tape is stitched, remove stitching carefully.*

STEP SEVEN: Dry the tube thoroughly, if you have wet it. With the sandpaper, abrade lightly the area you have marked off around the puncture, putting a small, solid object under the tube to support it as you rub it with the sandpaper.

STEP EIGHT: Apply a light coating of rubber cement to the area abraded. Let this coating dry to a hard glaze.

STEP NINE: Apply a patch of finest grade thin rubber to the tube over the puncture. Dust with talcum powder to prevent the tube from sticking to the casing.

STEP TEN: Reinflate the tube slightly with the hand pump. Check the area for further punctures. Deflate the tube.

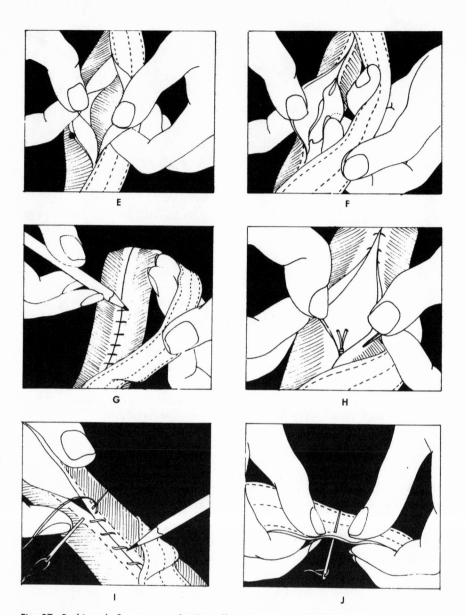

Fig. 87: *Pushing chafing tape aside (E), pull out inner tube (F), locate puncture, roughen tube with fine sandpaper, then apply thin layer of rubber cement. When cement is tacky or dry, peel protective paper from ultrathin tire patch made especially for tubular tires and apply patch over puncture. Dab fine powder over finished patch so rubber cement won't cause tube to stick to tire. When tube is repaired, with a black Pentel pen, draw (G) lines across area where thread holes match, to facilitate restitching. Don't try to resew chafing tape. When starting restitching, tie knot at one end and pull thread through first hole (H). Use special stitching thread, doubled. Lap new stitching over old machine stitch (I). When sewing, hold tire together with finger and thumb of one hand (J), with index finger of other hand between edges of the envelope, pressing down tube so it doesn't get caught in stitching, and keeping chafing tape in correct position. Push tire down on needle, rather than pushing needle through tire.*

STEP ELEVEN: Inspect the tire casing for damage, such as bruises, gouges, rips, tears, and the rare manufacturing defect. If the tire casing itself is damaged, I recommend relegating the tire to the spare-use-only category, because while the casing damage can be patched with a thin piece of canvas applied with rubber cement, if the bruise or hole is small, even this patch will bulge and cause the tire to "thump" annoyingly, especially at high speeds. Tubular tire repair kits do come with a special piece of canvas for this purpose, but I recommend its use for emergency situations only. Patched tires can, of course, serve ideally as spares.

STEP TWELVE: Sew up the tire, using the three-cornered needle and thread. In an emergency, a twelve-pound-test linen thread or double thread *silk* fishing line will do. Nylon line won't serve the purpose; it cuts into the tire. Start by sewing back about a half-inch over the cut stitching. Use a simple overhand stitch (Fig. 88) to finish the stitching, running the thread about a half-inch through *existing* holes left from the manufacturer's original stitching. Don't make new holes. Pull stitches firm, but don't overdo it or you'll cut the tire casing.

STEP THIRTEEN: Apply rubber cement over the area revealed when you peeled back the protective tape over the stitching and on the tape itself (Fig. 89). Let dry. Carefully lay tape back in position.

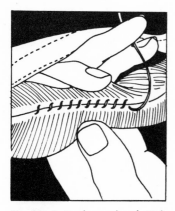

Fig. 88: A simple overhand stitch is all you need use when repairing tubular tires.

Fig. 89: Use rubber cement over restitching and on base tape. When dry, press base tape carefully over stitching so it lies flat without wrinkles. If base tape doesn't quite cover, use tape from an old tire to patch missing section.

STEP FOURTEEN: Mount the tire, inflate to riding pressure, and check again for leaks. Leave inflated so rubber cement has a chance to dry thoroughly.

Tubular versus Tube Tires

Many experienced cyclists prefer tubular tires because they are much easier to change than conventional tires. The advantage of tubulars for touring is that you can carry four or five complete tires and tubes rolled up with you. They are light, very flexible, and extremely compact, and, with care, they'll last 4,000 miles or more. However, if you are going to tour with tubulars, buy only the heaviest weight, the twelve- to sixteen-ounce type. I prefer the Clement "Olympic," but if you can't find the Clement line, the Vittoria 201-B with butyl tube is excellent. The butyl tube is a good idea, because it will hold tire pressure for weeks. Tubulars without butyl tubes need some air added daily because tube walls are so thin that they "exhale" air. Remember, if you go the tubular route, buy a few valve adapters (twenty-five cents each) so you can use American service station air hose outlets.

If most of your cycling is going to be back and forth from work or touring in a big city, however, I recommend you use conventional "wired-on" tube tires (Figs. 90 and 91). These are much more resistant to punctures than tubulars. City streets have on them a good deal of broken glass, bits of sharp metal, and assorted other tire-puncturing junk that is always located where you must cycle for safety. The problem is that you usually don't have room to maneuver away from or around such hazards, because

Fig. 90: *Tubular and wired-on tube tires compared. Tubular tire is at left. Center tire is suitable for touring, as is the heavier wired-on tire at right. Reprinted with the permission of Temple Press Ltd. from "The Cycling Book of Maintenance."*

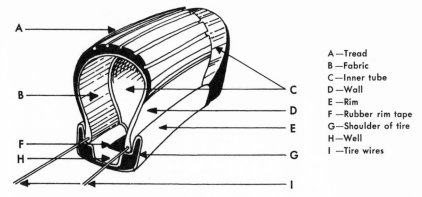

A—Tread
B—Fabric
C—Inner tube
D—Wall
E—Rim
F—Rubber rim tape
G—Shoulder of tire
H—Well
I—Tire wires

Fig. 91: *How a wired-on tube-type tire fits on rim.*

of the flow of motor vehicles around you; so, while city cycling can be quite safe if you know how to cope with it (see pages 20-21), you are often forced to run into areas where you can get punctures. If you cycle at night in the city, you can't always see puncture hazards in time to get away from them.

I have two complete sets of wheels—one set of tubulars for touring and country cycling, and one set with wired-on tires for city cycling. When you change wheels, you might also have to readjust the brake shoes because the rim diameter might be slightly different from a touring clincher wheel to a racing tubular rim. Make sure the brake blocks contact the rim properly. You cannot interchange tubular and wired-on tires on the same rim. Each type of tire requires its own rim design.

Tips on Fitting Tubular Tires to Rims

Although tubular tires are quick and easy to change, there is a best way, as follows:

STEP ONE: Make sure there are no spoke heads protruding from the rim. If there are, file them down flush with the spoke nipple, so they won't puncture the tire and tube.

STEP TWO: Apply a very thin layer of tire cement (shellac for track racing, road-tire cement for road racing and touring) to the rim and tire base tape and allow it to dry to a tacky state (Fig. 92). The cement is

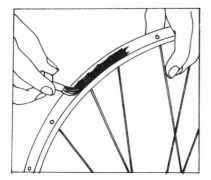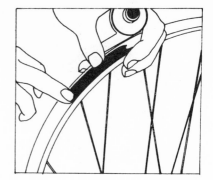

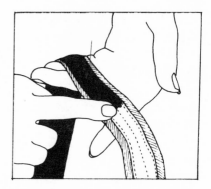

Fig. 92: When mounting tubular tire to rim, apply special rim cement to both rim and tire base tape, so tire won't slip off rim under high speed. Smooth down cement with finger. If cement is thin, apply two coatings (one on tire).

essential for safe cycling, because tubulars can be pushed off the wheel rim under the stress of cornering and other maneuvers, which at high speed can be embarrassing, if not downright unsafe. Also, if rim cement is not used, tubular tires tend to "creep" around the rim and bulge up around the valve, causing a thumping effect and eventually tearing the valve from the tube (Fig. 93).

A handy alternative to rim cement is double-sided sticky rim tape. Cyclo-Pedia has French Jantex rim tape No. T-80 (fifty cents a package), which should be enough for a couple of wheels. Rim tape is a lot handier than rim cement, especially on a tour.

If you are on the road and you wish to change a tire quickly, you can get by without adding more cement to the rim, and just use the tacky effect of the old cement until you get home. It is a good idea to remove all old cement before applying fresh cement, to prevent cement buildup and bulge spots on the rim. Any good shellac solvent, or even paint remover liquid (be careful not to get this on the bicycle frame!), will do.

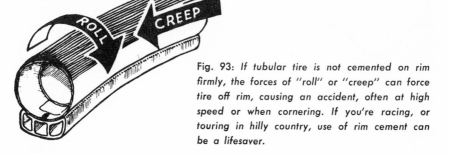

Fig. 93: *If tubular tire is not cemented on rim firmly, the forces of "roll" or "creep" can force tire off rim, causing an accident, often at high speed or when cornering. If you're racing, or touring in hilly country, use of rim cement can be a lifesaver.*

STEP THREE: Deflate tire almost completely, having just enough air to give the tire a little body. Hold wheel in an upright position and insert valve through the valve hole in the rim (Fig. 94).

STEP FOUR: With the valve at the top of the wheel and the wheel on a soft pad on the floor (or on the grass), stand behind the wheel and with both hands push the tire downward onto the rim, finishing on the side opposite the valve (Fig. 95). Hold the rim away from your body while you're doing this—or wear old clothes.

STEP FIVE: With the tire on the rim as far as possible, force the remainder of the tire onto the rim with both thumbs (Fig. 96).

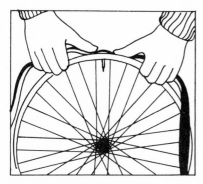

Fig. 94: *Start mounting tubular tire by placing valve in rim valve hole.*

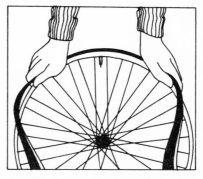

Fig. 95: *Then, with rim upright, start pushing tire over rim from both sides at once.*

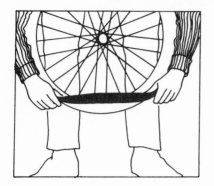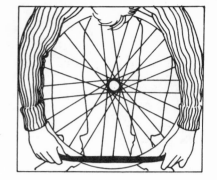

Fig. 96: *When you reach bottom, lift tire and rim up, continue pressure.*

STEP SIX: True up the tire with your fingers (Fig. 97) so that it sits evenly all the way around the rim and tire tension is even all the way around. Inflate the tire partially and inspect it to make sure that it is seated evenly. Leave the tire inflated for a few hours, if possible, before using it, to give the rim cement time to dry and become fixed.

How to Carry Tubular Spares

Because tubulars do take time to repair, you should always carry at least one spare on any trip. A convenient way to carry the spare is to fold the tire so that the tread is on the outside and not folded back on itself (Fig. 98). Wrap the tire under the seat, behind the seat post, with a strap (Fig. 99).

Fig. 97: *If tire is very tight, grip tire between knees and use both hands to push tire on rim. Then, blow the tire up a little—enough to give it its tubular shape. Work around checking that the center of the tread is central to the wheel and that uneven stretching is not causing bulging. Finally blow up hard.*

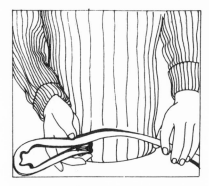
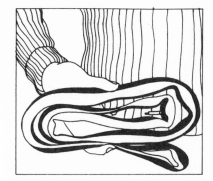

Fig. 98: *Spare tire can be folded as shown for carrying under saddle or elsewhere. Be sure valve is in position shown, where it can't chafe tire.*

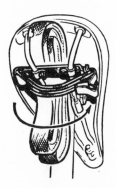

Fig. 99: *Here's how to carry spare tire under saddle, secured by rubber bands. Tire carrier is made by Vittoria. If you can't find this carrier, use old pedal strap.*

How to Repair Tube Tires

In the bicycle trade, conventional tires are called "wired-on" tires because they depend on metal wire beads around the two lips of the tire for rim adhesion. These tires are open inside, and the tube is removed easily from the tire for repair.

STEP ONE: If the tire goes flat overnight, you may have either a tiny puncture or a slow leak through the valve. You can check for a valve core leak by removing the valve cap, inflating the tire to normal pressure, and putting a bit of soapy water in the valve. If the valve leaks, you will see bubbles. In this case, all you need to do is tighten the valve core. If the valve still leaks, replace the valve core with a new one. You will need an old-fashioned metal valve cap to tighten or remove the core. This is available from any bicycle shop and most service stations.

STEP TWO: To repair a tube puncture you will need two flat-end tire levers, or two dull-edge, broad-blade screwdrivers, to pry the tire off and put it on. First, remove the valve core from the valve, with a valve cap. If there is a locknut on the valve stem, remove it from the stem.

STEP THREE: Although you don't need to remove the wheel, it is usually easier to do so. However, if you're on the road and touring, with saddle-bags or carriers in the way, you can attack the repair by removing the tire in the vicinity of the puncture, pulling out the tube, and patching it as described below. Otherwise, remove the wheel and, with the two tire levers, pry one side of the tire away from the rim until one side is loose enough to pull all the way off. Remove the tire by hand from the other side of the rim.

STEP FOUR: Inflate the tube and rotate it near your ear until you find the location of the puncture by hearing the hiss of escaping air. Draw a circle around the puncture with a piece of chalk. If you can't find it by listening for escaping air, immerse the tube in a tub of water and watch for bubbles as you rotate the tube in the water. Hold your finger in the puncture area while you dry the tube off thoroughly. Mark the puncture with a piece of chalk.

STEP FIVE: With a piece of sandpaper or the metal abrader that comes with tire repair kits, scrape the tube around the puncture and put a thin layer of rubber cement around it, extending outward about a half-inch in all directions. Let the rubber cement get tacky, pull the paper backing off the appropriate-sized tube patch, and press the patch firmly down onto the coated area over the puncture. Be careful, in handling the tube patch, not to finger the patch over the coated area where you have removed the paper covering. Hold the patch carefully by the edges until you have pressed it into place over the puncture.

STEP SIX: While the rubber under the patch is drying, check the outside of the tire carefully and pry out any embedded glass, nails, and the like. Remember, *something* caused that tire to go flat, and that something is most likely still embedded in the tire. Then, spreading the tire apart as you go, check the inside walls for any breaks. Breaks, if not too bad, can be patched with a tire patch. However, if the tire has bad cuts or bruises, discard it and buy a new one. Check for loose spokes, and tighten them. Remove the rubber strip inside the wheel and check to make sure all spokes are flush with the spoke nipples. File down any protruding spokes to prevent a later puncture, and replace the rubber strip. Realign the rim, if necessary, as discussed on page 304.

STEP SEVEN: Install the tire on the wheel. First, make sure most but not all the air is out of the tube. Tuck the tube carefully back into the tire. Put the valve into the valve hole in the rim. Next, starting at the valve, with hands on either side of the wheel, push the beaded edge of the tire all the way around until one side of the tire is on the rim. Then push the other side of the tire on the rim in the same manner. You should not need to use the tire levers to install the tire. But if you do use them, make sure that when you have the lever pushed up under the tire, you do not pinch the tube between the lever and the rim and cause a puncture. Inflate the tire and check for leaks before remounting the wheel.

Tips for Westerners (and Easterners, Too)

If you live where cactus or other thorny bushes abound, you may have already found that you have to buy special thorn-resisting tubes for your conventional tube tires. Or, if you're an Easterner planning a cross-country tour through cactus states, you should plan to use thorn-resisting tubes, or prepare yourself for a lot of tire repairs.

In any case, a good thing to do after every ride is to rotate the wheels slowly and check for thorns and other puncture-causing debris embedded in the tire casing. This is a good procedure for any cyclist, by the way.

Tips on Tubular Tire Care

The hints and tips that follow will greatly prolong the useful life of your expensive tubular tires (the sew-up types).

Do not leave spares folded on bicycles longer than two weeks. Remove the spare, inflate lightly, let it stand overnight, deflate, and reroll. This prevents spares from taking a "set" on the folds. In refolding, fold the opposite way so that the part that was on the inside is now on the outside. However, always fold so that the tread is on the outside. When folded, mount the spare so that it cannot rub or chafe anywhere. Ideally, you should carry it in a plastic bag.

Valves should be protected against dirt with a light plastic dust cap. Remember to close the valve on the spare. Open, it can be easily bent.

Extra spares should always be stored lightly inflated, in a warm, dry place. Be very careful not to store tubulars that have become wet, unless you inflate them so they can dry out.

For safety, particularly if you do a lot of riding, check rim cement frequently. If you are on a tour, check rim cement at least weekly, because this cement can dry out and flake off. Rim cement is absolutely essential to keep tires from creeping and crawling.

Prevent punctures by using a "thorn puller" or "nail puller" (Fig. 100), a tire accessory that weighs only a half-ounce and that can be fitted to the caliper-brake center bolt over the tire to scrape off nails, thorns, and other impedimenta stuck to the tire, before they can puncture the tube. Check treads regularly and pull out foreign material embedded in the tire.

If you realign your rim, remember that retensioning spokes can cause spoke heads to protrude and puncture the tire. Remove the tire, and check and file off any protruding spoke heads.

If you carry your bicycle, be careful not to let the tires rub on any metal or wooden parts. Check the placement of wheels against car seats, carrying racks, toe straps, and tie-down straps.

On an airplane trip, if you bring your bicycle, remember to half-deflate your tires, because if your bicycle is stored in an unpressurized baggage compartment, the low pressures at high altitudes may permit the high pressures inside the tire to cause a blow-out.

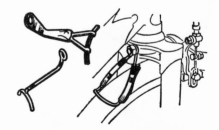

Fig. 100: *Nail catchers, installed on brake pinion bolt and adjusted to ride lightly over tire, can save many a flat by pulling out nails, pieces of glass, or bits of stone before they can cause a puncture. Three types of nail catchers are shown here. The Reg type, lower left, is most popular in the United States. Other types shown: Pelissier, upper left; Carlton, right.*

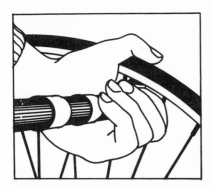
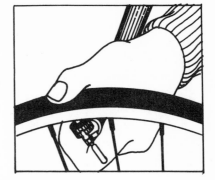

Fig. 101: When inflating tire with "Presta" valve, first open valve stem by turning it counterclockwise, jab valve stem up for a second to free it, then apply pump firmly. Hold pump onto valve with thumb and forefingers. For tubular tire only.

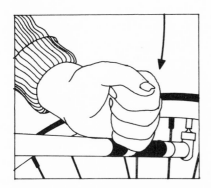

Fig. 102: When finished pumping tubular tire, knock pump off valve by quick, firm downward jab with side of fist. Don't try to wiggle or pull pump off valve.

Add a little air every day to tubular tires. Walls of tubes are so thin that they "breathe" a little air, so make up for the loss by adding air daily. Five or ten strokes of the pump should do. Use a gauge to find the correct pressure.

Use the pump correctly. Do not push it on from side to side, or pull it off slowly and erratically. You do not need adapters to convert European valve stems to American stems if you use the press-on type of bicycle pump. I prefer the Campagnolo hand pump (Fig. 101), which can be carried on the bicycle. Be sure to knock off this press-on pump from the valve by a sharp blow with the side of your hand (Fig. 102).

Keep oil from the tire. Do not oil the tire pump; use light grease. Oil can be blown into the tire, grease cannot. And oil will eat away and ruin the entire tube, making it necessary to junk the tire (on sew-ups).

12

PREVENTIVE MEDICINE FOR BICYCLES — A COMPLETE MAINTENANCE GUIDE

Until just recently, before we grown-ups caught on to what wonderful fun, relaxation, and healthy exercise bicycling is, bikes were mostly for kids. The bicycle industry in America today still, for the most part, thinks of them as toys. But, even the cheapest bicycles need maintenance and repair. The more costly and complicated (as well as the more pleasurable) machines are really worth your tender loving care.

Given proper attention, the better bicycles will last you a lifetime, with just a few of the running gear parts having to be replaced from time to time.

WHO SHOULD DO THE MAINTENANCE

Unless you are absolutely all thumbs and your mind boggles at the slightest thing mechanical, you should do much of your own bicycle maintenance, for at least three reasons.

In the first place, good bicycle mechanics are very scarce. About all most bicycle stores can do competently are fix flats (on tubular tires only, not on sewn tires), repair coaster brakes, and do other minor nut-and-bolt-type work. When it comes to aligning precision ten-speed derailleur mechanisms, and doing other work on foreign, high-quality, more expensive bicycles, or even on the less expensive, lower grade ten-speed models, getting a good mechanic can be a real problem.

I have found, and everyone I know who has had a lot of cycling experience confirms this fact, that most bicycle stores today simply cannot be depended on to do an adequate job of bicycle repairing.

If you have a good bicycle with a ten-speed derailleur, but you are absolutely all thumbs with tools, you can generally find a good enough mechanic by looking in the classified telephone directory for a bicycle store that advertises foreign-made bicycles such as Carlton, Frejus, Gitane, Bobet, and the like. Also, the larger Schwinn dealers can sometimes be counted on to have good mechanics, because Schwinn has an aggressive full-time training program for bicycle mechanics, with factory- and field-training schools. In general, you should avoid the smaller family-type bike shops, especially if they are involved in other businesses, such as lawnmower repairing.

Another good way to find a qualified bicycle mechanic is to check with a bicycle club in your area. For a list of the bicycle clubs of America, see pages 315-16. Also, check with your local AYH chapter.

A good bicycle mechanic is always hard to find. For example, in a large city like Chicago there are no more than four or five bicycle shops that handle high-quality lightweight road and track bicycles. If you live far from a big city, you will probably have no choice but to do your own maintenance.

In the second place, bicycle stores today charge $7.50 or more an hour, plus parts, for repairs. You will save a lot of money by fixing your own bicycle, especially if there is more than one bike in the family. For example, a new ten-speed derailleur mechanism can be bought for as little as $6.50 and installed in less than a half-hour. A bicycle store would charge you at least $15.00 for the job.

Also, while bicycles are easy to maintain and repair, with the better machines, fine adjustment and tuning of the various parts can be an art— an art you will want to learn in order to get the most out of your bicycle. With a little practice you can do your own work faster and a lot better than 90 percent of the so-called bicycle mechanics in bike stores. And if you go in for touring, long trips, youth hosteling, and the like, you should at least know how to make emergency repairs.

TOOLS YOU WILL NEED

Most foreign-made bicycles, as well as American-made bicycles using foreign-made parts such as derailleur gears (all derailleurs are foreign-made), caliper brakes, and the like, use metric nuts and bolts and there-fore require metric tools.

Below is a list of tools and their uses. If you think they are expensive, remember that most bike repair shops charge $7.50 an hour and up for repairs, and many do a fairly poor job, especially on the more expensive foreign-made bicycles where precise adjustment and alignment are vital to get the performance you have paid for. A good bicycle is truly a life-time investment, and the right tools will help you keep your investment in tip-top shape. Most of the tools listed here are light enough to go along with you on extended tours, so for all but the most serious prob-lems, you can be mechanically self-sufficient, no matter where you go.

DERAILLEURS, FRONT AND REAR: For Campagnolo derailleurs, a combina-tion Allen and Socket wrench, costing $1.75. For all other derailleurs, a Mafac ultralight (7½-ounce) tool kit, containing spanners and wrenches that also fit all brake nuts and many other smaller metric parts. Cost: $3.00 (Fig. 103). (I consider the Mafac kit in its plastic bag a must for road trips.)

CHAIN RIVET REMOVER: On the ³/₃₂-inch-wide chains used on derailleur-equipped bicycles, you cannot use a master locking link as you can on the ⅛-inch-wide chains used on coaster-brake and three-speed hub bi-cycles such as the Raleigh Sturmey-Archer hub and Schwinn Bendix two-

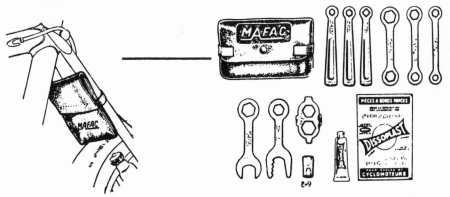

Fig. 103: *This Mafac metric tool kit fits most parts on most European bicycles, as well as American-made bicycles using European components. Includes kit of tire patches for tubular or wired-on tires.*

and three-speed hubs and coaster brakes. The $\frac{3}{32}$-inch chain must fit between the closely spaced cogs on the five-speed freewheel, and the extra width of a master link would cause the chain to hang up on one of the cogs, with resulting considerable damage to the derailleur and, if you've been going fast, possibly to you.

So, to remove the $\frac{3}{32}$-inch-wide chains on derailleur-equipped bicycles, you'll need a combination rivet extractor and rivet-installing tool, for $1.75 (Fig. 104). Buy a replacement pin and screw for this tool for seventy-five cents.

Note: All the tools mentioned here can be bought from any good bicycle dealer or one of the specialty mail-order houses, such as Cyclo-Pedia in Cadillac, Michigan (see Appendix). I use them for most of my foreign bike parts, because their prices are considerably lower. However, they do not carry everything; for a list of specialty bike-part and tool mail-order houses, see pages 317-18.

FREEWHEEL REMOVER: You'll need to remove the freewheel on the rear wheel of a derailleur-equipped bike to clean it, so a remover is necessary, at $1.00 for a Benelux freewheel (Fig. 105), or $2.00 for French Atom and Schwinn Spring freewheels (Fig. 106). You can tell these freewheels apart because the Atom and Spring freewheels have a splined interior (sight along the axle into the freewheel). Most other freewheels can be removed with the Benelux tool.

METRIC ALLEN WRENCH SET: A set of metric Allen wrenches is invaluable. Sears sells such a set as a "Metric Hex Key Set" for about eighty-five cents, in a plastic pouch, that will fit anything you'll find on a bike using Allen nuts and screws. This includes most derailleurs.

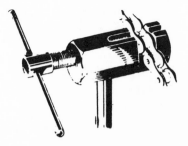

Fig. 104: *Chain rivet remover. Also used to replace or reinstall rivets. An essential tool for any bicycle owner.*

Fig. 105: *Freewheel removing tool. In use, apply tool to freewheel with wheel mounted in bicycle, tighten axle nuts or quick-release slightly to hold freewheel tool onto free-wheel and turn counterclockwise to remove freewheel from hub.*

Fig. 106: *Another type of freewheel remover, for Schwinn hubs.*

WHEEL HUBS: Two offset thin wrenches for adjusting the hub cones of standard and racing wheels are very handy. A set of 13 x 14 and 15 x 16 millimeters costs $3.95 from Wheel Goods (see Appendix).

PEDALS: Good pedals should be dismantled, cleaned, and regreased several times a year. You'll save time by using a special wing-nut pedal wrench to fit the small nut holding the pedal on its axle. Fifty cents from Wheel Goods.

Derailleurs Maintenance and Adjustment

Derailleurs are simple and easy to keep in efficient operating condition. But they are not toys. The better makes are as finely constructed and as precision-machined as the parts of the finest automobiles, and they are just as deserving of your care and attention.

A properly aligned, adjusted, and lubricated derailleur reduces drag, wear and tear on gears and chain, and makes the bicycle far easier to pedal. If you go on trips, you should at least know how to make the basic adjustments on derailleurs yourself.

Derailleur Gear Changers

The derailleur type of gear-changing mechanism has been developed over the past quarter-century or so until today it is just about the most efficient and foolproof gear switcher made for bicycles.

However, the mechanism is exposed, and people, particularly young people, damage even the sturdiest of the derailleur breed by careless handling or improper use. (See pages 108-09, for instructions on how to change derailleur gears quickly, safely, and without damaging the mechanism.)

Derailleur is a French word meaning, literally, to "derail," or to push a bicycle chain from one gear to the next larger or smaller gear. While we're at it, let's get acquainted with more derailleur terminology—the various parts of front and rear derailleurs and how they work. All of the popular makes of derailleurs—two French, one Italian, and one or two Japanese—operate on the same basic principle.

The rear derailleur mechanism (Fig. 107) consists of the gear-shifter mechanism, and four, five, or six gears. The gears are mounted on a freewheel unit, which means the cyclist can stop pedaling without stopping the bicycle (coasting). The freewheel unit with its gears threads onto the rear wheel hub. The gear derailer is mounted on an "ear" or adapter bracket on the rear drop out and can be removed with only a metric wrench.

Since derailleurs are exposed to the elements, they can easily get knocked out of alignment or adjustment if the bicycle falls on the derailleur side, or if too much dirt and dust get into the mechanism. I have had derailleurs shoved out of whack by so simple a thing as an inexperienced cyclist running into my derailleur from behind. (After this happened, I decided to ride behind novice cyclists.)

How Derailleurs Work

To see how the derailleur mechanism works, hang your bicycle from two ceiling hooks, or turn it upside down. Then, turn the pedals and

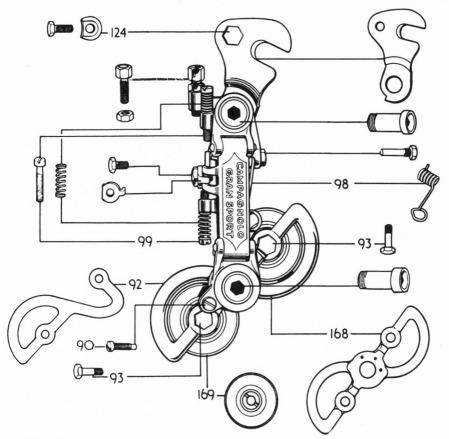

Fig. 107: *Typical derailleur mechanism, in this case the Campagnolo "Gran Sport" unit. Parts are as follows (major ones only): 90-peg stop; 92-inner roller plate; 93-bolt to jockey roller; 98-traverse spring; 99-limit stop adjuster bolts (top bolt is for low or larger gear limit travel, lower bolt is for high or smaller gear limit travel); 124-chainstay bolt; 168-outer roller pate; 169-tension roller*

move the rear derailleur gear-shift lever up and down. Look at the mechanism. You'll see that while a four-sided cage moves from side to side, its sides always remain parallel. This is known as the parallelogram-changer principle, and its purpose is to keep the two small wheels in the derailleur and the chain parallel to the vertical plane of the freewheel gears. (Note: The terms "gears," "cogs," and "sprockets" refer to the same thing; we'll use "gears" because it's more familiar.)

The top wheel in the derailleur gear shifter is called the "jockey" wheel because it "jockeys" the chain from one freewheel gear to the other. The lower wheel is called the "tension" wheel because it keeps the chain under constant tension even though different lengths of chain are required, depending on what combination of rear and front derailleur gears and chainwheel you are using. Obviously the lowest (largest) rear gear and the highest (largest) front chainwheel will use up more chain than the opposite combination. The derailleur mechanism must therefore not only derail or move the chain from one rear gear to another of larger or smaller diameter, but it must also maintain constant tension on the chain. The derailleur keeps the chain taut by spring-loaded shafts which keep the jockey and tension wheels under constant pull toward the rear of the bicycle. This tension is adjustable.

Figure 107 shows a typical rear derailleur mechanism. Study this photo to learn the names of the parts. Figure 109 shows two typical front derailleurs, a Campagnolo "Valentino" and a Huret "Allvit."

Derailleur Troubles and Their Solutions

Derailleurs can behave badly not only because of their own malfunction, but also because of trouble in the parts associated with them. In this section, therefore, we will also treat maintenance of the chain, the freewheel, and the chainwheel. The freewheel is the four- or five-geared

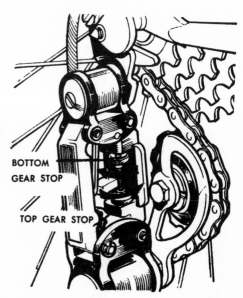

Fig. 108: *Adjust the Simplex "Prestige" derailleur as follows: top knurled nut is for large-gear chain travel limit; bottom knurled nut is for high-gear travel.*

BOTTOM
GEAR STOP

TOP GEAR STOP

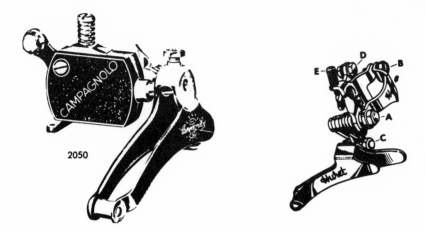

Fig. 109: *Two typical front derailleurs or front changers. On the left, a Campagnolo "Valentine," and on the right, a Huret "Allvit." Spring-loaded nut "E" adjusts large chainwheel travel limit. Derailleur cage should just pass above large pinwheel by about a quarter of an inch. To move unit up or down for this adjustment, loosen bolts "A" and "B."*

widget on the rear wheel hub. The chainwheel is the big sprocket up front next to the right pedal crank.

1. PROBLEM: Gear changes while riding.

   CAUSE: Gear-shift control lever too loose.

   SOLUTION: Tighten gear-control-lever thumbscrew (wing nut), or use a screwdriver on nut type. Caution: Tighten just enough so lever feels slightly tight. Do not tighten so hard that shifting becomes difficult.

   On Schwinn children's bicycles using a "Stik-Shift," and other similar machines with this shift, tighten the lever-adjusting nut under the shift cover somewhat. Do not overtighten or the shift will not operate smoothly.

2. PROBLEM: Gear changes erratically, slowly, and noisily.

   CAUSE: Derailleur jockey and tension sprockets are not lined up in the same plane as rear gears.

   SOLUTION: Turn bike upside down. (Note: I prefer to hang the bi-cycle from the ceiling by hooks attached to the saddle [seat] and handlebars, which puts all parts at eye level or close to it.) Sight along a vertical line to check that tension and jockey wheels are parallel to rear hub gears, as shown in Fig. 110.

Another indication of misalignment is chain rub marks on the inside of the derailleur cage. If derailleur wheels do not line up with rear hub gears, check first to make sure the derailleur itself is positioned correctly. Some derailleurs' top shafts are screwed into a threaded opening in the rear drop out, or the top shaft can be fitted into a threaded opening in a mounting bracket that fits into the rear drop out and is held on by a mounting screw and the wheel axle bolt or quick-release skewer. In any case, do not attempt a manhandling cure by hitting the side of the derailleur chain cage with a hammer. If the chain cage is badly bent due to abuse (such as dropping the bicycle on the derailleur side), it can be replaced by a new chain cage, which you can order from one of the mail-order shops listed on pages 317-18. If the cage is only slightly bent,

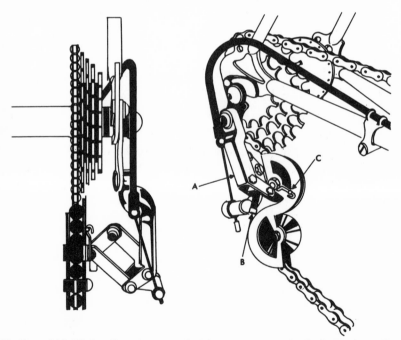

Fig. 110: *Huret "Allvit" derailleur (two views). Adjustments are A for high-speed (smallest gear) and B for low-speed (largest gear). Chain tension is adjusted by placing terminal spring loop in one of the four tension bolts in outer cage plate C.*

gripping it with an adjustable open-end wrench and twisting it gently can often bring the chain cage back into alignment. Use a steady "levering" action.

On Campagnolo derailleurs, use an adjustable wrench over the outside of the heavy casting (the part that has "Campagnolo" stamped on it), and gently twist it back into alignment.

On Huret Allvit derailleurs, and many others, if the derailleur arm is out of alignment, the jockey wheel will not track down the center of the chain but may, instead, press on the side of the chain and cause a grinding noise. To remedy this, give a slight twist of the derailleur arm with an adjustable wrench, first putting the derailleur in the low-gear (large-gear) position. Remember, in this case the derailleur "arm" (see Fig. 110) is *not* the derailleur main body we mentioned above. On the Huret Allvit, it is the arm that comes out from the bottom of the derailleur body next to the low-gear adjusting screw (see Fig. 110). This arm is bent out of alignment relatively easily, particularly when the bike is used carelessly.

A good reason for having everything in correct alignment on derailleur mechanisms, aside from the noise and extra wear and tear caused by misalignment, is that a good deal of energy-wasting friction can also result from such misalignment.

Check the alignment of the derailleur itself by sighting a line down the middle rear gear to the chainwheel (the big gear up front, next to the pedals). The middle of a five-gear freewheel should be directly in line between the two front chainwheels (Fig. 111).

Note: On three-chainwheel clusters, line up the center chainwheel and the middle rear freewheel gear (on five-gear clusters). Three front chainwheel clusters are a compromise at best, and you're going to have to accept the fact that fifteen gear choices are not going to work equally well in all gear selections. The smaller chainwheel with thirty-two or thirty-six teeth, coupled with an "Alpine" rear gear of thirty-six teeth, will permit you to climb very steep grades, but do not expect the smaller chainwheel to work too well in the smaller rear gears.

Note: If you have everything aligned correctly, make sure that if you take the wheel out for any reason, you put it back in exactly the same position. Use wheel stops (small metal chocks that fit in the rear drop out where the axle goes), which go behind the axle and are adjustable. After you have aligned everything, lock the wheel stops in position behind the axle so the next time you remove a wheel, all you need do to replace it

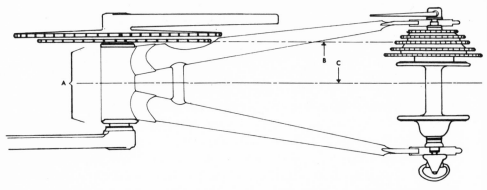

Fig. 111: Front and rear gears must line up precisely. Center of five-gear rear cluster, for example, must line up (B) at midpoint between double front chainwheel or on center of a triple chainwheel. A line (C) drawn between center of bottom bracket (A) should also be on center of entire rear axle sprocket assembly and on center of distance between rear-wheel drop-outs. Misalignment is a common cause of poor derailleur operation and excessive wear of gear teeth and chain.

in the right spot is to pull it snugly up against the wheel stops and fasten the axle nuts, or quick-release skewer. Incidentally, another cause of misalignment can be a bent derailleur mounting bracket on bicycles where the derailleur is bracket-mounted and not screwed into a threaded hole in the rear drop out. If it is not bent too badly, you can straighten the bracket by gently applying an open-end wrench. Otherwise, you'll have to buy a new bracket.

Although this discussion about alignment might seem forbidding and complicated, I assure you that it is really very simple. Read it two or three times if necessary, and refer to the appropriate parts of the derailleur mechanism as you read. You'll find that the picture will become clearer and the working relationships of the parts will fall into place in your mind (along with the necessity for accurate alignment of all moving parts).

Shimano derailleurs (Japanese-made, used on many American bicycles), five-speed derailleur mechanisms, are very similar to better European makes, and have low- and high-gear stops that may need adjustment from time to time. The Shimano "Skylark" is a pretty good mechanism, easy to adjust and sturdy, but you'll need a Phillips-head screwdriver to turn the adjusting screws.

3. PROBLEM: Chain keeps riding up on the low-gear sprocket (the largest rear gear). This can cause the chain to bind in the spokes, with disastrous results.

CAUSE: The low-gear derailleur adjustment screw needs readjustment.

SOLUTION: Make this adjustment. On Huret Allvit and Sprint derailleurs used with most Schwinn and other American-made bicycles, the low-gear (large-sprocket) adjustment screw is located at the bottom of the derailleur, next to the cable pivot bolt and nut. On Simplex "Prestige" and "Raid" derailleurs, the low-gear adjustment is the top of the two thumbscrews in the center of the derailleur body. On Campagnolo derailleurs, the low-gear adjusting screw is at the bottom of the derailleur, as it is also on the Cycle Benelux P.2 derailleur (English). This takes care of the popular makes of derailleurs. The low-gear adjuster keeps the derailleur from moving too far inward and derailing the chain beyond the largest gear into the spokes. Adjust so the chain will not climb beyond the large gear.

4. PROBLEM: Chain runs off high-gear (small) sprocket.

CAUSE: High-gear adjusting screw is moved out of place because of vibration.

SOLUTION: Readjust the high-gear adjusting screw. Turn wheel so that the chain is on the large front chainwheel and small rear gear. If the chain has jammed between chain stay and gear, be careful that in pulling it out you don't bend it or the derailleur. If necessary, loosen the quick-release skewer or axle nuts and push the wheel forward, or rotate it gently backward. Turn the high-gear adjusting screw until the chain will not slip off high gear. On Huret Allvit derailleurs, the high-gear adjusting screw is the small screw about two-thirds of the way down the outside face of the main housing bracket, recessed into a small hole in the bracket. On Campagnolo derailleurs, the high-gear adjusting screw is located about halfway down, at the rear of the main housing casting, and points toward the ground. On Benelux derailleurs, the high-gear stop is at the bottom of the unit, pointing toward the ground, and on the Shimano "Skylark," it is at the bottom of the two Phillips-head screws at the center rear of the derailleur. Figure 109 shows Huret derailleur front mechanism adjustments. Figure 108 shows Simplex derailleur mechanism adjustments.

Note: Every time your bicycle is knocked over on the derailleur side, you should check high- and low-gear stops on the rear derailleur. If you've parked (and locked) your bicycle where people can get at it, curious passersby may have played with the gear shifters. If this is the case, look at the position of the gear-shift handle, move it back about where it was when you parked, and start off by pedaling very gently, while, at the same time, adjusting the gear-shift levers. Otherwise, if you take off with the chain on one and the lever in position for another gear, you can catch the chain between gears and damage the derailleur. This goes for the front (chainwheel) derailleur too.

If you've had your bicycle for some time (six months or so), or you've ridden on sandy or dusty roads, sand or dirt can get into the derailleur linkage arms and clog the derailleur up. It is a good idea to clean the mechanism about every hundred miles, and relubricate pivot points and linkage with light oil. If the chain hangs up on a new bicycle, especially on the high gear (small gear), loosen the linkage bolts slightly.

5. PROBLEM: Chain skips while pedaling, usually in high gear.
   CAUSE: Insufficient chain tension.
   SOLUTION: Varies with type of derailleur.

HURET ALLVIT DERAILLEUR: Move the chain tension spring back a notch.

SIMPLEX DERAILLEUR: For more spring tension on a Simplex derailleur, remove the screw and dust cap from the bottom pivot bolt, and insert a metric Allen wrench in the hole you'll now see. Then, while you hold the locknut between the pivot bolt and the cage (the bracket with two half-moons holding the two small derailleur wheels), with a wrench (metric), turn the Allen wrench toward the rear of the bicycle for more chain tension, or toward the front for less tension. (Note: Use as little tension as possible to reduce drag, wear and tear, and make pedaling easier. This applies to all derailleurs.)

CAMPAGNOLO DERAILLEUR: To increase chain tension on a Campagnolo rear derailleur, remove the chain cage stop-bolt (the thin bolt with a small round head that looks like a water tower lying on the ground, and that keeps the cage from rotating too far clockwise). Let the cage unwind until no more spring tension can be felt. Then, with an Allen wrench, remove the cage pivot bolt (the bolt that holds cage to derailleur), located at the bottom of the derailleur, and remove the cage from the spring end. Turn the cage slightly forward until the end of the spring fits into the next of the three holes. Replace the pivot bolt and cage assembly and tighten the pivot bolt. Wind the cage assembly counter-clockwise one-half to one-and-a-half turns, hold it in this position, and reinstall the cage stop-bolt. (Make sure the cage assembly is right side up by checking that the top roller is the one that has the inner side exposed. The bottom roller has the cage on both sides of the wheel, the top wheel has the cage on the outer side only.)

Replace the chain (with rear wheel in place) and check the shifting while pedaling. (Always check the bicycle on the road, not hanging from the ceiling.) Be sure to check high- and low-gear adjustment screws.

SHIMANO SKYLARK DERAILLEUR: Increase chain tension by removing the chain cage stop-bolt and by winding the cage assembly forward one turn and replacing the stop-bolt.

BENELUX DERAILLEUR: Cable tension adjustment is similar to the Campagnolo.

CAUSE: Burrs on teeth of freewheel gear.
SOLUTION: File or grind burrs off.

CAUSE: A chain link too tight or binding.
SOLUTION: If you've removed and reinstalled the chain, check the link involved. Or check *all* the chain links. If a link binds or is tight (when you move it up and down), twist the chain gently from side to side. Of course, if your chain is rusty, don't bother with this procedure; simply install a new chain.

CAUSE: Excessive wear in chain or gears.
SOLUTION: Chains and gears do wear, and old chains stretch as a result of wear. Always replace worn loose chains (an old chain always breaks when you're miles from a bike shop). Do not replace an old chain and leave worn gears. Replace both at the same time. Old gears are identifiable by a slight hook on the inner lip of the gear teeth, which can catch the chain and make it "skip." Check the most used gears first, using your fingernail. Hooks can be filed or ground off. Removing a gear from the freewheel is a very difficult job, which

most people should leave to a bicycle mechanic. Therefore, I will not describe this procedure here.

CHECK CHAINWHEEL TEETH: Chainwheel teeth can also wear. They show this wear on the "lands" of the teeth; that is, by wearing away the face of the curvature of the gear teeth on the side toward the rear of the bicycle, away from the direction of rotation of the chainwheel. If the chainwheel is worn this much, it should be discarded and replaced with a new one, to avoid rough pedaling and erratic drive. Also, a worn chainwheel will soon wear out a new chain. If you're in doubt about chainwheel wear, check the chainwheel as follows: wrap a chain around the chainwheel and pull the chain down into the teeth by holding the ends of the chain snugly together. If the chain links fit tightly into the chainwheel teeth and cannot be picked away from the wheel at any gear, the wheel is in good shape. But if the chain climbs up on the teeth without being lifted up by you, mark this point of climb. Then try a new chain and repeat the procedure. If the new chain comes up at the same point, the gear is worn and should be replaced. However, if the new chain fits nicely, the old chain is shot and should be replaced.

Remember that a chain doesn't actually "stretch," but because the parts wear and "give," it acts as though it *has* stretched. It takes only a few thousandths of an inch of wear on each of the rivets to make the chain stretch a half-inch. (This is why frequent cleaning and lubrication are important in chain maintenance.)

Another check for the chainwheel and chain fit is to put the chain you intend to use on the chainwheel, already installed on the bicycle, and watch how the chain flows over the chainwheel teeth. There should be no "lifting" or sticking of the chain to the chainwheel teeth.

See pages 286-87 on crank axle maintenance for instructions on replacing the chainwheel.

6. PROBLEM: Gear won't-shift all the way into low (onto rear, large sprocket).
   CAUSE: Low-gear adjusting screw is out of adjustment.
   SOLUTION: Readjust as per instructions above.

   CAUSE: Cable has stretched, or has slipped in the cable pivot bolt (where it is fastened to derailleur).
   SOLUTION: Shift derailleur into high gear while turning pedals. Cable should have small amount of slack. If too loose, take up slack by

turning the adjusting barrel on the derailleur, or, if there is no barrel on your machine (many good bicycles don't have one), loosen the cable pivot bolt-nut, pull some of the cable through, and re-tighten. Be sure to leave a little slack in the cable.

If the gear-shift cable breaks while you are on a trip, you can at least avoid having to pedal all the way home in high gear by screwing the high-gear adjustment to keep the chain on the first or second gear up from the highest (small-sprocket) gear.

7. PROBLEM: Chain slips off small front chainwheel sprocket.
   CAUSE: Low-gear limit screw is out of adjustment.
   SOLUTION: Turn pedals and shift front derailleur to small chainwheel. Readjust low-gear limit screw. On Huret Allvit front derailleurs, this screw is on the body of the derailleur, just under the righthand (chain-side) clamp bolt, facing toward the chain guide. On Campagnolo front derailleurs, the low-gear adjusting screw is the inner (closest to seat tube) screw, just forward of the cable anchor screw. Remember, the function of the chain guard is to derail or move the chain from one chainwheel sprocket to the other. There is no tension adjustment to the front derailleur; this is taken care of by the rear derailleur. To avoid confusion, I must also point out that on rear derailleur freewheel gear clusters, the smaller the gear the higher the gear ratio (for high speeds) and the larger the gear the lower the gear ratio (for climbing steep hills). Gear sizes and ratios are the other way around for front derailleurs; the small chainwheel is for low speed (hills) and the big chainwheel is for high speed.

8. PROBLEM: Chain won't stay on large chainwheel (front derailleur).
   CAUSE: High-gear adjusting screw is out of adjustment.
   SOLUTION: Since there are only two adjusting screws on front derailleurs (chainwheels), and we have already told you where the low-gear adjustment screw is on all popular front derailleurs, all you need do is shift the front derailleur lever to the high position (toward the rear of the bicycle), while turning the pedals, and adjust the chain guide over the large chainwheel with the high-gear adjusting screw. If shifting from small to large chainwheel after this adjustment is hard, bend the upper front corner of the inner part of the chain guide (cage) slightly inward, toward the chainwheel.

If, however, the chain tends to jump off the chainwheel toward the outside (away from the bicycle), bend the upper front corner of the outer chain guide slightly toward the chainwheel. To find the exact spot where you bend the chainwheel guide, turn the pedals (cranks) by hand while the bicycle is off the ground and move the front shift lever until the chain just starts to lift off the chainwheel teeth. The part of the chain guide (cage) to be bent is touching the chain at this point.

9. PROBLEM: Chain won't shift onto large front chainwheel.
   CAUSE: High-gear adjusting screw is out of adjustment.
   SOLUTION: Readjust screw so chain guide will push chain up onto large front chainwheel.

   CAUSE: Cable has stretched.
   SOLUTION: Push front derailleur control lever all the way forward while turning pedals (cranks). Cable should be nearly tight. If it is loose, unscrew cable bolt (the bolt that holds the cable to the front derailleur shifting mechanism), pull cable through, and retighten cable bolt.

10. PROBLEM: Front derailleur chain cage rubs on chain. Chain rattles.
    CAUSE: Low- or high-gear adjustment screws have vibrated out of adjustment.
    SOLUTION: Readjust screws.

    CAUSE: Front derailleur mechanism not aligned so chain cage is parallel with chainwheel.
    SOLUTION: Loosen the two bolts that hold the front derailleur mechanism to seat tube (frame) and turn the derailleur mechanism left or right to align the chain cage parallel to the chainwheel. While you've got the mechanism loose, make sure it is as close (low) to the chainwheel as possible, so that the outer plate of the chain cage just clears the teeth of the large chainwheel.

    CAUSE: Crooked or wavy chainwheel. Chain rattles.
    SOLUTION: Straighten chainwheel by prying it back into position with a long, square-shanked screwdriver. To avoid bending the chainwheel more than you want to, use as fulcrum (levering) points the bottom bracket cup (holding chainwheel axle in frame bottom), inside the right crank and chain-ring mounting bolts,

with chain on large chainwheel. To judge which way to bend the chainwheel, sight through the front derailleur chain cage, and use the inside plane of the chain cage as a guide.

Another good way to straighten a chainwheel is to use the rear fork as a guide, turn the chainwheel, and mark the high and low spots (near and far distances from rear fork) on the chainwheel with a china-marking pencil or a piece of chalk. If a high and low spot are opposite each other (directly across the chainwheel), using adjustable wrenches and pulling on the low point and pushing on the high point will usually bring the chainwheel back into true.

To protect chrome plating or finish on the chainwheel, use a piece of rag between the paws of the wrench. Take it easy as you push—don't overdo it. It is far better to make too slight a push than to give it all you've got and shove the chainwheel out of true in the other direction.

If, however, there are two high points opposite each other, and two low points opposite each other, all you need do is push the two high points inward toward the frame simultaneously.

If the chainwheel is wavy, the straightening job is going to be tougher. Use an adjustable wrench at the point where the wave peaks or bottoms out and press gently in the required direction. Move around the wheel and adjust all waves or bends in this manner. If you can't bring the wheel back into true, you'd better buy and install a new chainwheel. Find out what rough treatment bent the chainwheel in the first place so this won't happen again. (If you have to replace it with a new chainwheel, see pages 287-89 for instructions on removing and installing chainwheels.)

11. PROBLEM: Pedals turn, crank turns, chain turns, freewheel turns, but the wheel doesn't turn.

   CAUSE: Pawls inside the freewheel mechanism are stuck open by a piece of dirt or by the use of too heavy a lubricating oil in the freewheel.

   SOLUTION: Remove the freewheel and soak it in kerosene to remove dirt and/or heavy oil. Oil again with a light oil such as No. 5 SAE.

HOW TO REMOVE THE FREEWHEEL: If you have a quick-release, remove the bicycle wheel. Then remove the quick-release skewer from the hollow axle by unscrewing the plastic-covered skewer-adjusting nut located opposite the skewer-release handle. (Be careful not to lose the two small springs.) With the wheel now out of the bicycle, insert the freewheel remover in the freewheel and reinstall the quick-release skewer, and hand-tighten it snugly, but no tighter, against the freewheel remover. With an adjustable wrench, turn the freewheel remover counterclockwise (left-hand thread) until it comes loose. Remove the skewer and freewheel tool; you should be able to remove the freewheel by hand or with the free-wheel tool. Do not try to use the freewheel tool alone if the freewheel is tight—you'll only strip the tool.

To replace the freewheel, screw on by hand till tight, insert the free-wheel tool and skewer, and carefully pull up tightly. It is not necessary to bear down on the tightening job because the pull of the chain when you start riding will do the rest. When you reinstall the skewer, remember that the spring must go in *small* end first, toward the hub.

Routine Derailleur Maintenance: Lubrication

CHAIN: Every 200 miles (or more frequently, if you ride dusty roads), remove the chain, soak it in kerosene, and relubricate with a heavy oil or with Lubricate grease, made by Fiske Brothers Refining Company, New-ark, New Jersey, and available from most hardware and bicycle stores.

In order to remove the chain, you'll need a rivet-remover tool (Fig. 104, see page 232). When pressing the chain rivet out with the tool, be careful not to press the rivet out all the way. Stop when the rivet is part way out, remove the tool, and see if you can complete the job by prying the chain apart with a small screwdriver or by twisting the chain away from the rivet. Ideally, you should leave just a bit of the rivet end showing inside the chain link, so that when you reinstall the chain, the small section of rivet can be popped back into the link hole. The job can be completed by pushing the rivet home with the same tool you used to push it out. If you should push a rivet all the way out of the hole by accident, it will be simpler to go to the next link and remove that rivet, rather than try to fuss around putting the rivet back again. One more or less shouldn't make too much difference.

Incidentally, if you're installing a new derailleur $\frac{3}{32}$-inch-wide chain, remember that some new chains (I have never been able to figure out why) come with a master link, just like the $\frac{1}{8}$-inch-wide chains used on three-speed and coaster-brake bicycles. You should remove this master (or spring-connecting) link by prying it off, and discard it along with the link it was supposed to hold. If you use the master link, it will rub on the gears.

DERAILLEUR: Lubricate pivot points every thirty days or every 200 miles. Every month, clean off dirt and grease from the derailleur with a brush dipped in kerosene (remove the wheel first so you don't drip kerosene on tires, and keep kerosene from brake pads), and relubricate the derailleur wheels with a light oil. Better yet, and this is best if you're finicky about performance, remove the entire derailleur mechanism from the bicycle and soak it in kerosene. Remove the small wheels from the cage (place them on a rag on the bench so as not to lose the small ball-bearings). Use Lubriplate grease inside the small wheel cones and stick the ball-bearings back in place. Reassemble derailleur.

If the derailleur wheels have worn smooth, replace them with new wheels, which you can order from Wheel Goods Corporation or Big Wheel, Ltd. (see Appendix).

Selecting Correct Chain Length

Spence Wolfe writes in *American Cycling* (now *Bicycling!*) that for optimum performance, the chain should be no longer than is necessary to do the job. But how long is this? And why are different lengths of chain needed anyway? To answer the second question first, chain lengths vary because different combinations of gear ratios (gear teeth) are used on different bicycles and to suit individual needs. (See the discussion of gear ratios on page 118.) Different derailleurs use different lengths of chain.

As for the first question, Mr. Wolfe recommends "using the maximum length possible (while still retaining tension), when the chain is on the smallest freewheel cog and on the smallest chainwheel" (up front).

Wolfe also cautions you to make sure that on Campagnolo derailleurs, the roller cage has not rotated so far forward that the cage stop-bolt has touched the lower body of the cage (the knurled part). If you need more chain tension, follow the procedure on pages 242-43 for increasing tension on Campagnolo derailleurs.

Another way to check for correct chain length is to shift the chain to the large front chainwheel and the largest rear gear, and leaving a slight excess (a half-inch to an inch of chain) to allow you to shift out of this gear freely.

Chain Wear

Spence Wolfe recommends still another good way to check chain wear. "Assuming that the bike concerned is the derailleur type, a good method to check the chain is to put it on the large freewheel cog and on the large chainwheel. Then have someone put pressure on the pedal as though the bike were being propelled. Measure twenty-four links of the taut top run of the chain. If this measurement is as much as twelve and one-sixteenth inches from the center of the first pin to the center of the twenty-fifth pin the chain should be replaced."

If you continue to use a worn chain, you will find yourself buying new freewheel sprockets and, still worse, the more expensive front chainwheels.

If you ride in the rain, be sure to apply penetrating oil to the chain immediately after your ride, to make sure rust will not set in, and to force out any accumulated moisture. Then apply light motor oil with a penetrant such as STP added, and work it into the chain.

If you keep the chain well lubricated at all times, the oil will "float" dirt away from working parts. But remove the chain and clean as described above every couple of weeks—every week if you ride a lot. Never use gasoline to clean the chain. Use kerosene and a little elbow grease with a small wire brush to get dirt out from between links.

Wolfe recommends dousing the chain in hot No. 90 SAE transmission oil, then hanging it up overnight or until the oil is cold. But watch out for fire during this process!

BRAKES

Caliper Brakes

Caliper brakes have been around in one form or another for a long time, certainly (in an efficient form) since the early 1920s. With minor mechanical modifications and improvements, these are the brakes found on "lightweight" or "touring" and high-quality road (and many other types) of bicycles today.

You may find combinations of front caliper brakes with rear coaster-brake hubs or two-, three-, or four-"speed" rear hubs. This combination is a good one if you like multiple-gear hubs and coaster brakes, but want good brakes. A coaster brake on the rear wheel alone is like a car with only rear brakes (which went out of style in the 1920s).

Caliper brakes operate very much like disc brakes on modern automobiles; that is, they squeeze down on both sides of the wheels so that a rubber pad, like an auto disc pad, grips the side of the rim and reduces forward wheel motion by pressure and friction.

Although there are dozens of makes of caliper brakes, there are only two basic types: center pull (see Fig. 13) and side pull (Fig. 14). Center-pull brakes are easier to adjust and tend to stay adjusted longer than the side-pull type, but they cost more and are found only on better bicycles.

You can tell center-pull brakes by the wire that comes down over the brake and attaches to a piece of metal called a "cable anchor" (see Fig. 13). From the cable anchor another cable runs to both sides of the caliper brake assembly so that when the hand lever is squeezed, both sides of the caliper brake are pulled together.

Side-pull brakes, on the other hand, have a control cable that attaches directly to one of the caliper arms, usually the lefthand arm.

There are three type of hand-operated caliper brakes, each of which apply to both center-pull and side-pull brakes. Center-pull brakes come with or without hooded brake levers (Fig. 112 and Fig. 113). Side-pull caliper brakes may also have hooded levers, on turned-down (racer-type) handlebars, or they may have "tourist" levers on conventional handlebars.

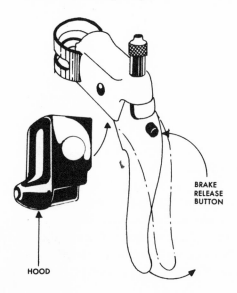

BRAKE
RELEASE
BUTTON

HOOD

Fig. 112: *Many center-pull brakes come with a rubber hood for hand comfort and buoyancy and a brake release button, which springs brakes apart to facilitate wheel removal. This Weinmann brake has both, plus an adjuster.*

Fig. 113: *Brake shoes, as on this rear center-pull brake, are closed at front end and open at rear, so action of rim on brake can't force brake shoe out of brake block. When replacing blocks, make sure open end is toward rear of bicycle, as shown here.*

Most of the better center-pull and side-pull caliper brakes also come with a quick-release button, which is located either on the front of the hand lever, or on the side-pull brake itself. The quick-release lever button, when pushed in, releases the two brakes by opening up the caliper arms, only for the purpose of making it easier for you to get the wheel on and off. By no means should you think of the quick-release lever as another adjustment. It is there just so that you don't have to struggle so hard to get the tire and wheel out of the bike to fix a flat or make an adjustment on the wheel.

Replacing the Caliper Brake Pad

Eventually the rubber brake shoe on any caliper brake will wear out or, through age and lack of use, harden so that its characteristic rubbery friction is lost. If you're thinking about buying a used bike with caliper brakes, run your fingernail into the rubber brake shoe. If it feels hard and unresilient, fresh new shoes should be installed.

You can install the rubber shoe alone, which costs a few cents less than the rubber shoe in its metal holder. I prefer to buy a new block plus shoe because it doesn't cost much more, and you get a new nut and lock-washer in the bargain, which is important if threads on the old shoe are worn or partially stripped. The new brake block and shoe cost about forty-five cents each, and you can save a couple of dollars in the twenty minutes or less it takes to replace all four brake pads.

To install a new brake shoe, squeeze the brake lever slightly, and press its quick-release mechanism so that the brakes open wide. This feature is designed to permit the brakes to open farther than usual in order to facilitate installation by making room for the side bulge of the tire to pass through the brake pads as the wheel is pulled from the fork. If you don't have a quick-release unit, disregard this step.

Next, using a small adjustable wrench or the proper-sized socket wrench, unscrew the nut holding the brake shoe on the caliper brake lever. Remove both brake shoes in this fashion.

Before replacing the new brake shoes, examine one. You'll notice that one end is closed and one end is open. *Always replace the brake shoe with the closed metal end toward the front of the bicycle.* Otherwise, forward pressure as brakes are applied will push the brake pad out of the holder, and you will be left with no brakes just when you need them most.

Adjusting Center-Pull Brakes

Center-pull brakes on the better twenty-seven-inch-wheel lightweight bicycles, such as the Schwinn Paramount, the more expensive Frejus, and other Italian, French, and Belgian makes, have brake-shoe adjustments in both vertical and horizontal planes. By adjusting the locknut on the brake shoe, you can move the shoe so that its surface lines up exactly in the plane of the wheel rim. Incidentally, the rubber brake block is supposed to rub on the metal wheel rim edge and *not on the tire,* when brake control levers on the handlebar are squeezed. You'll get stopping power if the brake rubs on the tire, but your tire won't last long, because the brake block will soon chew a hole right through the tire sidewall.

After you have the brake shoes lined up so they are hitting the wheel rim side evenly, hold the brake control lever on the handlebars down tightly, and tighten the brake-shoe nut. When you release the brake control lever, the brake pad should be an eighth of an inch from the wheel on both sides. If it is not, you can loosen the brake-shoe nut and move the shoe in toward the wheel on brakes such as the Mafac center-pull. If your caliper brakes have only one brake-pad adjustment, as on most Weinmann, Philip, and other popular makes used on most of the less-expensive lightweights, you'll have to adjust the brake cable by turning the adjusting barrel.

New cables will stretch after awhile, so you may not be able to take up the slack by turning the adjusting barrel. If this is the case, you will have to pull some of the brake cable through the brake and snip off the unused end. If brake-cable length is the problem, simply loosen the anchor screw that holds the cable clamped to the cable holder (Fig. 114), pull the cable through about a quarter of an inch, retighten the cable-bolt nut, and slip the cable holder back onto the inner brake cable.

Adjusting Side-Pull Caliper Brakes

Side-pull brakes are adjusted in much the same manner as center-pull brakes. The brake cable is connected directly to the caliper arm instead of to a cable anchor, as in center-pull brakes. If you can't take up the slack in the brake cable and bring the brake pads back to around an eighth of an inch from the wheels by loosening the retaining nut on the adjusting barrel and turning the barrel, you'll have to loosen the anchor nut that holds the brake cable in place and pull the cable through a bit more. Be careful not to let the cable slip out of the anchor-bolt hole, because most cables will be frayed a bit at the end, and you'll find it all

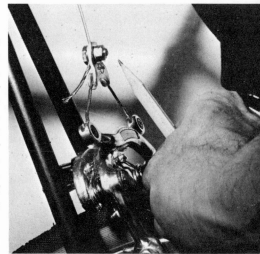

Fig. 114. Where pencil is pointing is the location where you can take up the excess cable length on center-pull brakes. Rear center-pull brake anchor bolt assembly (at top) is fed through fixture attached to the seat-post adjusting nut, just visible at top of photo. When you loosen seat-post locknut to raise or lower seat, you should hold the hangar in the original position; otherwise, as you tighten seat-post locknut, the hangar will move out of position and cause brakes to bind on rim.

but impossible to put the cable back in the hole. This will call for a trip to the bike store for a new cable. Incidentally, most stores will try to sell you a complete new rig, the metal housing plus the cable for $1.25 or so, when all you need is a cable for about seventy-five cents. The professional shops, which do repair work on top-quality machines, will have the cables alone. Do not try to cut a cable before installing it—the cable wire ends will fray out, and you will wind up again having to buy a new cable. Bicycle repair shops have a special tool for cutting wire, but unless you want to spend the $5.00 or so that such a tool costs, stick to your old scissors or cutting pliers to cut the cable *after* you have it installed and the cable-bolt nut is tight. Make sure, when you buy a new cable for English bikes such as the Raleigh, that the cable has the correct leaded ends. Show the old cable to the salesman to make sure you get an exact duplicate.

Caliper brakes can be adjusted as described on bicycles of any make— American, English, Japanese, Austrian, Dutch, and any others sold on the American market.

Hub Brakes

Hub brakes are usually found only on tandem bicycles used in mountainous terrain, where their superior braking leverage is required. Hub brakes are far heavier and more costly than caliper brakes and are unnecessary unless you have a tandem and plan a lot of riding in the Rockies, the Alps, or other mountain areas. However, a few words about adjustment may be useful.

Hub brakes use a brake "shoe" mechanism, much like conventional automobile brakes. To adjust them, it is vital that the metal clip which holds the cable anchor plate to the frame or fork be kept tight. If it is loose, the cable will not be able to pull the brakes tight enough for good braking.

To adjust the brake lever which controls the hub brake, tighten the nut through which the cable passes until the brake binds (rotate the wheel to test), then slacken until the wheel revolves freely.

If the cable is too loose, loosen the locknut on the cable (located just under the clip securing the anchor plate to the bicycle frame), and rotate the adjusting nut until the play is removed. Then tighten the locknut.

Caliper Brake Levers

All caliper brake levers are pretty much the same, the difference being only a matter of shape, according to whether they are used on turned-down "racing" handlebars (Fig. 29) or on conventional "touring" handlebars (Fig. 26). If your brake levers are not located in just the right position for your hands and arm length, you may want to move them on the handlebars. The brake lever should be where you can get at it quickly. The reason for having the brakes adjusted, incidentally, so that the rubber shoes are about an eighth of an inch from the wheel rim, is that you will get fast results when you squeeze the brake lever. If the brake pad is too far away from the tire, it will take longer for your squeeze to stop the bicycle. In an emergency, this could be dangerous.

To move the brake lever on hooded levers on turned-down handlebars, pull up the rubber hood, and if you have a quick-release brake, push the release button and open the brake lever all the way. Underneath the lever, through the body of the lever mechanism, you will see a nut or pull-up bolt which tightens the clamps holding the brake-lever unit on the handlebars. By turning this nut counterclockwise, you will loosen the brake handles so that you can reposition them to suit yourself.

On "tourist" (conventional) handlebars, the pull-up bolt is on the outside of the pull-up grip.

Replacing Brake Cables

Eventually your brake cable, like a shoelace, will wear and break. It is a good safety measure to replace frayed cables before they break so that you can always stop safely. The cable replacement procedure for all caliper brakes is pretty much the same. Loosen the cable-bolt nut where the cable fastens to the caliper cable anchor on center-pull brakes, or where the cable fastens to the caliper arm on side-pull brakes. Pull the cable out of the cable bolt and out of the cable housing.

Pull the cable out of the hand lever by pushing up from underneath. You'll see that the cable end comes out of a rotating slotted brass or steel cable holder in the handle. To replace the old cable with a new one, slide the *large* leaded head end into the larger of the two holes in the slotted cable retainer in the brake handle. Then push the brake cable through the housing into the cable-anchor bolt, and tighten the anchor-bolt nut slightly. Check to make sure the brake pads are about a quarter of an inch from the wheel rims. If they are not, pull the cable through the cable bolt, or slacken it off as necessary. Remember, new cables stretch after a while, so it will be necessary to readjust brake shoe clearance as described above, from time to time.

Note: On center-pull brakes, the rear cable-anchor bolt, and nut mechanism, (see top of Fig. 114 for a partial view) are sometimes attached to the seat-post adjusting nut by a metal hanger. If you've adjusted the seat up or down, make sure that, in the process, the hanger is at the same angle as when you started. Otherwise the rear brakes will bind, because the cable will have been tightened by the hanger being too far up or down.

Brake Tips: Do's and Don'ts

WHEEL RUB: If your wheel is out-of-round, you'll find that you probably cannot adjust the brake shoe as close to the rim as an eighth of an inch. You should then realign the wheel as described on page 304 before adjusting the brake shoe clearance.

Untrue wheels will also cause excessive tire wear. As the rim brake grabs the distorted portion of the rim, it tends to grip more tightly there than on other parts of the rim. This can cause a skid mark, and the tire will wear excessively in that one spot.

CABLE SIZE: When you must buy a new cable, take your old cable and the old cable housing with you to insure an exact duplicate. Brake cables vary in diameter (thickness), and you must be sure to get a cable that will fit easily through the cable housing. If the choice is between a cable that fits stiffly or a little loosely in the cable housing, select the smaller of the two cables. When inserting the cable in the housing, coat it lightly with Lubriplate or another light grease so that it will slide in easily.

You should also check the cable housing carefully; if it's broken so that any part of the inside of the housing rubs on the cable, you will have a recurring cable breakage. If this is the case, replace the cable housing.

REPLACING WHEEL SIZE: If you want to replace or rebuild your sporting or tourist twenty-six-inch wheel-size bike into a twenty-seven-inch wheel-size machine, you can, but remember that most side-pull caliper brakes can't be adjusted far enough upward to accommodate larger wheels.

You'll have to buy a new set of brakes, preferably Mafac or other good quality center-pull, for $12.95 a pair, including levers, hoods, and sleeves.

LUBRICATING BRAKE MECHANISMS: A few drops of oil on fulcrum points (pivot bolts) every few weeks will be sufficient for lubricating your brakes. Before oiling, remove accumulated dust and dirt with a clean rag (this is especially important if you do not have fenders).

Do not lubricate any part of hand levers.

Do not lubricate the wheel rim or get oil on the brake shoe rubber!

Caliper Brake "Symptoms" and Cures

- FRONT BRAKE "DRAG": If you can't eliminate drag by adjusting the brake shoes, check the front pivot bolt. This is the main bolt that holds the brakes to the frame. If it's bent, replace it.

- SIDE-PULL CALIPER BRAKES DO NOT RETURN TO POSITION, BUT "DRAG": Lubricate the pivot points. If the arms drag (rub) on each other, bend the arms so that they clear each other. (Caution: Do not try to bend cast-aluminum brake arms, because they'll break off. Bend forged arms only.) Use an emery cloth or fine file to eliminate friction between the arms. If the arms do not pivot freely, adjust the center bolt and the locknuts. If the side-pull brakes are hard to center, so that one brake block does not drag on the rim, release and bend outward the spring on the side that drags, and reinstall the spring against the arm.

- HAND LEVERS ON HANDLEBARS BIND: Check to find the exact location of the binding. If sides of brake lever rub against the brake block, use a thin screwdriver to gently pry the lever inward (or bend the lever slightly inward). Check to make sure the cables aren't binding and that the cable housings (the spaghetti tubing through which the cables run) curve gradually from the levers to the frame and from the frame to the brakes.

- CENTER-PULL BRAKE ARMS DO NOT PIVOT FREELY ON TRUNNIONS (CENTER BOLT): If the center bolt or trunnion fits too tightly, ream out a small hole in the arm with a drill. Or sand the trunnion to a smaller diameter. If the arms are too thick, file at the pivot area so that the pivot bolt sits against the trunnion without binding the arm. Loosen the pivot bolt; if the arm moves freely, the arm is too thick.

* UNEVEN BRAKING: Check for out-of-round or dented rims. Sometimes the brakes will grab unevenly, and at the same time, "shudder" or "judder." Juddering means that the entire brake assembly is loose on the trunnion bolt holding it to the frame. The brake assembly must be rigid. Loosen the locknut, take up on the adjusting nut, and re-tighten the locknut. The brakes should have no front-to-rear play; they should pivot freely but not loosely. If the brakes still "judder," check the head bearing play on the front fork, and readjust (see pages 296-99).

* SQUEALING BRAKES: Squealing is usually the result of vibration. Check the brake blocks for hardening due to old age. If the blocks have hardened, replace them with new rubber. Sometimes the only way to prevent looseness that causes squealing in the caliper-brake system is to cut away the rubber brake shoes at the front, causing them to "toe in" slightly. This puts pressure on the brake arms by causing them to bend slightly as the brake is applied. Also, check the brake shoes to make sure particles of grit are not embedded in the rubber, which is another cause of squealing.

WHEEL HUB MAINTENANCE

English and some American bicycles (Figs. 115, 116) have oil fittings on the hub so that you can squirt oil into the wheel bearings from time to time. The better European hubs do not have such fittings, because they are precision machined and designed to be taken apart from time to time for cleaning and greasing.

All hubs, oilable or not, should be torn down, cleaned, and regreased approximately twice a year, and those with oil fittings should be oiled once a month, depending on how frequently the bike is used. Oil isn't as successful a lubricant as thin grease, because oil is easily washed off bearings by water (as when you ride in the rain). Also, oil is too thin to stand up under long, hard, dusty rides.

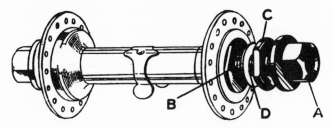

Fig. 115 *Typical British front-wheel hub. Parts are (a) axle and axle nuts and washers; (b) adjustable cone; (c) locknut; (d) oil hole under spring-clip cover.*

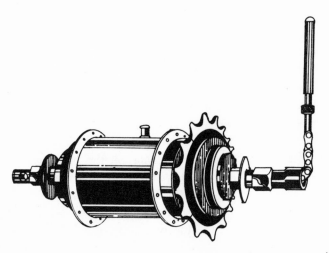

Fig. 116: *A rear Sturmey-Archer hub showing the oil fitting. Lubricator cap and opening.*

The instructions below on wheel hub, axle, and bearing maintenance apply pretty much to all hubs, of any make. There are minor exceptions, such as in the finer hubs like those made by Campagnolo, but this exception involves only a dust cap that is fitted over the bearings. This cap can be prized out carefully to make the bearing removal and replacement easier.

Tools Needed for Hub Maintenance

You will need a special, thin cone wrench or offset cone pliers to hold the adjustable cone while you tighten the locknut with a crescent wrench. Pliers cost about $3.00 and a cone wrench, about $2.70. You will need two cone wrenches—a thirteen- or fourteen-millimeter wrench for front hubs and a fifteen- or sixteen-millimeter wrench for rear hubs—plus a six-inch adjustable crescent wrench. The cone pliers may be better for you to buy if you have a variety of types of bicycles in your family, because they can be adjusted to fit any hub cone.

Hub Assembly and Disassembly (Front and rear derailleur only)

STEP ONE: Remove the wheels from the bicycle.

STEP TWO: Put one end of the wheel in a vise, gripping one of the locknuts. If this is a rear wheel, grip the freewheel locknut side. If you have a three-speed or coaster-brake hub, do not take the hub apart; you will find a mess of gears and sundry other parts all over the place, and it isn't worth the trouble. The only maintenance needed by Sturmey-Archer, Bendix, and other multispeed and coaster-brake hubs is a monthly oiling with a medium-weight (20 SAE) oil. (We are dealing here with any front hub and only with derailleur rear-wheel hubs, both of which are assembled and disassembled in the same manner.)

STEP THREE: If you are disassembling a derailleur-equipped bicycle wheel with a rear freewheel gear cluster, note very carefully the position of any spacers and washers as you remove the axle. These spacers and washers must go back in *exactly* the same position to preserve the alignment of the gear cluster with the chainwheel (see pages 237-38 for a discussion on alignment).

STEP FOUR: Remove the locknut, lock washer (the washer that fits into a spline on the axle), and the adjustable cone. Holding the wheel assembly *by the axle*, loosen the vise and set the wheel down on a rag or piece of paper on a workbench. Remove the axle and, at the same time, catch any bearings that come loose. Remove all bearings after removing the axle. If you have an American-made bicycle, the bearings may not be loose but will be in a cage or retainer. If this is the case, simply pull off both the retainers as you would a ring from a finger.

STEP FIVE: Clean the entire assembly—axle, bearings, and hub cone—thoroughly with kerosene.

STEP SIX: Inspect the balls for rust or cracks, the cones for galled spots (shiny spots indicating wear), and the axle-bearing surfaces. If any of the balls are rusty or cracked, replace the entire set of balls. Check the axle for alignment by rolling it down a sheet of cardboard and watching both ends of the axle. If either end of the axle shows signs of being out-of-round, you need a new axle.

STEP SEVEN: With the wheel on its side on the table, put a layer of all-purpose grease inside the hub race and lay the loose bearings in the grease. The grease will hold the bearings in place until you insert the axle in place from underneath (which you should do next).

STEP EIGHT: Put a layer of grease in the top hub race, insert the rest of the bearings in the race, and screw on the adjustable cone until it is snug. Then back it off a quarter-turn. Put the wheel back in the vise as described in Step Two.

STEP NINE: Insert the lock washer and locknut, and screw the locknut tight, while holding the adjustable cone in position with a cone wrench or cone pliers.

STEP TEN: Check the axle for side play by grasping the wheel in your fingers while the axle is held by a locknut in a vise, and move wheel from side to side. If end play is apparent, loosen the locknut, tighten the adjustable cone with the cone wrench or cone pliers about an eighth of a turn, and retighten the locknut. Continue this procedure until the end play is removed.

STEP ELEVEN: Check for bearing tightness. Remove the wheel and axle from the vise. Twist the axle between your thumb and forefinger. If it feels tight or binding, loosen the locknut, back off the adjustable cone about an eighth of a turn, and retighten the locknut. Ideally, the wheel should spin so freely that the weight of the tire valve (if it is at the nine or three o'clock positions) is enough to move the wheel. At least, if you spin it, the wheel should come to rest gradually, and indicate a delicate enough balance so that the tendency is for the valve to come to rest somewhere between the eight and four o'clock positions.

STEP TWELVE: The above steps also apply if you have an American-made bicycle with caged bearings. However, if the cage is worn so that the bearings fall out of the cage, replace the cage and bearings. The cage (or retainer) should have a part number stamped on it, which you should use in purchasing a replacement. When replacing caged bearings, make sure the correct side of the cage faces the cone. The balls should bear against the cup cage, not the cage itself.

STEP THIRTEEN: You may find it impossible to remove all end play and at the same time have the wheel turn freely, with the less-expensive American-made bicycle hubs. If this is your problem, a little end play won't hurt so long as the wheel turns freely. However, with precision-machined European hub assemblies, you should be able to adjust the cone for zero end play and at the same time achieve free wheel motion. This is what is meant by precision machining. Remember, if you own a more costly bicycle, you have paid a premium for performance. There is absolutely no reason why, with a little patience and care in adjusting the cones, you cannot get almost perfect wheel performance as far as the hub is concerned.

STEP FOURTEEN: Put back all the washers and spacers in the same position they were in when you removed the wheel, and reinstall the wheel in the drop-out.

Pedal Maintenance

As you can imagine, a good deal of stress and strain is imposed on pedals. As you will see when you take a pedal apart, pedals use small ball-bearings which, due to their location and use, are quite susceptible to wear and corrosion. This is why pedals should be disassembled, cleaned, and regreased twice a year, or more frequently if you do a lot of cycling.

The following tells how you disassemble and assemble various types of pedals.

American Pedals

Although there is a great variety of pedal construction used on conventional American-made bicycles, most of them are similar enough in construction to make these instructions valid.

STEP ONE: Remove the pedals. Bear in mind that the righthand pedal has a righthand thread (unscrews counterclockwise) and the left pedal has a lefthand thread (unscrews clockwise).

STEP TWO: If your pedal has a removable dust cap, follow the instructions under Continental pedals. If your pedals have no removable dust cap and the outer section is one piece, remove the two small nuts at the threaded end of the pedal axle, pull out the inside metal bracket holding the pedal rubbers, and remove the axle assembly.

STEP THREE: Remove the locknut, washer, and adjustable cone over a rag or cup to catch the loose bearings.

STEP FOUR: Clean the bearings, pedal cups, and races in kerosene. Examine the bearings and cups for wear. Check the axle for straightness. Check the rubber for wear. Replace any damaged or worn parts.

STEP FIVE: Put a layer of grease such as Lubriplate Type A in the pedal cups; stick the bearings back in place and reassemble.

STEP SIX: Run the adjustable cone down snugly, and back off a quarter-turn. Insert the washer and locknut, and tighten the locknut.

STEP SEVEN: Check the pedal for tightness and side play. Loosen the locknut if the pedal is too tight and does not spin easily, back off the adjustable cone with a small screwdriver about an eighth of a turn, and retighten the locknut. Repeat until the pedal runs free. If the pedal has too much side play, loosen the locknut, tighten the adjustable cone an eighth of a turn, and retighten the locknut. Repeat until side play is eliminated.

Continental Pedals

British standard pedals (Fig. 117) and European-made rattrap pedals (Fig. 118) generally have a removable (righthand thread) dust cap. A basic difference between these pedals and American pedals is that the rubbers have to be removed on American pedals before the pedal bearings can be removed. Also, on European pedals, all you have to do to get at the pedal locknut, washer, and adjustable cone is to remove the dust cap.

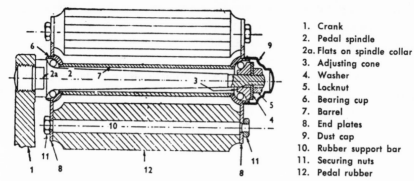

1. Crank
2. Pedal spindle
2a. Flats on spindle collar
3. Adjusting cone
4. Washer
5. Locknut
6. Bearing cup
7. Barrel
8. End plates
9. Dust cap
10. Rubber support bar
11. Securing nuts
12. Pedal rubber

Fig. 117: *Standard assembly-line pedal used on British three-speed bicycles. See legend for part identification. Reprinted with the permission of Temple Press Ltd. from "The Cycling Book of Maintenance."*

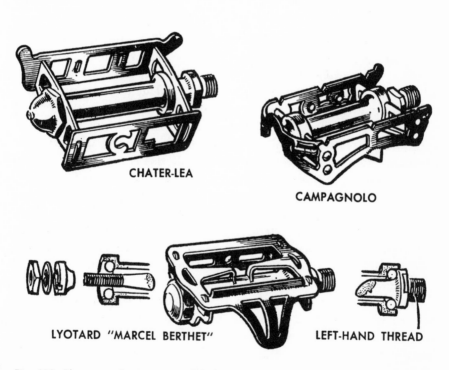

CHATER-LEA

CAMPAGNOLO

LYOTARD "MARCEL BERTHET"

LEFT-HAND THREAD

Fig. 118: *Three popular rattrap pedal designs: top left, Chater-Lea; top right Campagnolo; bottom, Lyotard "Marcel Berthet." Lip on the Lyotard makes inserting foot easier and faster.*

A very handy little tool to use with European pedals is a pedal wing-nut wrench which fits most pedal locknuts and which can be purchased for only fifty cents from any of the bicycle mail-order houses (see pages 317-18). Another very handy tool, indeed, if you do much bicycle mainte-nance, is a pedal wrench with thin jaws, which fits most pedals and which sells for around $3.00, from one of the bicycle mail-order houses.

Once you remove the dust cap, the rest of the steps in the maintenance —regreasing and assembly—follow Steps Three, Four, Five, Six, and Seven above.

HUBS

Multispeed and Coaster-Brake Hub Maintenance

There are four makes and a wide variety of one-, two-, three-, and five-speed integral rear hubs in common use on bicycles in this country. There is even an adapter kit to convert multispeed integral rear hubs into a six- or nine-speed machine, using a derailleur. A Japanese manufacturer makes a twelve-speed combination rear hub and derailleur which, if used with a double front chainwheel, will give you twenty-four speeds, and with a triple front chainwheel, thirty-six speeds. I don't know what you'd do with more than twelve or fifteen speeds, but if you want them, they're available. More on these combinations later in this chapter.

I am not going to attempt to give you detailed take-apart and assembly instructions for all these hubs; there are simply too many makes and models to make this practical. Hubs are a rather complicated assemblage of gears and mechanisms. (If Figure 119 doesn't scare you off, nothing will!) Many require special tools to assemble or disassemble, and the majority of bicycle dealers are competent to deal with most of them.

This section, therefore, will be limited to routine hub maintenance, ad-justment, and tips on correct usage. If you follow these instructions, your hub should last the life of the bicycle and seldom, if ever, need to be taken apart. However, if you really want to disassemble your rear hub, either out of curiosity or because you can't find a bicycle mechanic who knows how to fix it, you can obtain step-by-step illustrated assembly and dis-assembly instructions, complete with a list of spare parts, from the hub manufacturer or the bicycle manufacturers.

Bendix Rear Hubs

Bendix coaster-brake and multispeed hubs are used on Schwinn and some other makes of American bicycles, so we'll start with these hubs.

Bendix Automatic Coaster Brakes

The Bendix automatic coaster brake is a two-speed unit which contains both coaster brakes and a set of internal gears. This type of hub permits the cyclist to change gears by back-pedaling slightly, or to brake by back-pedaling, both without removing hands from the handlebars. It is well suited for a young rider, up to age twelve. There is a 32 percent decrease in gear ratio between high and low gears on this hub—enough to enable a young rider to negotiate hills fairly easily.

There are two types of Bendix coaster-brake two-speed hubs. The standard model is marked with three yellow bands around the hub shell. The other, which is marked with three blue bands around the hub shell, is the overdrive automatic unit. This has a direct drive and a high gear with a 47 percent gear ratio increase, which makes cycling a bit easier on hills. It is used on Schwinn Sting-Ray bicycles, among others.

Lubrication

Because all the working parts are inside the hub, these hubs don't require much maintenance, beyond regular lubrication about every month, and after long trips. Use a fairly light oil, equivalent to No. 20 SAE viscosity motor oil. Squirt about a teaspoonful into the hub through the hub hole provided for this purpose.

Also, once a year you should take the bicycle into the dealer and have him disassemble and regrease the hub and check for any worn or broken parts.

Since coaster brakes (*unlike* caliper brakes) need grease for proper operation and for long life, if you've made extensive tours in hilly country involving a lot of braking, it's a good idea to have your dealer disassemble the hub and regrease it when the tour is over, rather than wait until the year is up.

If the hub does not shift properly, makes grinding noises, shifts into low without back-pressure, or if the brakes fail, this means that new in-

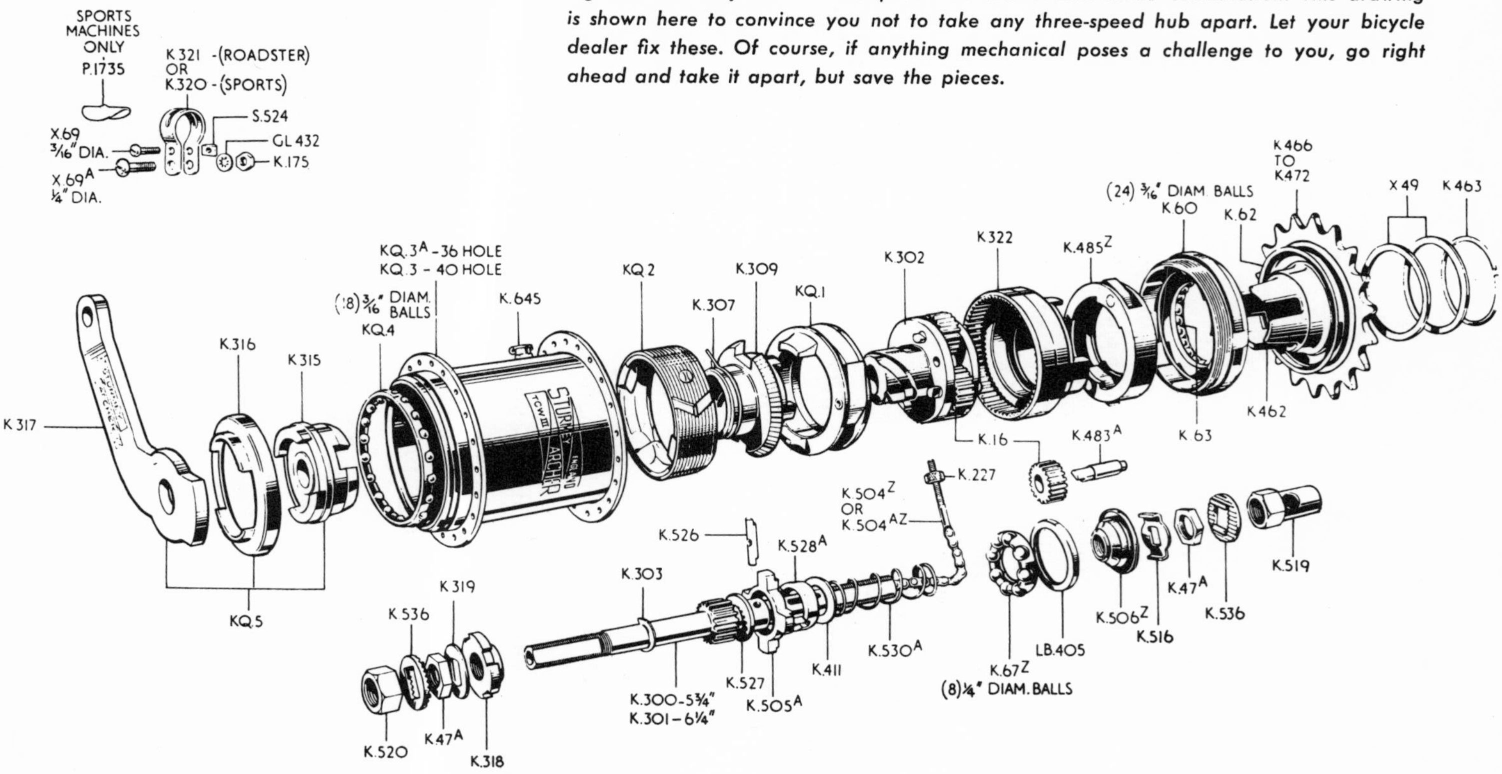

Fig. 119: Sturmey-Archer three-speed hub and coaster-brake combination. This drawing is shown here to convince you not to take any three-speed hub apart. Let your bicycle dealer fix these. Of course, if anything mechanical poses a challenge to you, go right ahead and take it apart, but save the pieces.

LEGEND

Part No. Description

Part No.	Description
GL432	Shake-proof Washer
K16	Planet Pinion
K47A	Cone Locknut
K60	Right Hand Ball-Ring
K62	Sprocket Dust Cap
K67Z	Ball Retainer—(8) ¼'' Ball
K175	Nut for X69A Bolt
K227	Locknut
K300	Axle 5¾''
K301	Axle 6¼''
K302	Planet Cage
K303	Axle Circlip
K307	Brake Actuating Spring
K309	Thrust Plate
K315	Left-Hand Cone
K316	(Chromium) Dust Cap for Left-Hand Cone
K317	Brake Arm
K318	Brake Arm Locknut
K319	Lock Washer
K320	Clip for Brake Arm (Sports)
K321	Clip for Brake Arm (Roadster)
K322	Gear Ring
K411	Thrust Washer
K462	Driver
K463	Driver Circlip
K466	Sprocket 16 Teeth
K472	Sprocket 22 Teeth
K483A	Planet Pinion Pin
K485Z	Gear Ring Pawl-Ring
K504Z	Gear Indicator Rod and Coupling. For 5¾'' Axle.

Part No. Description

Part No.	Description
K504AZ	Gear Indicator Rod and Coupling. For 6¼'' Axle.
K505A	Clutch
K506Z	Cone
K516	Right Hand Cone Locking-Washer
K519	Right Hand Axle Nut
K520	Left Hand Axle Nut
K526	Key
K527	Clutch Sleeve
K528A	Thrust Ring
K530A	Clutch Spring
K536	Serrated Axle Washer
K645	Lubricator
KQ1	Planet Cage Pawl Ring
KQ2	Brake Band
KQ3	40 Hole Shell and Left Hand Ball Cup Assembly
KQ3A	36 Hole Shell and Left Hand Ball Cup Assembly
KQ4	Ball Retainer—(18) 3/16'' Ball
KQ5	Brake Arm/Left Hand Cone/and Dust Cap Assembly
LB405	Dustcap
S524	Nut for X 69 Bolt
P1735	Strengthening Pad—For Sports Machines only
X49	Sprocket spacing Washer (1/16'')
X69	Clip Screw, 3/16'' Diameter
X69A	Clip Screw, ¼'' Diameter

ternal parts will be necessary. These can be installed by your bicycle dealer.

No routine operating adjustments are required on any Bendix hubs, making them even better for children and more child-proof than other hubs, which have wires attached to them.

All you need to remember, if you remove the rear wheel, is to refasten the coaster-brake clamp arm which clamps onto the rear fork stay.

Sturmey-Archer Multispeed Rear Hubs

Sturmey-Archer multispeed rear hubs are perhaps the most widely used of all hubs. They are used on Raleigh bicycles and other brand-new bicycles made by Raleigh such as Robin Hood, Hercules, and private label brands.

There are three- (Fig. 119) four-, five-speed and combination coaster-brake and three-speed Sturmey-Archer rear wheel hubs in use today. All of them have a number of things in common, one of which is that proper gear shifting is greatly dependent upon proper adjustment of working parts.

Lubrication is also very important. In fact, oil can evaporate from a hub between the time the bicycle leaves the factory and when you buy it, so be sure to have the dealer add a tablespoonful of *light* oil to the hub before you ride off.

When changing gears with any Sturmey-Archer hub, ease pedal pressure slightly, and change gears quickly.

Sturmey-Archer Trouble-Shooting

PROBLEM: Gears slip; they won't stay put in the gear selected.

SOLUTION: Adjust the indicator rod. Check your hub so you know which type you have, and follow the instructions on the indicator rod adjustment for your particular hub.

TCW, AW, AB, AG, and SW Hub Indicator Rod Adjustment

STEP ONE: Put the gear-shift lever in No. 2 position (or S5 five-speed hubs in third gear) (Fig. 120).

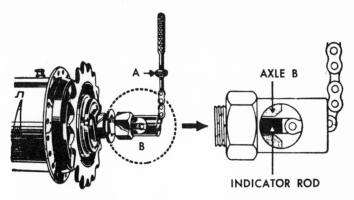

AXLE B

INDICATOR ROD

Fig. 120: *Cable adjustments for SW-TCW hubs, including locknut (A), and knurled section of cable (B). Indicator rod should be where shown for proper hub operation. Courtesy of Raleigh Industries, Limited*

STEP TWO: Unscrew the locknut (A, Fig. 120).

STEP THREE: Adjust the knurled section of the cable (B, Fig. 120) until the end of the indicator rod is exactly level with the end of the axle (B, Fig. 121). Check the location of the indicator rod through the "window" in the *righthand* nut on the axle (B, Fig. 120).

STEP FOUR: Tighten the locknut.

STEP FIVE: If you can't obtain enough adjustment with the cable connection at the hub, unscrew the nut and bolt holding the cable on the top tube (X 90, Fig. 122) and move the cable forward or rearward, as required. This step is known as "changing the fulcrum point" of the cable.

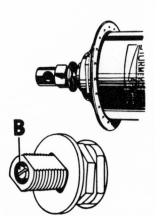

Fig. 121: *Rod "B" on a Sturmey-Archer hub should line up with end of axle for proper cable adjustment of Sturmey-Archer hubs.*

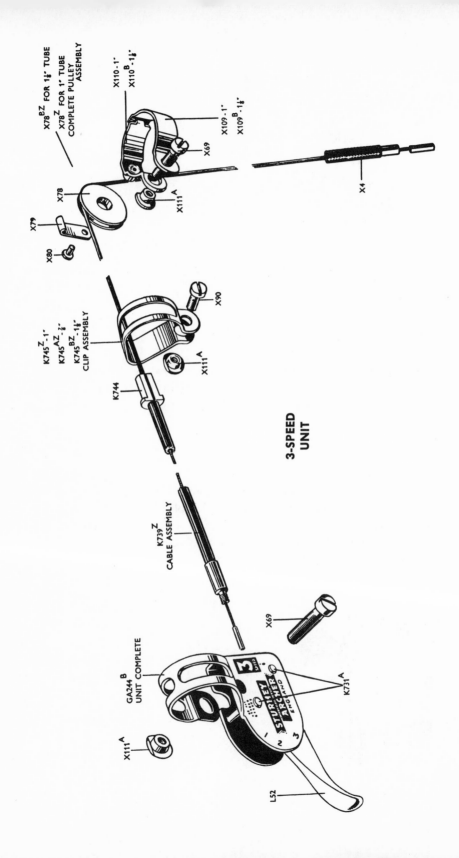

X78^BZ FOR 1⅛" TUBE
X78^Z FOR 1" TUBE
COMPLETE PULLEY ASSEMBLY

X110-1"
X110^B-1⅛"

X109-1"
X109^B-1⅛"

X69

X78

X79

X80

X111^A

X4

K745^Z-1"
K745^AZ-⅞"
K745^BZ-1⅛"
CLIP ASSEMBLY

X90

X111^A

K744

3-SPEED
UNIT

K739^Z
CABLE ASSEMBLY

X69

GA244^B
UNIT COMPLETE

K731^A

X111^A

STURMEY
ARCHER
ENGLAND

3

1 2 3

L52

Code No. Description

K739Z   Trigger Cable assembly—Give length of
        both inner and outer cable
K744   Fulcrum Sleeve
K745Z   Fulcrum clip complete 1″ diameter
K745AZ Fulcrum clip complete ⅞″ diameter
K745BZ Fulcrum clip complete 1⅛″ diameter
X90   Clip Screw
X78Z   Pulley complete for 1″ tube
X78BZ   Pulley complete for 1⅛″ tube
X69   Clip Screw
X78   Pulley Wheel only
X79   Pulley Arm
X80   Pulley Arm Screw
X110BZ Clip with Pulley Stud (1⅛″ tube)
X109B   Half-clip (1⅛″ tube)

	3-SPEED UNIT	4-SPEED UNIT	
			Description
	GC3B	GC4A	Trigger Control complete less pulley
	GA244B	GA246A	Trigger Unit
	L52	K723	Trigger Lever
	K731A	K731A	Pivot Pin
	L55	K722	Trigger Pawl
	L56	K738	Trigger Spring
	X69	X69	Clip Screw
	X111A	X111A	Clip Screw Nut

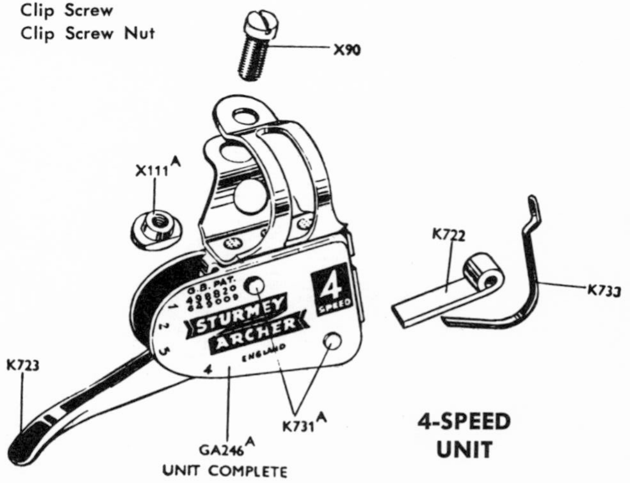

4-SPEED UNIT

K733

K722

X90

K731

GA246
UNIT COMPLETE

X111

K723

Fig. 122: Trigger control gear-shift lever for 3- and 4-speed Sturmey-Archer hubs. If you cannot get enough adjustment with the cable locknuts at the hub, loosen nut X90 and slide clip assembly further forward about a half-inch, and retighten.

AM, ASC, and AC Sturmey-Archer Hub Indicator Rod Adjustment

The only difference between indicator rod adjustment for these hubs and other Sturmey-Archer hubs lies in the location of the indicator rod adjustment indicator. On AM, ASC, and AC hubs, the indicator rod is in the correct position when the end of the rod is level with the end of the axle on the *lefthand* side of the hub. This is the side opposite the chain, or left side as you face the front of the bicycle.

Adjustment of the indicator rod should be made as shown above.

If gears still slip or change noisily after the indicator rod has been adjusted, wear on the internal parts in the hub is indicated. Take the bicycle to your dealer for repairs, or, if you wish to make them yourself, write to the bicycle manufacturer or see your dealer for assembly and disassembly instructions and the special tools that are needed.

Cable Change on Sturmey-Archer "Sportshift"

Sturmey-Archer also makes a gear-shift mechanism for their three-speed hubs, which is mounted on the top tube. Follow these steps to change cables:

STEP ONE: Loosen the locknut on the hub cable at the hub, and unscrew the knurled ferrule until the cable is free at the hub end.

STEP TWO: Remove the center screw from the control unit (gear-shift unit) and remove the cover from the plastic cover plate.

STEP THREE: Push the control lever to the No. 3 position, and remove the old cable. Pull the old cable through the slot of the cable anchorage and over the pulley wheel to remove the entire cable.

STEP FOUR: Readjust the cable by moving the lever to the No. 2 position and adjusting the cable ferrule at the hub end until the indicator rod is in the correct location for the type of Sturmey-Archer hub involved. (TCW, AW, AG, AB, and SW hubs have a different adjustment from AM, ASC, the AC Sturmey-Archer hubs. See page 270 for details.)

Here are common symptoms of Sturmey-Archer hub problems, their causes and their solutions. If hub needs disassembly, I recommend you let your bicycle shop do it.

PROBLEM: Sluggish gear change.
CAUSE: Cable binding or worn toggle link chain.
SOLUTION: Lubricate or replace cables. Lubricate gear-shift unit.

PROBLEM: No gear at all; pedals turn, wheel doesn't.
CAUSE: Internal pawls stuck or held in place by too heavy oil.
SOLUTION: Add light oil. If this does not free up, dismantle hub. Clean parts. Reassemble and oil again.

CAUSE: Bent axle.
SOLUTION: Dismantle hub. Replace axle.

CAUSE: Distorted axle spring.
SOLUTION: Replace spring (requires hub disassembly).

PROBLEM: Hub runs stiffly, drags on pedals when free-wheeling, wheel seems to "bind."
CAUSE: Chain stay ends not parallel. When the axle nuts are tightened, this causes the axle to be "sprung" out of true, which, in turn, makes the internal hub parts "bind."
SOLUTION: Straighten the chain stay ends, or add packing washers on the lefthand side to align.

CAUSE: Corrosion of hub working parts due to nonlubrication.
SOLUTION: Disassemble the hub. Check and replace worn parts. Re-lubricate. Follow lubrication instructions above.

PROBLEM: Slips in any gear.
CAUSE: On S5 hubs, this could be a kinked gear cable. On other hubs, internal parts are worn or incorrectly installed.
SOLUTION: Replace cable or reassemble hub with new parts as needed.

PROBLEM: On TCW (coaster-brake and three-speed) hub combinations *only,* brakes are noisy or "shudder" when applied.
CAUSE: Loose brake arm clip.
SOLUTION: Tighten clip nuts and bolts.

PROBLEM: On TCW hubs only, internal brakes in hub "grab" on application.
CAUSE: Lack of oil in rear hub.
SOLUTION: Add good quality *thin* oil, SAE 20 or thinner.

General Instructions

Sometimes even when you take the steps to correct any of the problems listed above, you will still not have corrected them. If this happens to you, there is probably wear in the internal parts of the hub. Disassemble the hub, clean it, and inspect the parts. I do not recommend that the average bicycle owner attempt to replace any of the interior parts of these hubs. But, if you want to anyway, trouble-shooting charts and hub assembly data can be obtained from the manufacturers.

In any case, do not attempt to adjust the rear wheel cones on multi-speed hubs. If the wheel binds, or shows side-play, and you think that cone adjustment is the answer, let your dealer do it. Some hubs have factory-adjusted cones, and you can ruin the hub if you try to adjust them yourself, without following a detailed instruction manual.

Sturmey-Archer Trigger (Gear-Shift) Control Maintenance

There isn't much that can go wrong with a gear shift (Fig. 123) unless you bend it accidentally. If you do, it should be replaced.

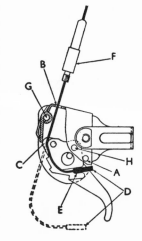

Fig. 123: *Typical Sturmey-Archer gear shift. To remove control wire, it is not necessary to remove control from handlebar if the lever can be pulled back far enough to allow cable nipple to pass between pawl and ratchet plate. Procedure is (1) detach inner wire from indicator chain at hub, and (2) outer casing from fulcrum clip. Pull cable ferrule (F) upward until screw engages that of control casing at (B), then unscrew ferrule. Pull lever right back beyond bottom gear position to stop (A), push inner wire through to detach nipple from ratchet plate, then pull wire out between pawl and ratchet at (C) and finally through threaded hole (B).*

To fit control wire, pull lever right back beyond bottom gear position to stop (A) and insert wire through threaded hole (B) and between pawl and ratchet plate at (C). Wire nipple (D) is then fitted into notch (E) and cable ferrule (F) screwed into (B) until it rotates freely. Keeping tension on wire, push lever forward into top gear position. Control is then ready for reconnection.

Cables do fray, wear, and break, however, and you should know how to replace the gear-shift cable (or cables, on an S5 five-speed hub).

Trigger Control Cable Replacement, Three- and Four-Speed Hubs

STEP ONE: (Note: You do not have to remove the control mechanism from the handlebars if you can pull the lever back far enough to permit the cable nipple to pass between the pawl and ratchet plate.) Remove the inner wire from the indicator chain at the hub.

STEP TWO: Remove the outer wire casing (the spaghetti tube) from the fulcrum clip on the top tube (or, if it is a woman's model, from the top of the two down tubes).

STEP THREE: Pull the cable ferrule upward (so that the metal sleeve is entering the gear shift) until the ferrule screw (which you can't see because it's in the control casing) engages the control casing. Then, unscrew the ferrule.

STEP FOUR: Pull the control lever back beyond the bottom gear position as far as it can go. Push the cable (inner wire) through so you can remove the cable nipple (leaded end) from the ratchet plate, then pull the wire out between the pawl and ratchet and through the threaded hole.

STEP FIVE: To replace an old cable with a new one, reverse Steps One through Four, above.

Fitting Gear-Shift Cable to Frame (Sturmey-Archer)

When you install a new cable and its spaghetti cover on the bicycle frame, be sure to have the cable and cover long enough so you can turn the handlebars through their full movement in both directions. However, do not overdo it. Make it just long enough for adequate handlebar movement.

Standard control wire length for most bicycles with Sturmey-Archer multispeed hubs and handlebar controls is 54½ inches with a spaghetti cover length of 17½ inches. For controls mounted on the top tube, standard lengths are thirty-two, thirty-four, and thirty-six inches.

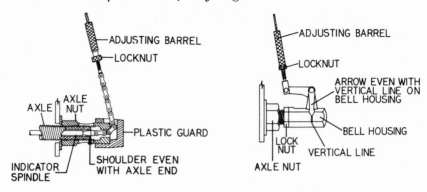

Fig. 124: *Right- and left-hand gear-shift cables for Sturmey-Archer five-speed hubs.*

For Sturmey-Archer Five-Speed Hubs

When installing new cables on Sturmey-Archer five-speed rear hubs (Fig. 124), follow this procedure:

STEP ONE: For the righthand gear-shift lever, follow the same procedure as for standard handlebar flick control. Screw down the locknut (Fig. 124).

STEP TWO: For the lefthand lever, push the lefthand lever to the forward position, and screw the cable connector to the bellcrank (the metal connecting piece between the cable and axle, held onto the axle by a nut). Screw the cable connector (1) to the bellcrank just two or three turns, no more.

STEP THREE: Push the lefthand lever to the backward position, and screw the cable connector until all cable slackness is eliminated.

STEP FOUR: With light pressure, push the bellcrank arm forward and, at the same time, turn the wheel backward or forward. If the gears are not fully engaged, the bellcrank arm will move farther forward.

STEP FIVE: Screw the cable connector as far as possible, and secure with the locknut.

How to Convert Sturmey-Archer SW or AW Hubs to Nine-Speed

If you're going on a tour, particularly if you are going to carry a load of gear and will have to climb hills, you can buy either a lightweight, ten-speed, derailleur-equipped bicycle with a wide range of gear ratios (see page 118 for discussion of gear ratios) or install a conversion kit on your Sturmey-Archer rear hub to give you a wider range of gears in both directions.

To convert your Sturmey-Archer rear hub to a nine-speed gear, you can install a Cyclo-Benelux Conversion Kit, which costs about $12.00. You will also need a three-gear sprocket, costing $3.75.

Since the Cyclo-Benelux Conversion Kit comes with complete installation instructions, which are fairly easy to follow, I will not repeat them here. A word of warning, though. Be sure to order the correct conversion kit for your hub. You can order a kit from any of the bicycle mail-order shops listed on pages 317-18. But you must specify whether your hub is an AW or SW model, and tell the bicycle shop whether you have a threaded or a splined driver. If your Sturmey-Archer three-speed hub is more than eight years old, it will most likely use a threaded driver. You can tell a threaded from a splined driver by checking to see if a split snap ring is in the center of the sprocket. If so, the driver is splined.

The Cyclo-Benelux Conversion Kit comes complete with a Benelux derailleur and gear-shift lever.

Note: Some rear fork stays are quite thick, which means you will have to have a longer axle fitted to your Sturmey-Archer hub. This job is best left to a bicycle mechanic.

You will also need two one-eighth-inch washers, one on both sides of the hub spindle, to push the fork stays out to accommodate the extra width of the gear cluster.

To install the conversion unit, you will need a chain rivet removing and installing tool (which costs about $1.75 and can be bought at any bicycle store or from any bicycle mail-order house), and an additional four to six extra links for your chain. Make sure you buy links that are the same make as your chain.

To determine how many extra links to add to your chain, see the discussion on chain length on page 249.

General Instructions on Maintenance, Adjustment, and Alignment of Hubs

STURMEY-ARCHER HUBS

For efficient cycling with minimum effort, as well as for proper operation of the rear hub, it is important that the rear sprocket of any rear hub, whether coaster brake or multispeed, line up with the front chainwheel.

For more information on alignment, see the discussion on pages 233-34 in the section on derailleurs.

To align Sturmey-Archer rear hubs, all you need do is change the rear sprocket a little, which is easy. You have an alignment adjustment of between 1½ inches and 1¾ inches in ¹⁄₁₆-inch increments. To change alignments simply follow these steps:

STEP ONE: Pry off the locknut (circlip) with a small screwdriver. (This is the round springlike clip that fits into a groove around the sprocket side of the hub—outboard of the sprocket.) Snap this ring out.

STEP TWO: Slide the sprocket off the hub, along with the washers on either side of the sprocket. To change alignment, you have a number of choices:

1. Face the dished (concave) side of the sprocket toward the outside of the hub. Put all the washers on one side or the other, or one washer on each side.
2. Put dished side toward the hub, washers as above. This gives you a total of six adjustments.

Incidentally, if you wish to change the gear ratio, up or down, on any Sturmey-Archer hub, simply ask your bicycle dealer to send to Raleigh of America in Boston for the sprocket with the number of teeth you desire. A larger sprocket with more teeth will give you a larger ratio (less speed in all gears but more hill-climbing ability), while a smaller sprocket will give you more speed, but hills will be more difficult to negotiate (all other factors, such as your physical condition, being equal, that is).

SHIMANO MULTISPEED HUBS

A number of American bicycle manufacturers use Japanese-made Shimano multispeed rear hubs. The Shimano hub, in my opinion, is every bit as good as any American or European multispeed hub and is a good deal easier to repair. If you plan to remove this hub, and disassemble and reassemble it, you will, however, need two special tools—a split snap ring remover and a ballcup remover—which you will have to order through your bicycle store.

The Shimano 3.3.3. three-speed hub is the most widely used of the Shimano units. Shimano publishes well-illustrated, easily understood, step-by-step disassembly, repair, and reassembly instructions. Repair parts are available in this country. However, since many of the bicycles sold in discount houses and department stores (American and foreign-made) use Shimano hubs, you may find that bicycle dealers are unwilling or unable to service them. This is why a knowledge of how to maintain them well is essential. Lubrication is very important. Use a light oil, adding about a teaspoonful every thirty days and after each long ride.

There are two types of Shimano gear-shift levers for this hub, both positive "click-stop" types. The first is a handlebar "twistgrip" similar to a motorcycle speed control, and the second is a lever, usually mounted on the top tube.

To remove a frayed wire from the handlebar twistgrip:

STEP ONE: Loosen the locknut on the handlebar twistgrip and remove the ferrule and wire.

STEP TWO: Remove the cable cover from the fulcrum stopper on the top tube.

STEP THREE: Unscrew the locknut on the bellcrank on the rear wheel and unscrew the knurled cable nut from the bellcrank lever. At this point, the cable and cable cover should be removable from the bicycle. Install the new cable and cover, reversing Steps One, Two, and Three.

STEP FOUR: The adjustment for both the twistgrip and the lever-type control should start with the shift in the "N" position. At this position, the red "N" on the bellcrank should be centered in the "window" of the bell-crank or, on older models of this hub, the arrow indicator should be centered over the indicating line on the bellcrank.

STEP FIVE: If the centering in Step Four cannot be made, move the fulcrum stop on the top tube forward or backward, as necessary, to make more or less cable slack as needed; then readjust at the bellcrank end by loosening the cable locknut and screwing the cable ferrule in or out as required. This step applies for both twistgrip and lever-type controls.

Note: Wire cables on any bicycle will stretch in time, so you will find it necessary to readjust the shift cable from time to time, as per Step Five.

PROBLEM: In the "H" shift position, the pedal skips or won't turn.
CAUSE: Pawl is worn or installed backward.
SOLUTION: Disassemble the hub and install new pawl and pawl spring (a job for the bicycle mechanic).

PROBLEM: Pedal skips at "N" position.
CAUSE: Planet cage pawl worn or broken, or pawl spring broken.
SOLUTION: Disassemble hub and replace defective parts (a job for the bicycle mechanic).

PROBLEM: Gears are stuck or do not change smoothly.
CAUSE: Broken parts are caught up in hub mechanism.
SOLUTION: Complete hub overhaul (a job for the bicycle mechanic).

PROBLEM: Hub is noisy.
CAUSE: Rusty mechanism due to lack of oil.
SOLUTION: If rust has proceeded far enough, a new hub may have to be installed. Try oiling the hub first. If this doesn't work, disassemble the hub and look for rusted parts. Install new parts as needed (a job for the bicycle mechanic).

PROBLEM: Erratic shifting.
CAUSE: Control cable not set correctly.
SOLUTION: Adjust as described under Steps Four and Five above.

The Shimano click-stop shift lever is used on a number of twenty- and twenty-four-inch-wheel bicycles, as well as on twenty-six-inch-wheel machines. It is described as a "Three on the Bar" shift by American advertising writers. To change the cables on the "stick" shift, follow these steps.

STEP ONE: Pry out the plastic dust cover on the round section at the bottom of the lever, which will reveal a screw in the center of the space.

STEP TWO: Remove the lever hub screw. The factory has this screw down rather tight, so use a good screwdriver and apply some elbow grease. Be careful not to lose the spacing washers under the nut, and to replace them in the same order.

STEP THREE: With the lever screw removed, the lever handle and wire will come off the lever slip in one piece. Remove the metal dust cover. Remove the cable nipple (leaded end) from its seat in the lever handle, and remove the cable and cable cover, replacing them with the new cable and cover by reversing the above steps.

The Shimano Combi-12 uses a combination four-speed derailleur and three-speed rear hub, for a total of twelve gear changes (twenty-four gear changes if a double chainwheel is used, thirty-six if a triple chainwheel is used).

Full instructions on the care, adjustment, and alignment of derailleurs are given on pages 233-49. Since the three-speed section of the Combi-12 is identical to the standard Shimano 3.3.3. three-speed hub, maintenance and adjustment instructions already given in this section for this hub apply to the Combi-12 hub unit. Cable-changing procedures for both lever gear shifts have already been described.

There is, however, a difference between the derailleur lever on the Combi-12 and the conventional derailleur gear-shift levers. Standard levers have no click stops. The rider must adjust the lever position so that the derailleur is not pushing the chain part way off a cog and causing a grinding noise from the rear wheel while under way. The Shimano lever has click stops, so fine adjustment of the lever cannot be made to prevent the chain from running part way off a cog and causing a grinding noise.

Most youngsters today seem to be able to cheerfully ignore all sorts of mechanical noises which would annoy experienced adult cyclists. The only time young folks complain about their bicycles is when the wheels stop turning, which is too late. Therefore, the Shimano click-stop lever shift is a real boon for the adult who has to fix his child's bicycle. Once the cable adjustments are properly made so the click stops and you move the derailleur to the correct position for each hub external gear, you don't have to make any further adjustment of the lever. All you have to do is watch out for later stretching of the cable. When it stretches—and it will —you'll need to readjust the cable position as follows:

STEP ONE: A stretched wire will cause an inaccurate setting of the click stop on the three-speed hub. Put the gear-shift lever in *top* position. If speed change cannot then be made to the *second* position, readjust by loosening the wire adjusting nut at the bellcrank and loosen or tighten the knurled ferrule on the cable as necessary. Then retighten the locknut.

STEP TWO: Make sure the indicator on the bellcrank is pointing directly to the red indicator line, with the three-speed lever in the "N" position.

To adjust the derailleur wire:

STEP ONE: Put lever in *top* position. If the cable is not tight (taut), cable tension is correct.

STEP TWO: Now move the pedals (the bicycle should be upside down or hung from the ceiling) and change the gears through the four gear changes. Make sure the derailleur moves the chain from highest to lowest gear and back, smoothly.

STEP THREE: If the lever cannot be put into the *second* position easily, tighten the wire by loosening the locknut at the camp on the seat stay and adjusting the knurled ferrule as necessary. Retighten the locknut.

STEP FOUR: Check adjustment by moving the lever to *top* position, as you turn the pedals. If the lever won't go into *top* position easily, loosen the wire slightly. Now, move the lever through all the gear ranges and adjust the cable as needed, if there is any noise in any of the gear-click stops.

TORPEDO DUOMATIC HUBS

Some American and imported bicycles are fitted with a West German-made two-speed hub with a foot-operated gear change and back-pedaling brake. This hub, which is called a Torpedo Duomatic, is similar in design to the Bendix automatic two-speed hub with coaster brake, and requires the same type of maintenance. Just follow the same instructions as for the Bendix unit (see pages 267-70).

I do not recommend your trying to dismantle this hub, unless you make sure you have complete step-by-step illustrated instructions, which can be obtained through your bicycle dealer.

Torpedo also makes a two-speed hub without the coaster brake, for use with caliper-brake-equipped bicycles. Maintenance instructions for this hub are the same as for the Bendix automatic hub; just feed it some light oil once a month after long trips, and if any strange sounds come from it, rush the bicycle to the nearest bicycle shop. If your mechanic can't (or won't) fix the hub, write to the Torpedo distributor or the bicycle manufacturer for the name of the closest *bicycle store* (not discount or department store) that can do this work.

As on most of the multispeed rear hubs used on bicycles in this country, the sprocket on the Torpedo hub can be easily changed to one with more teeth for touring in hilly country, or to one with fewer teeth for faster riding where the going is flat and easy. If you do change sprockets, remember that you must order the same make of sprocket as your hub, because sprockets are not interchangeable from one make of hub to the other.

Apropos of changing parts, parts from different makes of bicycles and bicycle components are more likely *not* to be interchangeable, except for mundane things such as tires, seats, and spokes. Be careful about ordering everything else!

A WORD OF WARNING

Before you take your multispeed rear hub to a bicycle shop, phone the shop to make sure it has the parts on hand or can assure you it is willing to go to the trouble to order them for you from its wholesaler. The problem is that hardly any bicycle shop can afford to carry the tremendous number of parts it would take to be able to service all American, English, and Japanese hubs that are popularly used in this country.

A related problem is that not all wholesalers carry all parts, and if the bike shop proprietor can't find what he needs from his own wholesaler, the chances are very good that he'll tell you they aren't available. If this happens to you, keep calling dealers until you find one who says he can and does repair the type and make of hub you have.

CRANKS

Crank Maintenance

The bottom bracket and crank assembly (Fig. 125), located at the point where the seat and down tubes meet, is one of the most highly

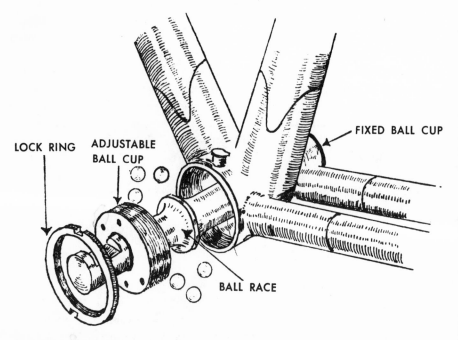

Fig. 125: *Typical bottom-bracket assembly. More expensive bicycles do not have an oil cup. Oil is well suited to pressures on bottom-bracket bearings. Grease is best, which means annual disassembly, cleaning, and regreasing of bottom-bracket components. Reprinted by permission of Temple Press Ltd. from "The Cycling Book of Maintenance."*

stressed parts of the bicycle. The entire assembly should be removed, cleaned, and regreased at least once a year. Side play must be removed by adjusting the ball cup nut or lock ring, depending on your type of bicycle. Above all, the chainwheel assembly must spin freely.

Occasionally you should turn your bicycle upside down or hang it from the ceiling and, after removing the chain, spin the cranks and listen for grinding noises from the bottom bracket. If you hear any such racket, regard it as a signal that the axle and its bearings need cleaning and regreasing.

Types of Bottom Bracket and Chainwheel Assemblies

There are three basic types of crank assemblies: one piece, three-piece cottered, and three-piece cotterless. American-made bikes, such as Schwinn (except Paramount), Huffy, Murray-Ohio, and others, use one-piece forged cranks with bearings in races.

European bicycles use either cottered cranks (Fig. 126), with a heavy steel cotter pin or key holding the crank on the axle, or cotterless cranks (Fig. 127), using more complicated and more expensive (but easier-to-remove) construction. Chainwheel and cranks can be either all steel or dural, a high-tensile, strong aluminum alloy metal. The better cranks and chainwheel assemblies, such as Campagnolo, T. A., Stronglight, and Williams, are of dural and cotterless design.

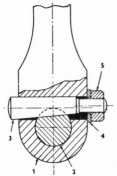

1. Crank (lefthand)
2. Bracket axle
3. Cotter pin
4. Washer
5. Nut

Fig. 126: *Typical cottered crank. Reprinted with the permission of Temple Press Ltd. from "The Cycling Book of Maintenance."*

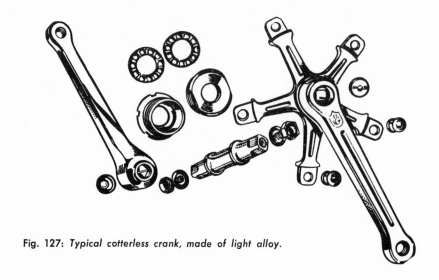

Fig. 127: *Typical cotterless crank, made of light alloy.*

American Bottom Bracket Maintenance

To remove the one-piece crank set from an American bicycle, you will need an adjustable ten-inch crescent wrench, a pedal wrench, a medium-sized screw driver, a six-inch punch with square end, and a hammer.

STEP ONE: Remove the chain guard, if you have one.

STEP TWO: Remove the left pedal, if you have a solid crank-spindle assembly. The English racers and European bikes have three-piece sys-tems—two cranks and one spindle—so it is not necessary to remove the left pedal on these. Remember, this pedal has a lefthand thread, so it must be removed clockwise.

STEP THREE: With the crescent wrench, remove the locknut on the bottom bracket. Then remove the lock washer, the adjusting cone, and the left ball-bearing retainer cage, with bearings inside.

STEP FOUR: Slip the bearing retainer out on the chainwheel side so that it slides down the axle. Then carefully maneuver the chainwheel and crank assembly out through the right side of the bottom bracket.

STEP FIVE: Examine the ball-bearing retainer and race. If the balls fall out of the retainer, or are cracked, or if race is damaged, replace the retainer and race with an exact duplicate (which can be obtained from most bicycle shops).

STEP SIX: Check the cups in the bottom bracket. If they are grooved, pop them out of the bottom bracket with a punch and a hammer, and replace them with an exact duplicate. Tap the new cups in place all around the circumference until the cup is seated squarely against the bottom bracket.

STEP SEVEN: After cleaning all parts, put a layer of any good quality heavy-duty grease (such as Lubriplate Type A) in the cups.

STEP EIGHT: Grease thoroughly and install the right bearing retainer on the crank assembly, making sure that the retainer is in the right direction, so that it fits snugly in the cup.

STEP NINE: Work the crank back through the right side of the hanger, making sure the right bearing retainer is in correctly and sits snugly against the right cone.

STEP TEN: Pack grease thoroughly into the left bearing retainer and install it on the crank, pushing it into the left cup. Screw on the adjusting cone till it snuggles up against the bearing retainer. Then, back it off about a quarter-turn.

STEP ELEVEN: Install the lock washer and locknut. Tighten the locknut.

STEP TWELVE: Install the left pedal. Grasp the cranks. If there is any side movement in the chainwheel, or if you feel any side movement (looseness) as you push the cranks from one side to the other, loosen the locknut, tighten the adjusting cone very slightly, and tighten the locknut.

STEP THIRTEEN: When the side play is removed, check for free-running by spinning the chainwheel with the chain slipped off. If the chainwheel does not turn freely, loosen the locknut, back off the adjusting cone very slightly, and retighten the locknut. Remember, it is better to have a little side play than it is to have the adjusting cones too tight.

European Cotter Crank Maintenance

European bicycles, and American bicycles that use European components, should also have their crank axle bearings disassembled, cleaned, and regreased once or twice a year (depending on bicycle use).

To remove cotter cranks, follow this procedure:

STEP ONE: Remove the chain.

STEP TWO: If you remove both wheels, the frame will be lighter and less awkward to handle. Put a heavy block of hard wood in a vise, V-notched so that the cotter key can be hammered out into the notch. *Hold the crank over the notch* (not the bottom bracket!), and unscrew the nut on the cotter key two or three turns. Loosen the cotter key with a sharp blow from a wooden mallet or hammer. Unscrew the cotter nut and remove it and the washer. If the cotter key is still tight, use a key punch very carefully so as not to damage the threads of the cotter key. Ideally you should be able to reuse the cotter key, because unless you are fortunate enough to find a cotter key with the exact flat of your original, you can have a problem filing and refitting another key. It is vitally important to use the hard wood support under the crank when hammering out the cotter to avoid damaging the bearings and axle.

Remove the cotters from the left- and righthand crank, and slide off both cranks and the chainwheel from the axle.

STEP THREE: Remove the locking ring, or locknut, with the special "C" wrench that came with your bicycle (or buy one from any bicycle shop). The "C" wrench has a special grip which fits into one of the notches on the locknut. The locknut has a righthand (normal) thread.

STEP FOUR: For this step I like to lay the bicycle on its side, over a large cloth or newspaper, to catch the free balls. Generally, European makes have balls free, rather than in races. (One important exception is Campagnolo, which manufactures balls within races.) When you take anything apart on European models, ball-bearings will run all over the place, unless you catch them as you disassemble. Remove the adjustable cone, and catch the balls as they come out of the bottom bracket. Try not to let the balls roll up the hollow bicycle frame. If they do you will have to tilt the frame until you roll them out, or buy new balls (which, incidentally, you can do from any of the bicycle mail-order houses, pages 317-18), if you know their diameter.

STEP FIVE: Clean the balls, cups, axle nuts, and the inside of the bottom bracket thoroughly with kerosene.

STEP SIX: Inspect the balls, axle races, and cups carefully. If there is any pitting in the axle or cup races, replace them. Balls should be clean and bright. If any of them show rust, pitting, or cracks, replace them with an entire set of new ones. You should also check the axle cotter notches for cracks and replace the axle if notches are apparent. In replacing the axle, balls, or cups, do not let the bicycle dealer sell you anything but an exact duplicate of what you need. If you have Japanese parts and your nearest bicycle store does not handle these parts, you can order them directly from Japan, if you know the name of the manufacturer.

STEP SEVEN: Put a layer of grease such as Lubriplate Type A in the righthand bearing cup in the bottom bracket (the bicycle should be lying on its right side). Insert enough balls in the cup (the grease will hold them in place) almost to fill the cup. You must have an equal number of balls on each side (unless there is a specific reason for them to be uneven). It is a good idea to count the balls as you take them out. Do not put in more balls than the cup will hold with a little room to spare. You can crowd almost one more ball than the cup should hold, but you will be short one ball for the lefthand cup, or if you have new balls, you will find that the axle won't fit snugly and you can't draw up on the adjustable cup properly. Put more grease over the balls once you have stuck them into the first layer of grease in the cup.

STEP EIGHT: Carefully stick the axle, long side first (the chainwheel side), into the bottom bracket and set it firmly against the balls in the righthand cup.

STEP NINE: Put a layer of grease in the adjustable cup, insert the remaining balls, add another layer of grease over the balls, and carefully thread the cup into the bottom bracket.

STEP TEN: Tighten the adjustable cup until it is just snug, and back off about a quarter-turn. Tighten the locknut.

STEP ELEVEN: Check the axle for side play, and readjust the cup and locknut as necessary. Check the axle rotation. It must rotate freely, without binding.

STEP TWELVE: Sight down the cranks for straightness. If they are bent, it is best to replace them with an exact duplicate.

STEP THIRTEEN: Slide the cranks onto the axle, with the cotter hole opposite the axle slot. Unless you have damaged the threads of the cotter key by banging them out with a hammer, you can reuse the old ones. If you have to fit a new cotter key, try to get a duplicate of the old one. Chances are you won't be able to buy an exact duplicate, for reasons I have never been able to learn. However, cotter keys are made of fairly soft steel, and you should be able, with a fine file, to file down a new key in a vise, to duplicate the old cotter key. Be careful, in filing, that you wind up with the cotter surface flat and not rounded off at the edges. And do not file off too much steel, because the cotter key will fit too far into the crank, and you won't be able to tighten up the cotter nut snugly on the crank.

STEP FOURTEEN: Insert the washers and the nuts on the cotter key and pull them up just enough to tighten the cotter down on the axle. The reason for the cotter nut is to hold a drive fit. If you simply try to tighten the cotter with the cotter nut and cycle off, you will find, after a few miles, that your cranks have worked loose, and, if you keep cycling, you'll need new cranks and a new axle.

STEP FIFTEEN: Using the same V-notched piece of hard wood in the vise that you used to drive out the cotter pins, support the bottom of each crank (in turn) on the wood and, with two or three firm blows, drive the cotter keys home. Then tighten the cotter nuts and give the cotter one more final blow with the hammer.

STEP SIXTEEN: With the chain still removed, spin the cranks by hand and check for binding. The cranks should revolve freely and come to a stop slowly. If they stop suddenly, or feel tight, loosen the locknut on the bottom bracket and back off the adjustable cup about an eighth-turn, and retighten the locknut. Check again for binding. Check also for end or side play by grasping each crank and pulling from side to side. Remove end play by readjusting the cup and the locknut, as outlined above. Reinstall the pedals and chain.

European Cotterless Crank Maintenance

Cotterless crank design varies by make, but axles and adjustable cups do not, so Steps Three through Twelve, above, apply also to cotterless cranks. There are major differences, however, in removing cotterless cranks and cotter cranks.

The first thing to remember about any make of cotterless crank (except for the axle, bearings, cups, and bolts) is that it is not made of steel; it is dural, an aluminum alloy. Therefore, you cannot take up on threads with the muscle you would use on a steel bolt and nut.

You will need some special tools to remove and reassemble cotterless cranks. Tools are made especially for either Campagnolo (Italian), Stronglight (French), or Williams (English) cranks. If you have T. A. Criterium (French) or Williams cotterless cranks, make sure your bicycle dealer sells you a special set of tools for removing them. Cotterless crank tools cost from $2.50 to $4.00 a set, depending on the make of crank they are to be used for.

Removing Cotterless Cranks

STEP ONE: Remove the chain.

STEP TWO: Remove the dust cap from the crank with a special tool designed for your particular make.

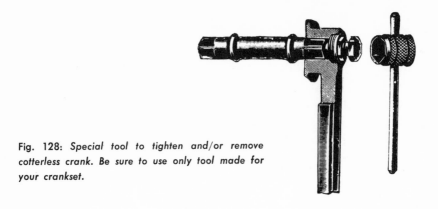

Fig. 128: *Special tool to tighten and/or remove cotterless crank. Be sure to use only tool made for your crankset.*

STEP THREE: Using your crank tools, remove the crank nut from each crank.

STEP FOUR: Use your extractor tool to press the crank off the axle. You will frequently find that cotterless cranks are on too tight for easy removal. Gene Portuesi says that racing cotterless cranks, in particular, are often too tight for removal with a crank tool. The problem, Portuesi states, is that if you try to draw the crank out by the leverage or force of the extractor alone, this tool, which is screwed into the crank, will pull off and ruin the threads inside the crank.

The cotterless crank tool is in two parts. One part, the socket wrench, is for removing the crank holding screw which screws into the axle. The other part of this tool is used to extract the crank off the axle. It works like a rear wheel remover on a car. After the holding screw is removed, the extractor tool is screwed snugly into the crank and taken up tight to force the crank off the axle. Opposing forces are between crank threads and axle.

If the crank is too tight, Portuesi recommends (and I think this is a good idea) that you push the extractor in tight, and tap it gently with a light ballpeen hammer. This should be continued by turning the extractor

⅛ turn after each tap and tapping again, repeating this until the crank "breaks" loose.

STEP FIVE: When reinstalling Campagnolo, Stronglight, and T. A. Professional cranks, lightly oil the crank bolt threads and washers, and the Stronglight axle surfaces.

STEP SIX: To disassemble, regrease, and reassemble the axle and bearing, follow the steps given above under instructions for cotter cranks.

STEP SEVEN: After every fifty miles, for the first 150 miles after reassembly of any cotterless crank, retighten the crank bolt on both cranks. It is very important to tighten after reassembly. If the cranks work just the least bit loose on the axle, the force of pedaling can destroy the fine-machined fit of the crank alloy, which is softer than the steel axle.

Do not disassemble these cranks any more often than necessary. They are dural, and can stand only so many tightenings. They will last a long time, however, if they are maintained properly.

T. A. Criterium Cranks

T. A. Criterium cranks are an interesting adaptation or compromise between a cottered and a cotterless crank. They have the advantage of not needing a special tool to remove the crank. These cranks also can be moved laterally on the axle by four millimeters to permit you to line up the crank and the freewheel as shown in Figure 111.

Before reassembling T. A. Criterium cranks, oil the surfaces that join (including the cranks) the axle and the three-piece cotters. Install the three-piece cotter so that the beveled surfaces of the sleeve and nut butt flat against the axle.

Note: The bolt must be inside the shallow indentation of the axle. Tighten the cotter tightly with a five-millimeter Allen wrench. Then install the left crank, positioned to clear the chain stay, and install the cotter as indicated above. Remember, you do not have to hammer this cotter home. Do not hammer at all.

THE HEADSET

Headset Maintenance

The headset consists of the front fork bearings and associated washers, adjusting nuts, cups, and cones. Once or twice a year you should dismantle the headset (Fig. 129) on your bike, clean it, and relubricate the bearings.

To lubricate the headset, follow this procedure:

STEP ONE: Loosen the expander bolt. This is the head bolt on the handlebar stem (Fig. 130). When you have loosened it about a quarter of an inch, tap the bolt down with a rubber mallet or a block of wood and a hammer. If you have caliper brakes, remove the front brake by loosening the nut at the rear of the fork and pulling the entire brake assembly away from the fork. If you have center-pull brakes, do not remove the brake assembly. Simply squeeze the brake closed, and remove the short cable connecting the brake yoke to the vertical brake cable. Remove the handlebars by twisting and pulling upward at the same time, holding the front wheel between your knees.

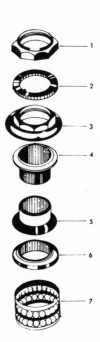

1. Locknut
2. Keyed washer
3. Adjusting nut
4. Headset top
5. Headset bottom
6. Bottom cup
7. Top and bottom bearings

Fig. 129: *Exploded view of typical headset. Bearings are usually loose, but in this new model Campagnolo headset, they are in a race, as they are on most American-made bicycles.*

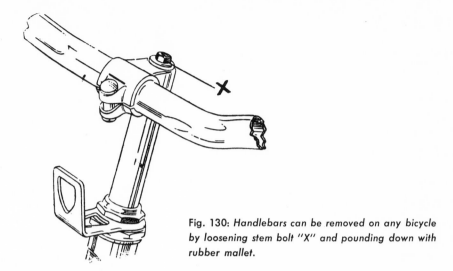

Fig. 130: *Handlebars can be removed on any bicycle by loosening stem bolt "X" and pounding down with rubber mallet.*

STEP TWO: With a large crescent wrench or monkey wrench, remove the locknut on the headset and the washer. Or, if the locknut has holes and is round, use a center punch and a hammer, gently.

STEP THREE: Remove the front wheel.

STEP FOUR: Lay the bicycle on its side, with the headset lying on a large cloth to catch loose bearings. Remove the adjusting cup from the top of the headset, and pull the fork out from the bottom. Remove any loose bearings that are still in the top or bottom cones.

STEP FIVE: Clean the headset cones and bearings with kerosene.

STEP SIX: Most American-made bicycles do not have loose bearings. They are held in a retainer or cage, so you don't have to worry about their dropping out of the bicycle and getting lost.

This also applies to the new Campagnolo headsets. If, when you re-move the caged bearing sets from the top and bottom of the headset, the bearing balls fall out of them, this means that the cage or retainer is worn and you should buy a new set of caged bearings. You can use loose balls if they are the same size as those in the retainer or cage set, instead.

STEP SEVEN: Check the cleaned bearings and cones for wear, galled spots, cracks, and rust, and replace any defective parts with new parts.

STEP EIGHT: Turn the bicycle upside down. Smear a layer of Lubriplate Low Temp or Texaco Starfak No. 2 grease in the bottom cone, and replace the bearings. Insert the front fork. Holding the fork in place by hand, turn the bicycle over so that the weight of the bicycle is on the front fork (to hold bottom bearings in place).

Note: If caged bearings are used, place them in the cone so that the curved, outer part of the bearings face into the cup.

STEP NINE: Put a layer of grease into the top cup, insert the balls or caged bearing, and screw down the adjusting cup until it is hand-tight. Then, back off about a quarter-turn. Insert the front wheel and turn the bicycle right side up.

STEP TEN: Adjust the headset by inserting a keyed flat washer and locknut, and tightening the locknut. Check the fork for play, vertically and horizontally, by turning it. If the fork feels stiff, loosen the locknut, back off the adjusting cup another quarter-turn, and retighten the locknut. If there is side or vertical play in the fork, loosen the locknut, tighten the adjusting cup a quarter-turn, and retighten the locknut. Repeat until the play is removed. The fork is ideally adjusted when it turns easily, and there is no vertical or horizontal play.

STEP ELEVEN: Reinstall the handlebars and front brake. Check the headset adjustment again by locking the front brake and rocking the bicycle back and forth. If you can feel looseness when you put your finger where the adjusting cup and the upper head cone meet, everything is in order, unless the looseness is quite noticeable. This is where you will have to exercise judgment.

If, when you turn the fork from side to side, you find it still binds, or you can't seem to get the ideal adjustment, you have probably either put one bearing too many in one end of the headset, and consequently are short one in the other end, or you are missing a bearing, because it has rolled up into the fork and stuck there on a spot of grease. In either case, you will have to dismantle the headset, following Steps One through Six, above, before you can adjust the headset properly. I would like to be able to give you a bearing count so you would know how many bearings you should have, but there are far too many bearing sizes and consequently too many different numbers of bearings in various makes of bicycles to make this practical.

Taping

See Figure 30, page 96, for taping instructions.

SPOKES

Good spokes are vital, especially on a long tour when you're carrying luggage.

I recommend the Robergel "Sport" high-tensile-strength steel, double-butted spoke. Double-butted means that the spokes are slightly thickened at the ends, where there is strain. The Robergel spokes cost about $6.00 per hundred, and for one twenty-seven-inch wheel you'll need thirty-six.

To make sure you get the right spoke size, remove an old spoke and bring it with you to the bicycle shop or mail it to your source.

How to Lace a Wheel

There are a number of reasons why you should know how to "lace" or respoke a wheel. A bicycle wheel can be bent, dented, or become flat in one spot because of an accident such as hitting a curb or pothole, or for any number of other reasons.

When a wheel becomes badly warped or develops a flat spot, the only remedy is to remove the old rim and lace on a new one.

Or you may wish to change hubs but keep the same rim—or vice versa. For whatever reason relacing is indicated, you may wish to, or have to, do it yourself.

Wheel lacing is simple enough if you follow instructions carefully. The steps that follow are for any thirty-six-spoke wheel, as found on most bicycles, although they can be used for the thirty-two-spoke front and forty-spoke rear wheels on English three-speed bicycles. (These instructions apply only to spokes "crossed over four," which means just that.)

STEP ONE: Remove the tire and rim strip.

STEP TWO: If lacing in the rear wheel, remove the freewheel gear cluster or gear on multispeed hubs, such as the Sturmey-Archer. (See pages 232-33 and 247-48 for derailleur freewheel removal, page 280 for Sturmey-Archer gear removal.)

STEP THREE: With a pair of wire clippers, cut all spokes and remove them from the hub and old rim. (Save the old rim, if it's for tubular sew-up tires, for use in checking flats or mounting spare tires for storage.)

STEP FOUR: Examine the hub. If it's a good one for derailleur bicycles, such as a Campagnolo hub, you'll notice that every other hole is countersunk (Fig. 131). If you think this countersinking is so that spoke heads can fit neatly flush into the hub, you're wrong. So was I, the first time I laced a wheel, and broke six spokes the first five miles. Actually, the countersinking is to permit the bent part of the spoke to curve gradually in the hub spoke hole, instead of knifing into a sharp bend where it can be weakened and break. The majority of spoke breaks occur at the point where the spoke leaves the hub hole at the bend. *Never spoke a hub so that the spoke head fits into the countersunk hole—the head must be on the noncountersunk side.* (If your hub does not have countersunk spoke holes, you can ignore this particular instruction.)

STEP FIVE: Holding the hub upright, insert a spoke into every other noncountersunk hole in the bottom flange of the hub. Spoke heads should be on the inside surface of the bottom flange. Fan out the spokes and lay the rim over the spokes so that the valve hole faces toward you. Turn the hub over so that the half-spoked flange is now on top. Find the first spoke hole in the rim to the left (clockwise) of the valve hole. Insert any

Fig. 131: *Be sure to insert spokes in wide-flanged or other type of racing hubs correctly, as shown here. Spoke head does not go into countersunk hole, but the other way around, so spoke can bend gradually upward to ease strain at this sharp bend area. Courtesy: Bicycling! (formerly American Cycling).*

WRONG   RIGHT

spoke from the hub into this hole. Screw on the spoke nipple three to four turns on this and all spokes as you insert them in the rim. From now on this spoke will be called Key Spoke A. Insert the first spoke in the hub to the left of Key Spoke A in the fourth hole in the rim to the left of Key Spoke A. Proceed around the rim as above, so that when you are finished, every fourth hole in the rim is filled, with four empty spoke holes in the rim between each spoke (Fig. 132).

STEP SIX: Insert one spoke in the first empty spoke hole in the top flange of the hub, to the left of Key Spoke A. This spoke will be called Key Spoke B. Key Spoke B's head should be on the outside of the top flange. Count off eighteen rim holes to the *left*, counterclockwise, of Key Spoke A, not counting Key Spoke A but counting all holes, filled or empty. Insert Key Spoke B into this eighteenth rim hole. The wheel should now look like Figure 133. The pencil points to Key Spoke B.

Fig. 132: When you are finished with Step Five in wheel lacing (see text), wheel should look like this.

Fig. 133: After completing Step Six, spoke should look like this. Pencil points to Key Spoke B.

STEP SEVEN: Following clockwise around the rim and hub from Key Spoke B, insert the spokes in the flange hub top, heads up, and into every fourth rim spoke hole, clockwise from Key Spoke B in the rim (counting all holes, filled or empty). When you have finished, all the top flange holes, and every other rim hole, should be filled, as shown in Figure 134.

STEP EIGHT: Turn the hub and rim over. With a spoke as a guide (Fig. 135), find the first spoke in the bottom flange, clockwise from Key Spoke A. Note that this hole is slightly offset, clockwise, from the Key Spoke A hub hole. This is done for added strength. Insert a spoke in this hub hole and into the first rim hole clockwise from Key Spoke A. We will call this spoke Key Spoke C. This hole will be countersunk on *top* face flange.

STEP NINE: Going around the rim and hub clockwise, insert a spoke into every hub flange and into every fourth rim hole, counting all rim holes, filled or empty. When Step Nine is complete, the wheel should look like Figure 136 with spokes in groups of three and one empty spoke hole separating each trio of spokes.

STEP TEN: Find the first empty hub flange hole clockwise to Key Spoke C in the hub. Put this spoke, which we will call Key Spoke D, into the first rim hole clockwise to Key Spoke C. (See Fig. 137. The pencil points to Key Spoke C.)

STEP ELEVEN: Insert a spoke in the hub, clockwise to Key Spoke D, and insert it four holes in the rim, clockwise to Key Spoke D. Proceed in this manner all around the rim and hub. When you have finished, the wheel should look like Figure 138 with spokes "crossed over" in groups of four. The wheel is now ready for alignment.

Fig. 134: Wheel should look as shown here after completing Step Seven.

Fig. 135: *This is a critical point in wheel lacing. Pencil points to Key Spoke B. Upright spoke is Key Spoke C.*

Fig. 136: *After completing Step Nine in wheel lacing, wheel should appear like this. Spokes should be in groups of three, with one empty spoke hole between each trio of spokes.*

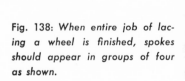

Fig. 137: *Pencil at bottom center points to Key Spoke C, vital to Step Ten.*

Fig. 138: *When entire job of lacing a wheel is finished, spokes should appear in groups of four as shown.*

Wheel Truing and Alignment

If you have ever respoked a wheel, or laced a new rim, you know that this is a job that requires a good deal of patience. Wheel truing is also a job that cannot be hurried.

There are two types of wheel-truing procedures: one that you use if you have just relaced a wheel, another for when you have either replaced a spoke or two, or simply wish to bring your wheel back to true. Since wheel truing after lacing is the more difficult procedure, I will go into it first.

Wheel Pull-Up and Truing after Relacing

Ideally, you should have a truing jig for this job, which you can buy from one of the bike mail-order shops for around $6.50, and which you can hold in a vise. However, an old front fork will do nearly as well, at least for front wheels.

The wheel is laced, with all the spokes in their correct holes.

STEP ONE: First, make sure the axle cones are properly adjusted, with no side play (see pages 261-62 for instructions on cone adjustment). All washers, spacers, and locknuts must be in place so that you can center the wheel properly (see the discussion of freewheel alignment with chain-wheel on page 239).

STEP TWO: Use a ratchet screwdriver to save time in pulling up the spokes. Tighten the inside spokes all the way around until only about five or six threads show under the nipples.

STEP THREE: Pull up the inside spokes as in Step Two.

STEP FOUR: Put the wheel in the truing jig, in an old fork, or, if it's a front wheel, back in the bicycle front fork. Starting at the valve hole, pull up all the spokes with a good spoke wrench (about thirty-five cents from any good bike store), about two or three turns. Be sure to use the same number of turns on each spoke.

If you're truing a rear wheel with a freewheel gear cluster, give the spokes on the freewheel side three or four extra turns at this time to make "dishing" easier. "Dishing" a wheel means flattening it on one side so that when the wheel is in the rear fork stays, it is also centered in line with the bicycle frame. The reason you "dish" or adjust the spokes so that the wheel is pulled over to one side is because the extra width of the freewheel gear cluster would put the wheel out of line with the bicycle if it were centered in the hub alone. If you trued the wheel in line with the centerline of the hub, the wheel would be way out of line with respect to the centerline of the bicycle.

STEP FIVE: At this stage, although the spokes can still be tightened, they should not be extremely loose. To test spoke tension, note that all the spokes should emit a "ping" when plucked, and all the spokes should give the same ping note.

STEP SIX: With the wheel in the truing jig, hold a piece of chalk close to the outer edge of the rim as you spin the wheel. The chalk will touch only that part of the wheel that is too far out of line. Start reducing out-of-roundness by pulling up the spokes opposite the out-of-round location, loosening them at the chalk mark if necessary. Continue this process, adjusting the spokes *a turn or two at a time* until the wheel is perfectly round.

STEP SEVEN: With the wheel in the truing jig, spin it and, with a piece of chalk, mark the outside edge of the rim, and note the side movement that needs to be corrected.

STEP EIGHT: Start at the valve hole and, with the spoke wrench, tighten the spokes one or two turns on the side away from the chalk mark. Correct for out-of-trueness on one side of the wheel at a time.

STEP NINE: If you are truing a rear wheel with freewheel gear cluster, dish the wheel so it is centered correctly. Assuming you have trued the wheel so that it is concentric and runs true, all you should have to do now to dish the wheel is loosen all the nipples of the spokes on the side opposite the freewheel one-and-a-half turns, and tighten the spokes on the freewheel side the same number of turns. Install the wheel back in the rear fork stays, and with all packing washers (if you use them) in place, the rim should be in the centerline of the bicycle frame.

STEP TEN: As a final step, check the correctness of dishing with a rim gauge. You can make such a gauge yourself. Remember, the adjusting bolt must be off-center so it just touches the hub locking nut or the outside packing washer.

Put the gauge over the rim, and set the adjusting bolt so that it just touches the hub locking nut or the last packing washer (if washers are used). Holding the same bolt adjustment, turn the wheel over and check the other side with the gauge. The adjustment bolt should just touch the wheel locking nut on the other side of the wheel (or packing washer, if used).

Campagnolo makes a dandy rim gauge for dishing any wheel, which costs $7.50.

To True a Wheel

If all you want to do is true your wheel for side alignment, simply follow the procedure in Step Six above. You may have to loosen the spokes that are opposite the side you want to pull the rim over.

A WORD ABOUT LUBRICATION

Although there are very specific instructions about when to lubricate various parts of the bicycle elsewhere in this book, it might be helpful for you to review this general summary of lubrication instructions.

Front-Wheel Hubs

- If the hub has an oil fitting, squirt in about a half-teaspoonful every thirty days.
- If the hub has a grease fitting, add one or two shots of a multipurpose grease such as Lubriplate Low Temp, which is especially good for winter cycling, or Texaco Starfak No. 2.
- Twice a year, disassemble, clean, and relubricate with grease.

Coaster-Brake Rear-Wheel Hubs

- Grease all new bicycle hubs immediately upon purchase, with two or three shots of Marfak No. 2 grease or, if an oil fitting, with two tablespoonfuls of No. 20 oil.
- Thereafter, lubricate as above every thirty days.

Multispeed Internal Gear Rear Hubs

- Add a tablespoonful of No. 20 good-quality motor oil to the hub immediately upon purchase (oil may have evaporated during shipment and storage), and thereafter every thirty days.

Chains

- Every thirty days, or more frequently if you ride on dirty or dusty roads, remove the chain, soak it in kerosene, then in No. 10 motor oil, remove excess oil, and reinstall.

Headset (Fork Bearings)

- Twice yearly, remove the headset locknut, adjusting cup and bearings, clean, and relubricate with Lubriplate Low Temp or Texaco Starfak No. 2 grease.

Bottom Bracket (Chainwheel Axle)

- Pedals are attached to pedal cranks, which are fitted to the axle, which is supported in the bottom by bearings and ball cups. Once a year, remove bottom bracket bearings, following instructions on pages 286-87; clean all parts and relubricate with Lubriplate Low Temp or Texaco Starfak No. 2 grease. The first time you relube, roll up a piece of an aluminum beer can to fit snugly inside the inner diameter of the bottom bracket to seal out dirt dropping down the seat and the tubes. Pack the bottom bracket well. If you do this, you can relube the bottom bracket every two years instead of yearly.

Note: You can buy a small, handy grease applicator, such as a Please

Grease Applicator, from most hardware stores. This is a good little gadget for general utility maintenance for bicycles and household appliances.

Cables

- Once a month, squirt a few drops of light oil, such as Lubriplate Spray-Lube "A," which comes in a handy "Spra-Tainer," on brake and gear change cables where they enter spaghetti tubing.

Caliper Brakes

- Every thirty days or so, squirt a few drops of light oil such as Lubriplate Spray-Lube "A" on brake pivot blocks and other brake moving parts. *Be careful not to get lubricant of any type on the brake shoes!*

Derailleur Mechanisms

- Every thirty days or so, put a few drops of a light oil on the moving parts of derailleur gear shifters, front and rear, including idler wheels of rear derailleurs and gear-shift levers.
- Once every six months, dismantle rear derailleurs, clean and regrease idler wheels with light grease such as Lubriplate Low Temp, and oil other working parts.

Freewheels

- Every thirty days put a few drops of light oil, no heavier than No. 5 motor oil, into the freewheel mechanism on derailleur-equipped bicycles. *Do not use heavier oil. Do not attempt to dismantle the freewheel.*
- Every six months (more often if you have been riding in dusty conditions), remove the freewheel, soak it in kerosene, and relubricate as above. (Review freewheel maintenance instructions on pages 247-48.)
- Do not use a lubricant—oil or grease—which contains graphite or molybdenum disulfide.

Pedals

- On conventional pedals squirt a few drops of No. 30 oil in *each* end of the pedal every thirty days.
- On rattrap pedals, dismantle the pedals every six months (according to mileage), clean the parts, and repack with grease such as Lubri-plate Low Temp. See pages 263-66 for instructions. This applies to rattrap pedals particularly. Do not oil rattrap pedals.

Bear in mind that one key to long life for a bicycle is cleanliness. After every long ride and once a week in the cycling season, wipe off all dust, dirt, and road soil from the frame and wheels and around the caliper brakes and pedals.

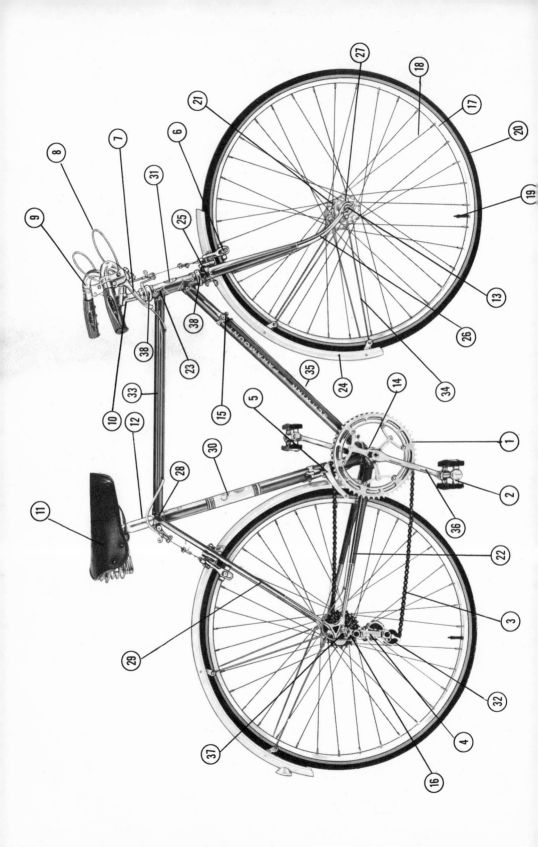

KEY TO BICYCLE PARTS:

1. Chainwheel
2. Pedal
3. Chain
4. Rear derailleur
5. Front derailleur
6. Caliper brake
7. Brake lever
8. Brake cable
9. Handlebars
10. Handlebar stem
11. Seat (saddle)
12. Seat post
13. Quick-release skewer (for instant wheel removal)
14. Bottom bracket
15. Gear-shift lever for rear derailleur
16. Freewheel gear cluster
17. Rim
18. Spoke
19. Valve
20. Tire
21. Hub (high-flange type)
22. Chainstay
23. Lug
24. Fender
25. Fork crown
26. Fork
27. Wheel dropout
28. Seat cluster lug
29. Seat stay
30. Seat tube
31. Steering head
32. Tension roller, rear derailleur
33. Top tube
34. Fender brace
35. Down tube
36. Cotterless crank
37. Rear drop out
38. Headset (top and bottom)

Appendix

A CYCLING DICTIONARY OF TERMS

ANKLING Technique of pedaling, in which the foot follows through 180 degrees or more.

BOTTOM BRACKET Short round tube holding axle, to which is brazed or welded both seat and down tubes.

BRAKE LEVERS Levers mounted on handlebars to actuate caliper brakes.

CABLE Wire to brakes or derailleur gears.

CALIPER BRAKES Hand brakes.

CHAIN Articulated drive unit which transmits power from chainwheel to rear wheel.

CHAIN STAYS Section of frame from bottom bracket to rear wheel drop out.

CHAINWHEEL Large wheel with gear teeth on right crank, which delivers power from crank, through chain, to rear wheel. Chainwheel can be single, double, or triple wheel.

COASTER BRAKES Foot-activated internal hub rear brakes.

COTTERPIN Holds cranks on bottom bracket axle in cottered crank designs.

CRANK Steel or dural member, one end of which is threaded to receive pedal, other end of which is fastened to bottom bracket axle. Righthand crank (facing forward) also is fitted with chainwheel.

CYCLOMETER Bicycle odometer for measuring mileage. Mounts on lower front fork.

DERAILLEUR From the French "to derail." A mechanism to derail or move chain from one gear to another on either rear wheel or chainwheel.

DERAILLEUR CAGE Holds rear derailleur idler wheels.

DOWN TUBE Part of frame extending from steering head to bottom bracket.

DISHING Truing a derailleur gear-equipped rear wheel so rim is centered over axle—*not* over hub. Wheel appears to be to right of hub center (on gear side).

FORK CROWN Flat or slightly sloping part at top of fork, just under steering head.

FRONT FORK Part holding front wheel drop outs, which is turned by handlebars to steer bicycle. Included in this unit is steering-column fork crown (inside head tube of frame), fork blades (round or oval depending on whether a track or road bike), and fork tips.

FRONT DROP OUT Lug brazed to front fork bottom tips into which front wheel axle fits.

HANDLEBAR STEM   Steel or dural piece, top section of which holds handlebars, bottom part of which fits into top of fork.

HUB   Front or rear wheel unit drilled to receive spokes and machined to hold axle and bearings.

JOCKEY SPROCKET   The top of the two rear derailleur idler wheels. This wheel moves the chain from one rear wheel gear to another.

MUDGUARDS   Fenders.

MUDGUARD STAYS   Fender braces.

PANNIER   Saddlebag for mounting on rear of bicycle, usually in pairs for balance. Smaller units may also be mounted on the front of bicycle.

QUICK-RELEASE SKEWER   Mechanism to permit removal of front or rear wheels in seconds.

RATTRAP PEDALS   All-steel racing and touring pedals.

REAR DROP OUT   Lug brazed or welded to seat stays and chain stays into which rear wheel axle fits.

RIM   Wheel, less spokes and hub.

SADDLE   Seat.

SEAT CLUSTER   A three-way lug into which is brazed or welded top and seat tubes and seat stays.

SEAT POST   A hollow cylinder made of dural or steel, the top end of which holds seat, the bottom section of which fits into seat tube.

SEAT STAYS   Part of frame extending from just under seat to rear wheel dropout.

SEAT TUBE   Part of frame in which seat is placed and which extends from under seat to bottom bracket.

STEERING HEAD   Large-diameter tube holding front fork and fork bearings, into which is brazed or welded top and down tubes.

TENSION ROLLER   Bottom of the two rear derailleur idler wheels. This wheel keeps correct tension on the chain.

TIRES, TUBULAR   Ultralightweight track- or road-racing tires. "Sew-ups" with tube sewn in all around inner periphery of tire.

TIRES, WIRED-ON   "Clincher" tires. Conventional type with tube easily accessible for repairs.

TOE CLIPS   Cage on pedals.

TOP TUBE   Horizontal frame member between seat tube and steering head.

TRUING   *See* Dishing.

VALVE   Where air is put into tire.

VARIABLE GEAR HUB   Rear hub containing two, three, or five internal gears and as many gear ratios, shiftable from external gear lever mounted on handlebars or top tube.

CYCLING ORGANIZATIONS

Amateur Bicycle League of America
4233 205th Street
Bayside, Long Island, New York
The ABL is the governing body of bicycle racing in the United States, and is a member of the U.S. Olympic Committee, an affiliate of the Union Cycliste International (the world governing body of racing), and an allied member of the Amateur Athletic Union of the United States.

American Youth Hostels, Inc.
20 West 17th Street
New York, New York 10011
Sponsors bicycle trips and tours both in the United States and abroad. Maintains hostels throughout the country, where members can stay at very reasonable rates. Provides touring information and maintains a stock of cycle camping gear sold from its catalog. Furnishes list of hostel locations and planned tours to members. Holds membership in International Youth Hostel Federation. Clubs located in principal cities throughout the United States. Membership: From $4.00 to $7.00, depending on age; family membership, $10.00.

Bicycle Institute of America
122 East 42nd Street
New York, New York 10017
Furnishes booklets, pamphlets, and information to those interested in starting cycling clubs and racing events, and in promoting bikeways (bicycle paths), locally and at the state level. BIA is the cycling trade association.

British Cycling Federation
26 Park Crescent
London W.1
England
Governs bicycle racing in England, although the BCF also offers assistance to members who wish to cycle-tour by providing itineraries, routes between youth hostels abroad, maps, accident insurance, and general advice. Membership: $4.50 if over eighteen, $3.00 under eighteen.

Canadian Youth Hostels Association
268 First Avenue
Ottawa, Ontario, Canada
Similar in scope and function to American Youth Hostels, Inc. The interna-

tional card issued by the AYH or the CYH enables you to use the facilities in hostels in all European countries.

Cyclists' Touring Club
Cotterell House
69 Meadrow
Godalming, Surrey
England

Similar in scope and purpose to the League of American Wheelmen, Inc., but furnishes infinitely greater touring service, including maps, guides, lists of hostels, and guided tours of England and Europe. Publishes bimonthly magazine, *Cycle Touring*, free to members. (See list of publications.)

League of American Wheelmen, Inc.
5118 Foster Avenue
Chicago, Illinois 60630

Current membership over 1,000. Sponsors local and national bicycling events and touring; issues informative monthly bulletin to members on various aspects of cycling. A close-knit organization, with members in forty-five states who visit each other, assist in tours, and promote cycling nationally. Dues: individual, $5.00; family, $8.00; sustaining, $15.00 (minimum). Dues include $1,000 death or dismemberment insurance, $2.50 medical with $25.00 deductible, and $50.00 dental.

International Bicycle Touring Society
846 Prospect Street
La Jolla, California 92037

Plans and conducts bicycle tours throughout the world. Operates famed "Huff-'n-Puff" tours.

National Bicycle Dealers Association
29025 Euclid Avenue
Wickliffe, Ohio 44092

The trade association of retail bicycle dealers.

Scottish Youth Hostels Association
7 Bruntsfield Crescent
Edinburgh 10, Scotland

Will help plan tours in Scotland and provide list of youth hostels for cycle tourists.

BICYCLE SUPPLY SOURCES

L. L. Bean, Inc.
Freeport, Maine 04032
The old standby. High-quality camping equipment at quite reasonable prices.

Big Wheel, Ltd.
310 Holly Street
Denver, Colorado 80220
Essentially the same catalog published by Wheel Goods Corporation (see below), except printing job is poor and hard to read.

Bike Riders Aids		W. F. Holdsworth, Ltd.
The Holdsworthy Co., Ltd.	or	132 Lower Richmond Road
London, S.E. 20		Putney, S.W. 15
England		England

Compact but quite complete list of cycling accessories and gear. If you're planning a European trip, you may want to order abroad for pickup in England to save shipping expense.

H. W. Carradice
North Street, Nelson
Lancashire, England
Full line of cycle bags, panniers, straps, and carriers.

Colorado Outdoor Sports Corporation
P.O. Box 5544
Denver, Colorado 80217
An elegantly printed list of fine camping equipment, much of which can be used by the cycle camper.

Cyclo-Pedia
311 North Mitchell
Cadillac, Michigan 49601
Publishes comprehensive list of bicycles of all types, as well as bicycle accessories, parts, and supplies. Catalog price: $1.00.

I. Goldberg & Sons
429 Market Street
Philadelphia, Pennsylvania 19106
Free 140-page camper's catalog.

Metropolitan New York Council
American Youth Hostels, Inc.
535 West End Avenue
New York, New York 10024

Catalog of camping needs, including cycle camping. Prices are quite reasonable and gear is pretested by AYH members, which is as good a qualification as any.

Wheel Goods Corporation
2737 Hennepin Avenue
Minneapolis, Minnesota 55408

One hundred-fourteen-page catalog on bikes, accessories, parts, and tools. Cost: $1.00.

Youth Hostels Association
29 John Adam Street
London, W.C. 2
England

Forty-eight-page cycling and camping equipment catalog, including panniers and carriers, tents and sleeping bags.

BICYCLING MAGAZINES

American Bicyclist and Motorcyclist
461 Eighth Avenue
New York, New York 10001
A monthly publication for the bicycle dealer. Little of interest to the cycling fan, unless he wants to start a bicycle shop. Subscription for a non-industry affiliated subscriber: $12.00 per year.

Bicycle Journal
P.O. Drawer 1229
Fort Worth, Texas 76101
For the bicycle dealer exclusively. Subscription: $3.00 per year.

Bicycling! (formerly *American Cycling*)
234 Montgomery Street
San Francisco, California 94104
The only magazine in the United States devoted exclusively to the bicycling enthusiast. Includes excellent articles on touring, racing events, and technical data on bicycle maintenance. Published monthly, March through December. Subscription: $6.00 per year.

Cycle Touring
69 Meadrow
Godalming, Surrey
England
Free to members of the Cyclists' Touring Club (same address as publication) or whatever the current American equivalent is of twelve shillings, sixpence ($1.50, early 1968), for six issues—December, February, April, June, August, and October. Well worth the money if you plan to cycle-tour abroad.

Cycling and Sporting Cyclists
161-166 Fleet Street
London, E.C. 4
England
Primarily for cycle-racing enthusiasts, although it also contains excellent articles on touring in England and Ireland and on the Continent. Published every Thursday. Subscription: six months, $8.25; one year, $16.50; three years, $25.00.

International Cycle Sport
Kennedy Brothers Publishing, Ltd.
Keighley
Yorkshire
England
An excellent publication covering the European and English competitive scene. Monthly. Subscription: $6.00 per year.

Le Cycliste
18, rue du Commandeur
Paris 14e, France
For the Continental cycling enthusiast, or for those who read and understand French. Even if you don't read French, this is a charming little publication, mostly on cycle touring in France, which should prompt you to learn the language just to read the material that goes with the beautiful illustrations. Subscription: $7.00 per year.

BIBLIOGRAPHY

BOOKS AND PAMPHLETS

Baranet, Nancy Neiman. *The Turned Down Bar*. Philadelphia: Dorrance & Company, 1964.

Benedict, Ruth and Ray. *Bicycling*. New York: A. S. Barnes and Company, 1944.

Bowden, Ken, and John Matthews. *Cycle Racing*. London: Temple Press Books, Limited (42 Russell Square, London, W.C. 1), 1965.

English, Ronald. *Adventure Cycling*. London: Nicholas Kay Limited (194-200 Bishopsgate, London, E.C. 2), 1959.

English, Ronald. *Cycling for You*. London: Clutterworth Press, 1964.

a'Green, George. *Story of the Cyclists' Touring Club*. London: Cyclists' Touring Club, 1953.

Kraynick, Steve. *Bicycle Owner's Complete Handbook*. Los Angeles: Floyd Clymer Publications, 1960.

Moore, Harold. *The Complete Cyclist*. London: Sir Isaac Pitman & Sons, Ltd., 1960.

Morehouse, Laurence E., and Augustus T. Miller. *The Physiology of Exercise*. St. Louis: C. V. Mosby Company, 1959.

Murphy, Dervla. *Full Tilt: Ireland to India on a Bicycle*. New York: E. P. Dutton & Company, Inc., 1965.

Pullen, A. L. *Cycling Handbook*. London: Sir Isaac Pitman & Sons, Ltd., 1960.

Shaw, R. C. *Teach Yourself Cycling*. London: The English Universities Press, Ltd., (102 Newgate Street), 1963.

Simpson, Tommy. *Cycling Is My Life*. London: Stanley Paul & Co., Ltd. (178–202 Great Portland Street), 1966.

Way, R. John. *Cycling Manual*. London: Temple Press Books, Limited, 1967.

Bicycle Dealer's Source Book. Dayton, Ohio: National Bicycle Dealers Association, 1967.

The Bicycle, Its Care and Maintenance. London: Iliffe Books Limited. (Dorset House, Stamford Street, London, S.E. 1), 1961.

Bicycle Riding Clubs. New York: Bicycle Institute of America.

Bike Racing on the Campus. New York: Bicycle Institute of America. (122 East 42nd Street, New York, N.Y. 10017.)

Bike Trails and Facilities (information kit). New York: Bicycle Institute of America.

Bike Trails and Facilities: A Guide to Their Design and Construction. West Virginia: American Institute of Park Executives, Inc., Walter L. Cook. (Oglebay Park, Wheeling, W. Va.), May, 1965.

321

Cycling Book of Maintenance. London: Temple Press Books, Limited, 1961.
Cycling Guide. Pennsylvania: American Youth Hostels, Inc. (2200 Pine Street, Philadelphia, Pa. 19141.)
Cycling in the School Fitness Program. Washington, D.C.: American Association for Health, Physical Education and Recreation, 1963.
The Family Hosteling Manual. New York: American Youth Hostels, Inc.
Gear Ratios. Cyclo-Gear Company, Ltd.
A Handbook on Bicycle Tracks and Cycle Racing. Dayton, Ohio: The Huffman Manufacturing Company, 1965.
Hostel Guide and Handbook. New York: American Youth Hostels, Inc. (20 West 17th Street, New York, N.Y. 10011), 1967–1968.
Know the Game Cycling. London: Educational Productions Limited (17 Denbigh Street, London S.W. 1), 1964.
Public Safety Memo 92, Bicycles. Chicago: National Safety Council, 1965.
Reynolds "531" Cycle Tubing (technical booklet). Reynolds Tube Company Limited.
Safe Bicycling. Boston: Committee for Safe Bicycling, Inc., 1965.
Traffic Accident Facts. Chicago: National Safety Council, 1967.

MAGAZINE ARTICLES

DeLong, Fred: "The Care and Use of Lightweight Bicycles." Philadelphia: Philadelphia Council, American Youth Hostels, Inc.
————. "Handlebars and Riding Position," *Bicycling!* (formerly *American Cycling*), April, 1966, p. 16.
————. "What Bicycle for Touring?" *American Cycling* (now *Bicycling!*), May, 1967, p. 12.
————. "What Length Cranks?" *American Cycling* (now *Bicycling!*), September, 1967, p. 14.
Duex-Roves. "Winter Cycling," *American Cycling* (now *Bicycling!*), December, 1966, p. 9.
Hartke, Vance. *The Congressional Conference on Bicycling in America.* Congressional Record, September 20, 1966.
Kepner, Paul R. "Cadence Chart." *Cyclo-Pedia,* 1967, p. 63.
St. Pierre, Roger. "Equipment Review: Witcomb Cycles and Jacques Anquetil Cycles," *American Cycling* (now *Bicycling!*), August, 1967, p. 17.
————. "Road Test, Raleigh RSW-16," *American Cycling* (now *Bicycling!*), June, 1967, p. 17.
Thomas, Vaugh. "Scientific Setting of the Saddle Position," *American Cycling* (now *Bicycling!*), June, 1967, p. 12.
Wolf, Spence. "Derailleur Maintenance," *American Cycling* (now *Bicycling!*), November, 1966, p. 23; December, 1966, p. 25.
————. "Front Hub Bearing Maintenance," *American Cycling* (now *Bicycling!*), September, 1966, p. 23.
————. "Tire Care," *American Cycling* (now *Bicycling!*), June, 1966, p. 19.

"The Bike's Comeback," *Sunset,* July, 1965, ER-191.
"Bikeways," *American Bicyclist and Motorcyclist,* February, 1967, p. 76.

"Cycling Clubs of the U.S.A.," *American Bicyclist and Motorcyclist,* May, 1967, p. 22.

"Here Are the First 12 Cities Awarded Federal Bikeways," *American Bicyclist and Motorcyclist,* August, 1966, p. 23.

"Here Comes the Federal Bikeway Boom," *American Bicyclist and Motorcyclist,* April, 1966, p. 31.

"LBJ Wants Bikeways Built Inside Cities," *American Bicyclist and Motorcyclist,* May, 1966, p. 26.

"Longest Bikeway in the World," *American Bicyclist and Motorcyclist,* June, 1966, p. 21.

"Of Bicycles, Parks and Recreation," *Park Practice Grist* (American Institute of Park Executives), May–June, 1966, S2-1.

DOCUMENTS

Natural Beauty of Our Country. Message from the President of the United States. House of Representatives, Document No. 78. February 8, 1965, p. 7.

S. 827 and H.R. 4865: Bills to Establish a Nationwide System of Trails. February 6, 1967. Washington, D.C.: U.S. Government Printing Office.

Trails for America: Report on the Nationwide Trails Study. U.S. Bureau of Outdoor Recreation. 1966, p. 119.

"Uniform Signs for Bicycle Routes," *American City,* May, 1967, p. 132.

INDEX